THE BIG 50
CINCINNATI REDS

The Men and Moments That Made
the Cincinnati Reds

Chad Dotson and Chris Garber

TRIUMPH
BOOKS

The previous edition has been catalogued by the Library of Congress as:

Names: Dotson, Chad, 1973- author. | Garber, Chris, 1973–
Title: The big 50 Cincinnati Reds : the men and moments that made the
    Cincinnati Reds / Chad Dotson and Chris Garber.
Other titles: Big fifty Cincinnati Reds
Description: Chicago, Illinois : Triumph Books, 2018.
Identifiers: LCCN 2016047884 | ISBN 9781629375410 (paperback)
Subjects: LCSH: Cincinnati Reds (Baseball team)—History—Juvenile
    literature. | Cincinnati Reds (Baseball team)—Biography—Juvenile
    literature. | BISAC: SPORTS & RECREATION / Baseball / General. | TRAVEL /
    United States / Midwest / East North Central (IL, IN, MI, OH, WI).
Classification: LCC GV875.C65 D67 2018 | DDC 796.357/640977178—dc23 LC record
available at https://lccn.loc.gov/2016047884

This book is available in quantity at special discounts for your group or organization. For further information, contact:

Triumph Books LLC
814 North Franklin Street
Chicago, Illinois 60610
(312) 337-0747
www.triumphbooks.com

Printed in U.S.A.
ISBN: 978-1-63727-571-9

Design by Andy Hansen
All photos are courtesy of AP Images unless otherwise indicated.

To Katie, Charlie, Luke, and Sam.
—CGG

To Sabrina, Reagan, and Casey.

And to my grandmother Dot, for collecting baseball cards with Cory and me, and for checking me out of school so I could watch the Reds on Opening Day.
—CSD

[Contents]

[Foreword]

The Cincinnati Reds are more than just a baseball team; they are an institution, a part of the very heartbeat of Cincinnati. From the team's inception as the first professional baseball club in 1869 to the glory years of the Big Red Machine and beyond, the Reds have been at the forefront of the sport. *The Big 50* sets out to describe the greatest men and moments in Cincinnati Reds history. Authors Chad Dotson and Chris Garber bring these moments to life in a way that both longtime Reds fans and newcomers will appreciate. This isn't just a history of the Reds; it's a celebration of the 50 most iconic stories of the club's past.

Long before I stepped onto the field in a Reds uniform or sat before a microphone for a Reds broadcast, I was raised a Reds fan. My youth coaches preached sprinting to first base after a base on balls, just like Pete Rose. We were told to polish our black cleats and wear our stirrups low, just like our heroes at Riverfront Stadium. I saw my first Major League game at Crosley Field and then played there a few years later with a CYO team for the city championship.

I was at Riverfront Stadium for the 1975 World Series, having driven non-stop from Tampa to Cincinnati with some of my college teammates for Game 4. We snagged standing room only seats, snuck down to four unused seats behind home plate and watched Luis Tiant beat my beloved Reds. An unlikely twist here is that I would later become a teammate of El Tiante when we played together for La Guaira in the Venezuelan Winter League.

So, as you read this collection of stories punctuated with detailed backstories, you will be transported to the pivotal moments in Reds' history: the magic of the 1990 Wire-to-Wire championship season, the tension of Tom Browning's perfect game, the joy of seeing Ken Griffey

Jr. on Father's Day, and the awe of witnessing Pete's record-breaking 4,192nd hit.

But the story of the Reds is more than just the big games and historic milestones. It's the story of the players who became legends, the managers who guided them, and the fans who lived and died with every pitch. It's about Joe Morgan's brilliance, Johnny Bench's farewell, and Joey Votto's modern-day mastery at the plate. It's about the unsung heroes, like the Stowe and Schwab families, who worked behind the scenes to help make the Reds what they are today.

One of the most compelling aspects of The Big 50 is how it reflects the evolution of the team through its greatest moments and players. From the very beginning of professional baseball to the championship years of the 1970s, from the heartbreak of missed opportunities to the celebrations of unforgettable victories, the book reminds us of how the Reds have continually shaped the game itself.

Whether you're reliving the triumphs of the past or discovering these moments for the first time, The Big 50: Cincinnati Reds will take you on an unforgettable journey through the team's most important and thrilling chapters. Every story in this book is a testament to the enduring bond between the Reds and their fans—a bond built on memories that will last a lifetime. So, turn the page, dive into the rich history, and celebrate the moments that made the Cincinnati Reds the legendary team they are today.

—Chris Welsh

Chris Welsh, "The Crafty Left-Hander," has been the color analyst for Cincinnati Reds broadcasts since 1993. He teamed with George Grande until Grande's retirement in 2009 to form the longest-running TV broadcasting partnership in Reds history. Welsh was named the 2022 Ohio Sportscaster of the Year by the National Sports Media Association. Chris created and operates baseballrulesacademy.com, an interactive website designed to teach the rules of baseball by use of video lessons and quizzes.

[A Note on Statistics]

"It was my understanding that there would be no math."
— Chevy Chase as President Gerald R. Ford,
Saturday Night Live, 1976

There's nothing to fear. We aren't statisticians, and this is not a statistics book. It's a book of stories, about people, places, and times; about a city, its team, and the larger-than-life characters who called it home. But you can't talk about baseball without talking about numbers. Whether they're old and straightforward (4,192 hits) or innovative and complex, baseball statistics are really nothing more than a way to objectively describe the events that took place in the ballgames.

One criticism of statistics is that they don't tell the whole story—that they ignore context. It's true that (at least for now) an infield single in the third inning of an August snoozer goes into the book as one base hit; exactly the same as a line drive with two outs in the bottom of the ninth.

This book provides that missing context, through firsthand accounts, hidden and forgotten stories, and yes, even through statistics themselves. A few in particular are used throughout the book. It's worth a couple of minutes to explain them, before moving on to the men and moments that define the Cincinnati Reds.

The Basics — Hitting

Often, we'll refer to the hitting statistics you see on the back of baseball cards: Batting Average (AVG), On-Base Percentage (OBP), and Slugging Percentage (SLG).

These are called a hitter's "slash" statistics, since they're often displayed with a "/" symbol dividing them, and always in the same order AVG/OBP/SLG: For example, in his MVP year of 2010, Joey Votto's AVG was .324, his OBP was .424, and his SLG was .600. That means that his slash line was .324/.424/.600.

You'll also often see reference to On-Base Plus Slugging (OPS), which is just what it sounds like—you add those two numbers together. Again using Votto's example, his OPS for 2010 was 1.024.

The last new number we'll use is On-Base Plus Slugging *Plus* (OPS+). This adjusts OPS so that we can compare players across eras and to account for the ballparks they play in. OPS+ is expressed in a very simple scale: A 100 OPS+ is league average, and each point up or down is one percentage point above or below league average. In 2010, Votto's OPS+ was a remarkable 171, which means that even after accounting for the fact that Great American Ball Park is friendly to hitters, Joey was 71 percent better than the average National League hitter that year.

The Basics — Pitching

Pitching won't be as complicated. We'll often tell you a starting pitcher's Win-Loss record and Earned Run Average (ERA), which looked like this for Jose Rijo in 1993:

(W-L, ERA)

(14–9, 2.48)

We'll also sometimes refer to a pitcher's ERA+, which is very similar to OPS+. It adjusts a pitcher's ERA for his ballpark, and expresses it on a scale where an ERA+ of 100 is league average. Rijo had a 162 ERA+ in 1993, 62 percent better than average.

Wins Above Replacement (WAR)

Wins Above Replacement (WAR) is the closest baseball statisticians have come to a single measure of a player's overall contributions. It includes a player's hitting, fielding, running, and pitching performance, and most importantly, compares him to a baseline—a scrub, or a "replacement player" who is readily available for league-minimum salary.

WAR is stated in terms of wins, so a 6 WAR player is significantly better (and much, much harder to find) than a 2 WAR player. Again, it's not perfect. Any time you're using just one metric you're oversimplifying, and some of the defensive data that goes into it is flawed.

But it's a great tool to compare different types of players within a season, or across history. Here's a rough scale:[1]

Scrub	0–1 WAR
Role Player	1–2 WAR
Solid Starter	2–3 WAR
Good Player	3–4 WAR
All-Star	4–6 WAR
Superstar	6–8 WAR
MVP	8+ WAR

As a last bit of context, here are the Reds (post-1919) single-season and career WAR leaders:[2]

Single-Season

Rank	Name	WAR	Year
1	Joe Morgan	11.0	1975
2	Dolf Luque	10.7	1923
3	Joe Morgan	9.6	1976
4	Ewell Blackwell	9.4	1947
5	Joe Morgan	9.3	1972
6	Joe Morgan	9.3	1973
7	Jose Rijo	9.2	1993
8	Frank Robinson	8.7	1962
9	Joe Morgan	8.6	1974
10	Johnny Bench	8.6	1972

Career

Rank	Name	WAR
1	Pete Rose	78.0
2	Johnny Bench	75.1
3	Barry Larkin	70.5
4	Joey Votto	64.5
5	Frank Robinson	63.7
6	Joe Morgan	57.9
7	Vada Pinson	47.7
8	Tony Pérez	45.5
9	Eppa Rixey	40.9
10	Dave Concepcion	40.1

---

1.   Scale derived from information provided by both FanGraphs and Baseball-Reference. Both websites are invaluable sources of statistical information and explanations. Each has its own formula for calculating WAR, The minor differences are beyond our understanding. This book uses Baseball-Reference's version (bWAR), mostly because we visit that site a little more often.
2.   We've excluded pitchers from the "dead ball" era, because they routinely made 40+ starts and threw over 300 innings in a season, making their WAR totals wildly inflated.

1

THE GREATEST WORLD SERIES GAME EVER PLAYED

Going into 1975, the Cincinnati Reds organization was starting to feel the pressure of unmet expectations. Yes, the Big Red Machine had averaged almost 95 wins over a five-year stretch. Yes, they'd won three National League West division titles and two NL pennants. But they hadn't won it all, and even the players were beginning to wonder if they ever would. To add to the pressure, they were picked by *The Sporting News* to win the 1975 World Series.

Their pitching staff was finally healthy. Gary Nolan (15–5, 1.99 ERA in 1972) had recovered after missing most of two seasons with shoulder problems. Don Gullett, still just 24, was maturing into one of the league's best left-handers. Veterans Jack Billingham, Fred Norman, and Clay Kirby served as a durable back half of the rotation, and a deep bullpen let manager Sparky Anderson earn his "Captain Hook" nickname on an almost daily basis.

The lineup would be largely the same as it had been at the end of 1974, with young Ken Griffey (who hit .282/.368/.418) in right field, allowing César Gerónimo to move back to his natural center, and Pete Rose in left.

The sole question mark was third base. The Reds hadn't been happy with third baseman Dan Driessen's 24 errors in 122 starts in 1974. General manager Bob Howsam explored trading first baseman Tony Pérez and moving Driessen across the infield, but Howsam wanted a slugging third baseman in return. After a trade for the Yankees' Graig Nettles fell through, the Reds started the season with light-hitting, but slick-fielding John Vukovich at third—Howsam and Anderson figured the Reds had enough offense that they could carry a weak hitter. With every returning starter carrying an OPS better than the league average, they were right. In short, the Reds were loaded.

With all that, they started the season just 12–12, and fell four games behind the Dodgers by May 2. There were positive signs—backup outfielder George Foster was murdering the ball in limited duty (.308/.333/.769)—but Vukovich wasn't working out at third.[1]

So Sparky tried one of the gutsiest moves in managerial history. He asked Pete Rose to move from left field to third base, which would solve the Reds' third base problem and get Foster's bat into the everyday lineup. Rose, an aging star battling to stay at the top, agreed.[2]

It was a deal built on years of trust between these two unique, competitive men. "I just want Pete to be adequate," Anderson said at the time. "I don't want him to be spectacular."

With hard work, Rose made himself adequate defensively, but the change made his team spectacular. From Rose's debut at third base until the All-Star break, the Reds went a mind-boggling 49–17, and turned a four-game deficit into a 12.5-game division lead. They ultimately won the NL West by 20 games, and then steamrolled the Pirates in the NL Championship Series, outscoring Pittsburgh 19–7 in a three-game sweep.

The Reds were highly favored over the Boston Red Sox in the World Series, and they grabbed a 3–2 series lead after a Game 5 blowout in Cincinnati, behind Tony Pérez's two home runs. Needing just one more victory, the Reds returned to Boston for Saturday's scheduled Game 6. A seemingly endless rainstorm delayed the game for three days, but finally, the teams took the field at Fenway Park on a soggy Tuesday night.

The Reds started the classic "Big Red Machine" lineup against Boston's Luis Tiant, who was riding an absurd hot streak. Tiant— the "Cuban of a Thousand Windups"—was already 3–0 in the 1975 postseason, including wins in Games 1 and 4, and had allowed only one earned run in his last 45 innings pitched at Fenway Park. He'd given up just 20 hits and eight walks over that stretch, while striking out 33. The Fenway stands were filled with "El Tiante" and "Tiant for President" t-shirts and signs. "Loo-eee, Loo-eee" chants echoed throughout the night.

Nolan got the start on the mound for the Reds. Anderson decided to go with his 15-game winner, even though it was Billingham's "turn" to start. The travel day, plus the three-day rain delay, gave Sparky the option of choosing any of his four postseason starters. Billingham wasn't

---

1. In the season's second week, Sparky pinch-hit for Vukovich the first time through the batting order. Vukovich, whose parents were attending the game, was not amused.
2. In 1974, Rose's batting average had dipped below .300 for the first time in a decade.

happy with the decision, but he also knew that Sparky planned to go to the bullpen early if Nolan got into trouble.

And that he did. After quickly retiring Cecil Cooper and Denny Doyle in the bottom of the first, Nolan allowed singles to Carl Yastrzemski and Carlton Fisk. Fred Lynn followed with a long home run to right-center. Boston 3, Cincinnati 0.

It didn't take Sparky long to show the 70 million television viewers just how he'd earned the nickname "Captain Hook." Both Billingham and Fred Norman were warming up in the bullpen in the first inning; Sparky pinch-hit for Nolan the first time his spot came up in the batting order.[3] The Reds eventually used a then-record eight pitchers in the game, saving only Clay Kirby and ace Don Gullett for Game 7.

The Reds offense got rolling in the fifth. With one out, Tiant walked pinch-hitter Ed Armbrister, who had hit only .185 for the 1975 season. Rose was next. After fouling off several pitches with a full count, Rose drilled a single to center, raising his Series average to .381. Armbrister hesitated rounding second, but then raced to third, surprising Lynn, who had trouble getting the ball out of his glove.

Up next, Griffey hit a Tiant off-speed pitch to deep left-center field, 379 feet from home plate. Lynn—who would soon collect both the 1975 Rookie of the Year *and* MVP awards—just missed the catch and crashed back-first into the concrete wall. The Boston center fielder lay in a motionless heap as Armbrister and Rose scored, and Griffey sped around for a triple.

Lynn stayed in the game, but the Boston crowd was silenced. The Reds had cut the lead to one, and had the tying run on third. One out later, Johnny Bench hit Tiant's first pitch—a low fastball—high off the Green Monster in left field. Yastrzemski, in his 15th season as the Red Sox left fielder, played the carom as he had hundreds of times before, holding Bench to an RBI single, but the Reds had tied it up.

Tiant escaped a two-on, two-out Reds rally in the sixth, and took the mound again in the seventh. He immediately worked himself into a jam for the third straight inning. Griffey led off with a single, and Joe Morgan followed with one of his own. After Bench flew out, Pérez lofted a fly ball to Dwight Evans in right, deep enough for Griffey to tag and advance to third.

---

3.   In the 1970s, the World Series used the designated hitter in even-numbered years.

Up next, Foster fell behind 0-1. With two out, Boston was conceding second base to Morgan, so he was running with the pitch as Foster drove Tiant's slow curveball off the center-field wall. Both runners scored easily on the double, and the Reds led 5-3. The lead was extended to 6-3 when Gerónimo led off the eighth with a home run—amazingly, Tiant was still in the ball game.

Pedro Borbon, by then in his third inning of relief for the Reds, allowed a leadoff single to Lynn to start the home eighth. After third baseman Rico Petrocelli walked, Sparky made his fifth pitching change of the night, bringing in his relief ace Rawly Eastwick. Eastwick quickly struck out Evans (avenging Evans' homer off Eastwick in Game 3) and got shortstop Rick Burleson to pop out to Foster in left.

The Reds were four outs away from their first World Series title in 35 years. The game and the Series seemed over. *Sport* magazine's Dick Schaap was distributing World Series MVP ballots in the press box.[4]

Analysis of thousands of games' worth of play-by-play accounts lets us estimate a team's typical chance of victory, given any particular game situation. In the situation the Red Sox found themselves (three runs behind, with two runners on and two outs in the bottom of the eighth), major league teams have won only 9 percent of the time. Long odds.

Boston manager Darrell Johnson called on his top left-handed bat off the bench, Bernie Carbo. Carbo, who won the 1970 Rookie of the Year Award as a member of the Reds, had slugged a pinch-homer in Boston's Game 3 loss. On this night, Eastwick got ahead in the count, then busted Carbo inside with a nasty rising fastball. Carbo barely fouled the pitch off, offering one of the ugliest and most defensive swings in World Series history. As Ron Fimrite described it in *Sports Illustrated*, Carbo "swung with all the power and grace of a suburbanite raking leaves."[5]

On the very next pitch, however, Eastwick left a mistake fastball out over the plate, and Carbo knocked it 420 feet into the center-field stands, tying the game and rousing a Boston crowd that had been silent since Griffey's double—and Lynn's crash into the wall—in the fifth.

"I remember everything then went blank for me," Morgan wrote in his autobiography. "I came to thinking only that we were tied, that the

---

4.   Eastwick was the favorite on the premature ballots. Rose was the eventual winner after Game 7.
5.   To *The New Yorker*'s Roger Angell, the swing looked "like someone fighting off a wasp with a croquet mallet."

SMELL A RAT?

The television replay of Fisk waving the ball fair, still a staple of highlight reels for 40 years, has become legendary. As with most legends, one has to choose how much to actually believe. In the version long told by NBC cameraman Lou Gerard and director Harry Coyle, Gerard was stationed inside the Green Monster and tasked with following the baseball with his camera. As Fisk came to the plate, Gerard was distracted by a menacing Fenway rat. Rather than pan the camera to follow the flight of the ball—and risk antagonizing the rat—Gerard kept the camera on Fisk, capturing the famous image of the waving, leaping Fisk. Both men stuck with that version until their deaths, but at least one other crew member says it was an exaggeration.

rug had been pulled out from under us just at the point where we were going to be world champs."

The Reds went down in order in the top of the ninth. Doyle led off the bottom half with a walk. Yastrzemski followed with a single, moving Doyle to third. The winning run was on third, with nobody out. Remember those probability tables we mentioned a couple paragraphs ago? Boston's probability of winning had jumped from 9 percent to 94 percent.[6]

With the game very nearly lost, Sparky called to the bullpen for Will McEnaney, his top lefty. McEnaney walked Fisk intentionally, loading the bases for the left-handed Lynn.

Lynn sliced a fly ball to very shallow left. Foster hustled over to the line and camped under the fly in foul territory next to the Fenway Park stands. Doyle tagged at third and, mistaking third base coach Don Zimmer's "No-No-No!" for "Go-Go-Go!" he broke for the plate. Bench made an athletic play to field Foster's brilliant one-hop throw and tag Doyle to complete the double play. Petrocelli grounded out to third and the game headed to extra innings.

Even as it was being played, Game 6 was recognized as one of the all-time classics. Longtime Reds TV announcer George Grande was working on the Red Sox crew covering the Series, and later said, "Everybody had the feeling that we may be a part of history, that this

---

6.   Remember, that's an average chance of winning. Given that the Sox had a future Hall of Famer and the reigning MVP (Fisk and Lynn) coming to the plate, their chances were even higher.

may be the greatest game ever played, that this may be the greatest moment in baseball, no matter who you're rooting for."

Even the players felt it. When he batted in the 10th, Rose chattered about it to the stoic Fisk: "This is some kind of game, isn't it? I don't think anybody in the world could ask for a better game than this."

Neither team scored in the 10th, but the Reds rallied in the 11th. Dick Drago, in his third inning of relief, hit Rose with a pitch to start the inning. Griffey tried to sacrifice bunt, but Fisk threw to second to force out Rose. Up next, Morgan got the fastball he wanted and blasted it into deep right, toward the three-foot high fence. Evans sprinted to the tricky right-field corner ("Whoa, where does he think he's going?" Morgan thought), and made a leaping, twisting, one-handed catch that robbed Morgan of at least a double, and probably a two-run homer.[7] Unfortunately for the Reds, Griffey was sprinting around the bases, thinking Morgan had hit a double (at least). Halfway between second and third when the catch was made, Griffey was easily doubled off first by the alert Evans.

In the top of the 12th, one-out singles by Pérez and Foster were wasted when 19-game winner Rick Wise, now on in relief, retired Concepción and Gerónimo in short order.

Cincinnati's Pat Darcy had pitched a perfect 10th and 11th. Although he had been used primarily as a starter during the 1975 regular season, Darcy had only pitched a handful of innings in the last month. Bench sensed that his pitcher was running out of gas.

"Pat's warming up, and he can barely get it over the plate," Bench said later. "I looked over at Sparky and shook my head. [Darcy] didn't have anything. His arm was sore. There was no chance."

The Boston hitters had also had two innings to watch Darcy. "I was just watching him throw and noticing that he was just throwing sinkers," Lynn said. "And both Pudge [Fisk] and I like low-ball pitchers, so it was really coming into our favor here."

Fisk, a native New Englander, led off the 12th, having already put together a pretty good night. He was one for three with two walks, and had made two great plays in the field: one on Griffey's bunt in the 11th and another catching a Bench foul pop in the 12th.

Darcy fell behind in the count 1–0. In the Reds dugout, Sparky asked pitching coach Larry Shepard how many pitches Darcy had thrown. The

---

7. Sparky called it the best catch he'd ever seen.

news wasn't what Sparky wanted to hear: Darcy had just thrown his 28th pitch. "Damn," Sparky said. "He ain't thrown that many in weeks."

Darcy's next pitch was one of those sinkers that Fisk loved. Fisk launched a long fly ball down the left-field line. It was definitely long enough to be a home run—the question was whether it would stay fair. Fisk hopped sideways down the first base line, never taking his eyes off the ball, frantically waving his hands to his right, willing the ball to stay fair. It bounced off the foul pole above the Green Monster, giving Boston a Game 7. Fenway Park organist John Kiley broke into Handel's "Hallelujah Chorus," and the church bells tolled in Fisk's hometown of Charlestown, New Hampshire.

Burleson told a teammate, "We just might have won the greatest game ever played." Rose agreed, and couldn't stop talking about how great Game 6 had been. But he also promised Sparky a win. In the Reds clubhouse, confidence reigned. "Beer tonight, champagne tomorrow," Morgan all but guaranteed.

2

WIRE-TO-WIRE REDS COMPLETE THE SWEEP

At 11:13 PM on October 20, 1990, downtown Cincinnati was eerily quiet, especially for a Saturday night. Police had begun gathering in the area a couple of hours earlier, but there was little to do, with just the occasional straggler wandering by.

Meanwhile, nearly 2,400 miles away, Reds first baseman Todd Benzinger settled under an easy popup. Just moments after the ball dropped softly into his leather mitt, a party broke out on Fountain Square.

People streamed into downtown from every direction, from homes and from bars. Some revelers brought brooms, emblematic of Cincinnati's just-completed sweep of the World Series. Some poured beer and champagne on each other's heads, despite the chill in the air. Seven were rowdy enough to get arrested for disorderly conduct.

In all, 12,000 ecstatic baseball fans came together—friends, neighbors, and complete strangers—to celebrate one of the most remarkable teams in the long history of the Cincinnati Reds.

Six minutes before that final out, José Rijo stood on the pitcher's mound at Oakland-Alameda County Coliseum and looked over at the visitor's dugout. Manager Lou Piniella hesitated, then began walking slowly in his pitcher's direction, hands stuffed in the pockets of his red jacket. It was the bottom of the ninth, Game 4 of the World Series, and the Reds were clinging to a slim 2–1 lead.

In the bullpen before the game, pitching coach Stan Williams was concerned that Rijo's fastball wasn't popping like it usually did. When the Athletics scored a run in the first inning, and Rijo struggled with command in the second—walking two hitters—those worries seemed to be founded. What no one could know at that time was that Jose Rijo was on the verge of becoming a Cincinnati Reds legend.

Rijo was nearly perfect for the rest of the night. He retired the next 20 Oakland hitters, striking out nine. The last of those strikeouts came at the expense of A's center fielder Dave Henderson, leading off the ninth. That's when Rijo looked over and saw his manager approaching.

With just two outs standing between Rijo and a complete game, Piniella approached the mound and asked his pitcher how he felt.

Rijo was calm. "I feel great," he said. "My arm feels great. But do what you have to do."

"Why not let Lou make the move he wants to make in that situation?" Rijo explained later. "He's got the Nasty Boys down there, and they've been nasty all year. This is a team effort, isn't it? That's how we got here."

Rijo was right. Piniella *did* want to make a move to that "nasty" bullpen, which had already thrown nearly 13 innings of scoreless relief so far in the Series' first three games—and he called on lefty Randy Myers.

The so-called "Nasty Boys," who dominated the late innings for Piniella's Reds, consisted of Myers, flamethrower Rob Dibble, and lefty Norm Charlton. More often than not, Myers was the guy Piniella counted on to close out games.

The first Oakland hitter to dig into the batter's box against Myers was pinch-hitter Jose Canseco, a four-time All-Star, former MVP, and one of the most fearsome sluggers in all of baseball. Though suffering from a bad back, Canseco had already hit one home run in the Series (and 37 for the season), and had the potential to tie Game 4 with one swing of his bat.

Myers looked in for the sign, reached back, and delivered a fastball, called strike one.

* * *

The game had not started well for the Reds. Rijo's early shakiness was the least of Piniella's problems. With one out in the top of the first, Cincinnati center fielder Billy Hatcher was hit in the hand by a pitch from A's starter Dave Stewart.

Hatcher had been a dynamo to that point, hitting .750 in the Series and reaching base in his first nine plate appearances.[1] Whether the pitch was intentional or not (some Reds thought it was), Hatcher's hand continued to swell. When it became apparent that Hatcher couldn't hold a bat, Piniella was forced to remove Hatcher from the game, replacing him with Herm Winningham.

---

1. Hatcher's .750 batting average broke Babe Ruth's World Series record, dating back to 1928.

Myers' second pitch to Canseco was another fastball, high and away, to even up the count at 1–1.

In the bottom half of the first inning, Cincinnati's left fielder and cleanup hitter, Eric Davis, suffered an injury of his own, one that would turn out to be much more serious than Hatcher's. With one away, Willie McGee hit a soft line drive between center and left. Davis sprinted into the gap, reached, and snagged the ball before crashing hard onto the ground.

The impact jarred the ball loose. Davis, clearly in pain, scrambled to get the ball and flip it to shortstop Barry Larkin before crumbling back onto the outfield grass. For four minutes, Davis was unable to get to his feet. His teammates stood and watched, shocked and silent.[2]

Losing Davis to injury would be a huge blow to the Cincinnati psyche, and he was desperate to stay in the game. Somehow, Davis convinced Piniella to permit him to remain, but when Rijo finally finished off the inning—McGee had scored to give the A's a 1–0 lead—Davis was having difficulty breathing. Spitting blood and in agonizing pain, Davis was rushed to the hospital; Hatcher went with him to get his hand X-rayed. Glenn Braggs was inserted into Davis' spot in the lineup.

The Reds had shocked the baseball world by winning the first three games in the 1990 Series, so the fourth game didn't start as a must-win scenario. But after losing two-thirds of their outfield in the first inning, the pressure was on Myers and the Reds to close it out. No one wanted to consider what would happen if the Reds had to play the rest of the World Series without Davis or Hatcher.

Myers' third pitch was a third fastball, and Canseco fouled it back. One ball, two strikes.

As Myers prepared to deliver another pitch to Canseco, third baseman Chris Sabo inched over toward the third-base line, attempting to prevent an extra-base hit down the line. Sabo, one of the truly unique players in Reds history, with his flat-top haircut, sports goggles, and all-hustle attitude, likely would have been the offensive story of the World

---

2.   Davis was this team's leader, as was evident in Game 1. It was Oakland's third straight World Series, and they were huge favorites after winning 103 games. With one swing of the bat, in the very first inning of the Series, Davis changed that narrative. With two outs and a runner on base, Davis launched a bomb to deep center field off Stewart, who was one of the most dominant pitchers in the game. With that home run, the Reds puffed out their chest a little, ultimately winning the first game by a score of 7–0. The A's were, in fact, mortal.

Series if it hadn't been for Hatcher's heroics. A seventh-inning double made Sabo 3-for-3 on the night. In Game 3, he had blasted two home runs to lead the Reds to an 8–3 win. His .563 average in the Series was the fourth-best in history to that point, and he collected at least one hit in all four games.

Myers' next pitch was another ball, high and away. Canseco shook his head and readied his bat again. The 2–2 pitch was again fouled straight back.

Until the eighth inning, the only time the Reds came close to scoring had been in the sixth. Larkin walked on four pitches. Piniella called for a hit and run, and Larkin advanced to third when Winningham singled into left-center field. One out later, Stewart walked Braggs, again on four pitches. With the bases loaded and one out, the Reds were in business.

Rookie Hal Morris—who had hit .340/.381/.498 that season—was up next, and all the Reds needed was a single to give them a lead. Even a fly ball to the outfield would have permitted Larkin to tag up with the tying run. Alas, Morris grounded to second base, and the A's converted the 4-6-3 double play. Inning over, and the A's still led 1–0.

Canseco stepped out of the box and bent over at the waist, his back clearly bothering him. The next pitch from Myers was ball three, just off the inside corner.

Full count. Myers got the sign from Oliver, went to the stretch, and pitched. Canseco took another big swing...and hit a chopper to Sabo at third. Two outs. The Redlegs were one out away from a world championship.

* * *

After retiring the A's in order in the bottom of the seventh, Rijo bounded off the mound. As he entered the Cincinnati dugout, he ripped his cap from his head and exhorted his teammates to score some runs. The Reds were running out of time.

Larkin led off the eighth with a line-drive single up the middle. On Piniella's orders, Winningham attempted to bunt Larkin, the tying run, into scoring position. Winningham fouled off his first bunt attempt, then took a called strike two.

CINCINNATI REDS

The baseball "book" says you can't bunt with two strikes, right? Well, Winningham laid down a gorgeous two-strike bunt, then hustled all the way down the line, beating the throw for a single.[3]

The Reds had runners on first and second with no outs and Paul O'Neill coming to the plate. Piniella signaled to third base coach Sam Perlozzo that he wanted another bunt, then walked over to Sabo in the dugout. "Can O'Neill bunt?" he asked. Piniella answered his own question: "I guess we'll see if he can."

O'Neill could, and did. Stewart fielded the bunt, but his throw pulled second baseman Willie Randolph off first base, and O'Neill was ruled safe. Bases loaded, no outs, Glenn Braggs at the plate.

Braggs hit a chopper to A's shortstop Mike Gallego, who threw to second for the force out. Larkin scored, and the game was tied 1–1.

Once again, Hal Morris had an opportunity to deliver a big hit. This was the seventh time in the series that Morris had batted with runners in scoring position, but he had come up empty each time.[4] This time, he lifted a high fly ball to right field. Winningham trotted home with the go-ahead run, and the Reds turned a 2–1 lead over to Rijo.

Herm Winningham and Glenn Braggs, backup outfielders who were only in the game thanks to untimely injuries, played crucial roles in helping the Reds to take the lead. It was a perfect example of what Rijo later called a "team effort."

"This was a very typical game for us," said Larkin afterward. "Our whole season has been a culmination of effort from 25 guys on the roster."

For their part, Winningham and Braggs would go down in Cincinnati lore. To this day, they remain fan favorites in the Queen City.

With two outs in the bottom of the ninth, right-handed hitting Carney Lansford—a former American League batting champion—took a ball, outside, from the lefty Myers. Myers took the return throw from his catcher and stalked all the way around the mound, adrenaline pumping.

The second pitch was another ball, not even close to the strike zone. Before throwing the ball back to Myers, Oliver stepped in front of the plate and motioned with his hands for Myers to calm down.

---

3. In the clubhouse later, Todd Benzinger crowed for everyone to hear: "Who bunts on an oh-and-two pitch? A team of destiny bunts on an oh-and-two pitch—and beats it out!"
4. He didn't make a habit of coming up empty. In his 13-year big league career, Morris hit .356 with the bases loaded.

Myers, excitable in the best of circumstances, took a deep breath to calm himself, but it was useless. When Lansford hit a little dribbler to the left side, foul by at least fifteen feet, Myers sprinted in the direction of the ball as if he were going to make a play on it. In the Reds dugout, players and coaches were pacing nervously. Some moved up to the top step, ready to sprint onto the field if Cincinnati's closer could get the final out.

Fastball. Lansford swung and popped it up in foul territory behind first base. Benzinger backpedaled, looked up, and the ball dropped into his glove. Cincinnati—who had been in first place every single day of the regular season, earning the nickname "Wire-to-Wire Reds"—had shocked baseball by sweeping the mighty Oakland A's in the World Series.

Players streamed from the dugout, jumping on each other in the middle of the field. Sabo leapt up and down, over and over and over, as if he wasn't sure what to do with himself. Hatcher, back from the hospital in a t-shirt (and with his hand wrapped) congratulated everyone he could find. Near the dugout, Piniella stood and watched for a moment, soaking in the scene, before joining his team on the field.

Rijo was named World Series Most Valuable Player after allowing just one run in two starts and striking out 15. The rest of Cincinnati's pitching staff was outstanding, as well. The A's collectively hit .207 and didn't score after the third inning in any of the games.

"These guys [the Reds] were on time, Jack," said Oakland closer Dennis Eckersley, in his inimitable style. "I don't think too many people could have beaten them."

Rickey Henderson, the Athletics' MVP leadoff hitter, agreed: "Somebody forgot to tell us it was the Reds' year."

Before the season, Eric Davis had talked wistfully about the possibility of winning a championship someday. "I'd like to drink champagne in October," he said. "I dream of that kind of stuff. You see the guys run out on the field, you know the excitement and joy they're feeling. I always picture myself pouring champagne on people's heads and jumping for joy and everybody's watching. That's prime time. That's where I want to be."

Now, Davis' teammates were engaged in precisely that sort of celebration, and he was stuck in the intensive care unit at Merritt Hospital in Oakland. Davis had suffered a lacerated kidney; he had to stay behind in the hospital while his teammates flew home. "That's the only thing that takes some of the luster off this," Piniella said.

"When he gets well," Hatcher added, "we'll all be back in Cincinnati and there'll be another party."

But two days later, Davis was still in the hospital, still in intensive care.[5] Back in Cincinnati, Reds fans came out on a rainy Monday afternoon, lined eight people deep in some places on Fifth Street for a ticker-tape parade and rally. An estimated crowd of 12,000 crammed close in Fountain Square to hear team president and CEO Marge Schott, Lou Piniella, and mayor Charles Luken make brief remarks.

Then the players took over. "You guys are the greatest!" yelled Rob Dibble. "You believed in us when nobody else in America did!"

Even the normally quiet Chris Sabo got excited: "We kicked their asses four straight! We got the ring!"

But the biggest cheers of the afternoon came when Reds coach Tony Pérez held up Eric Davis' No. 44 jersey.

Twenty-five years later, more than 30 members of the Wire-to-Wire Reds gathered at Great American Ballpark for a reunion and a weekend-long celebration of that glorious season. Fans packed the stadium to pay homage to the team that broadcaster Marty Brennaman called, "My favorite team of all time."

To one attendee, the reunion was particularly special, since he hadn't participated in the original party. In fact, it was noted that some of the biggest smiles of the weekend appeared on the face of Eric Davis.

5.   Davis would ultimately spend 11 days in hospitals following the World Series, eventually making a full recovery.

3

4,192

"Pete Rose is baseball."
— Major League Baseball commissioner Peter Ueberroth

September 11, 1985, shortly after noon: As he often did, Pete Rose wandered into Flanagan's Landing, a watering hole located on Second Street in Cincinnati. Rose shook some hands, slapped a couple of backs, and accepted the well-wishes of a few excited patrons. He then sat down and ordered a bowl of vegetable soup, which he tried to eat in silence.

Less than 24 hours later, Second Street would be renamed "Pete Rose Way."

2:30 PM: Pete arrived at Riverfront Stadium. Since being named player-manager the previous season, Rose had a physical office adjacent to the clubhouse. Things were quiet, more than five hours before game time, but no one let Rose pass without offering at least a brief "hello."

Rose had just spoken with his friend and legal advisor Reuven Katz. Katz had watched the previous night's game, when Rose went 0-for-4 in his first opportunity to get career hit No. 4,192, and break Ty Cobb's all-time record in front of the home fans.

"Last night," Katz told Rose. "That was the first time I ever saw you play when it looked like you weren't having fun. Have fun with it."

"He was absolutely right," Rose said later.

4:31 PM: As he always did before games, Pete met with the media. Over the last few months, the number of reporters at these pregame press conferences had swelled. The country was caught up in Rose's quest, which reached a fever pitch three days before, when Rose collected two hits against the Cubs at Chicago's Wrigley Field to tie Cobb's career mark.

Now everyone was on edge, waiting for the moment when baseball's history books would be rewritten. Rose had a prediction for the press. "I don't think I'll go 0-for-4 again tonight," he said.

5:23 PM: Finally, after answering every question, Rose dressed and stepped out onto the artificial turf. Painted hash marks were still visible from the Bengals' season opener three days earlier.

Pete took his customary spot at first base and loosened up his aging body with a few ground balls. He also tried to loosen himself up in a figurative sense, joking with photographers and trying to keep the tension at bay. Rose made a conscious decision: the game had been fun every single day for nearly 40 years. Why should that change now?

5:44 PM: Pete stepped into the cage for pregame batting practice with a smile on his face. It was a familiar ritual, practiced almost daily each summer since 1963.

Back then, Rose hit with the likes of Frank Robinson and Vada Pinson, by necessity. As a rookie, Rose had been frozen out by most of his Reds teammates, who had seen him as a cocky greenhorn trying to steal the roster spot of popular veteran second baseman Don Blasingame. They resented the "Charlie Hustle" attitude, and how Rose ran to first after getting walked. They called him a hot dog.

Robinson and Pinson, who were already established big leaguers, had taken Rose under their wing. As two of the first black stars for the Reds, they knew what it was like to be ostracized—how it felt to need friends and mentors. Rose never forgot the kindness they showed to a raw rookie, and he sought to return the favor to young players throughout his career.

On this day, Rose was hitting in a group with Eddie Milner, Nick Esasky, and Dave Concepción. After 12 minutes and a few rounds of swings, Pete headed back to the clubhouse, where he shut his office door. He would not get another quiet moment until many hours later.

"Pete is Mr. Cincinnati and Mr. Baseball."

—Reds president Marge Schott

"If my kid wanted to play sports, I'd bring him out to watch Pete Rose and tell him that's the way to play the game, whether it's baseball, football, basketball, or whatever."

—umpire Bruce Froemming

"It was like something from The Natural. *The Goodyear Blimp was directly overhead. There were a few clouds in the sky with a pinkish tint. It was a perfect setting. It was like it was meant to be."*

—umpire Ed Montague

7:46 PM: The game began more than 15 minutes late; there were long lines at the stadium gates, and the Reds wanted to make sure everyone could get to their seats before the first pitch. Finally, Rose, the first baseman, emerged from the Reds dugout, dribbling a baseball on the bouncy turf.

Moments later, Cincinnati's rookie left-hander Tom Browning delivered a first-pitch strike to San Diego's Garry Templeton, and the game was underway. Browning, en route to a 20-win campaign, made quick work of the Padres in the first.

7:59 PM: With one out in the bottom of the first inning, Rose approached the plate. The crowd rose to their feet in unison as Rose stood outside the batter's box, taking short practice swings. He settled into his familiar crouch on the first base side of the plate and took a ball from Padres starter Eric Show. As he had done so many times in his brilliant career, Rose stared the baseball all the way back into the catcher's mitt.

"If you have a lump in your throat, you're only human," said Reds TV play-by-play man Ken Wilson.

8:01 PM: With the count 2-and-1, Show delivered a slider on the inside part of the plate, and Rose lined it into left-center field for a single—hit number 4,192. Rose sprinted around first base, then returned to the bag. Fireworks exploded overhead and his teammates streamed out of the dugout in unison.[1] Tony Pérez and Dave Concepción, the last remaining teammates from the Big Red Machine, lifted Rose onto their shoulders.

Marge Schott presented Rose with a brand-new red Corvette that emerged from beyond the outfield fence. The license plate read: "PR 4192."

8:06 PM: Rose stood on first base, looking like the loneliest man in the world, just wanting the game to resume. The fans wouldn't let

---

1. One player even came out of the San Diego dugout to shake Rose's hand: outfielder Bobby Brown. "I wasn't going to miss this moment," Brown said. "I felt it was such a great accomplishment that I had to do something. I told him I was happy to be in the same park and on the same field with him."

that happen. The ovation got louder and louder, so Rose waved to the crowd over and over, then shifted his helmet from hand to hand. It was the first time Rose had ever appeared unsure of what to do on a baseball field.

Wave after wave of cheers from the 47,237 admirers rained down, as Rose fought his emotions. Eventually, he looked up to the chilly September sky. That's when the tears began streaming down his face.

"I was doing all right until I looked up and started thinking about my father," said Rose. Harry Francis Rose, who had been so instrumental in shaping Pete as a ballplayer, who had taught the youngster how to switch-hit, had passed away in 1970. "I saw him up there. Right behind him was Ty Cobb. Regardless of what you think, Ty *is* up there. My dad was in a front-row seat."[2]

He turned to first-base coach Tommy Helms, his longtime teammate and friend of 20-plus years. Helms was now the Reds' first-base coach, and the only other Red with business at first base. Rose buried his head in Helms' shoulder and sobbed. "I don't know what to do," Rose said.

"That's okay, Boss," Helms replied. "You're number one. You deserve it all."

In the dugout, Reds catcher Dave Van Gorder stood next to Rose's son, 15-year-old Pete Rose, Jr. "Obviously, the emotions at that point had reached a pinnacle. I said, 'Go out there, you have to go out there.'"

After six minutes of screaming, the applause had nearly died down when Petey Rose—wearing an identical No. 14 uniform as his father—emerged from the dugout. That set the crowd off again. Rose's tears returned as he embraced his son.[3]

As is so often the case in baseball, this was a night for fathers and sons. Just before play resumed, first base umpire Ed Montague reached over and shook Rose's hand. "He said he was thinking about his dad," Montague said. "I could appreciate him thinking about his father. I could feel that emotion."

Montague was thinking about his own father, Eddie, who he had just spoken with by telephone earlier in the day. The elder Montague, 80

---

2.   After the game, Rose talked at length about his father. "My dad would probably have said, 'Nice hitting, but why did you leave the guy on third base with one out?' He'd have patted me on the back and given me five, and kicked me in the butt for drinking champagne."

3.   Nearly 12 years later, on September 1, 1997, little Petey made his major league debut on that same field, hitting seventh and playing third base for the Reds. Wearing his father's No. 14 once again, the younger Rose went 1-for-3 with a walk.

September 11, 1985: Pete Rose laces a line drive for hit No. 4,192, breaking Ty Cobb's all-time record, in Cincinnati. (AP Photo/File)

years old at that time, had been a shortstop with Cleveland in 1928 when he played against Cobb, in the Hall of Famer's final season.

8:08 PM: Steve Garvey leaned over, patted Rose on the helmet, and said, "Thanks for the memories." Rose took his lead off first, and play resumed. Shortly thereafter, he was stranded at third.

8:38 PM: Rose received yet another standing ovation in the bottom of the third, when he again batted with one out. Show, seemingly rattled, issued a base on balls and Rose sprinted to first base. He advanced to third on Dave Parker's bloop hit into left field, then scored when Nick Esasky grounded a ball up the middle for a fielder's choice. Cincinnati led 1–0.

9:34 PM: As a brash rookie in 1963, Rose had failed to collect a hit in his first 16 plate appearances in the big leagues. Rose's confidence never waned. The day before his 22nd birthday, he finally collected that first major league hit, a triple leading off the bottom of the eighth against Pittsburgh hurler Bob Friend.

Now, more than 22 years later, Rose batted in the bottom of the seventh inning with the Reds still clinging to that 1–0 lead. Rose slapped a line drive down the left-field line. The ball bounced away from Padres left fielder Carmelo Martinez, and when the dust settled, Rose was standing on third with a triple. It was the 133rd triple of his career, and the 4,193rd hit.

Two batters later, Esasky lifted a fly ball to center field and Rose tagged and sprinted home. On a night that he would never forget, Rose had scored the only two runs of the game.

10:03 PM: With two outs in the ninth inning, Garvey popped a ball up into foul territory. Rose, hustling until the very end, made a valiant effort to reach over the railing in the Reds dugout, but was unable to come up with a spectacular play to end the game.

Until a moment later, when he did just that. Garvey grounded one hard into the hole between first and second. Rose dove to his right, stabbed the ball and—while lying on his back—made a perfect throw to pitcher Ted Power, who was covering first.

Rose had earned one final ovation.[4]

"This is beyond Pete Rose and beyond Cincinnati. This is for baseball, the whole game. This thing will last for eternity."
—former Reds manager Sparky Anderson

"I think of Pete Rose as somebody who has given his life to baseball.... He should bypass the Hall of Fame and go straight to the Smithsonian."
—Dodgers/Padres 1B Steve Garvey

"Woofs and licks, Schottzie."
—inscription on a punch bowl ladle given to Rose
by Schott in celebration of his achievement.

4. After the game, Rose received a telephone call in the clubhouse from President Ronald Reagan. "Sir," Rose said, "if you had been here tonight, you'd know why we think this is the baseball capital of the world right here in Cincinnati, Ohio."

4

PROFESSIONAL BASEBALL IS BORN

It wasn't an Opening Day like you would see today. No parades, no ceremonial first pitches. No mascots, no fireworks. No, there weren't all the bells and whistles, but it was an historic Opening Day nonetheless. For the first time, a baseball club fielded a full team of professional players.

The game was played at Union Grounds, located in front of the area now housed by the Cincinnati Museum Center.[1] Just a few hundred fans—mostly men, though there were some women wearing showy outfits and hats—had paid 25 cents, either in coin or paper "shinplasters," for admission. The spectators sat in the main grandstand—nicknamed "The Grand Duchess"—and a number of the patrons' carriages were parked on the field, on the right-field grass.

The Cincinnati Base Ball Club took the field clad in white flannel shirts with a "C" on the front, knee length knickers, and the famous long red stockings that had inspired the club's nickname. That afternoon, they would face a team who has been lost to history, the Great Westerns of Cincinnati.

The man who had put together the first all-professional nine, placing Cincinnati squarely at the forefront of the sporting world, was not a native Cincinnatian, or even an American for that matter. Harry Wright had been born in Sheffield, England, some 34 years before. Wright immigrated with his family to New York at age three and, following in his father's footsteps, displayed a keen talent for cricket as a teenager.

It was cricket that brought Wright to Cincinnati in 1865, when he was named the club professional for the Cincinnati Cricket Club. One year later, he was named the "captain"—essentially an amalgam of a current-day manager and general manager—of the newly-formed Cincinnati Base Ball Club, for whom he also played outfield and "change pitcher" (what we would call a relief pitcher today).

---

1. Union Grounds was originally used for cricket, and it was flooded in the winter to permit ice skating. During the 1869 season, it seated 4,000 fans, though thousands more crowded in for some games. There was no outfield fence; all three of Cincinnati's Opening Day home runs were of the inside-the-park variety.

CINCINNATI REDS

The Red Stockings had been enormously popular in 1868, going 36-7 under Wright's direction and establishing the team as one of the best in the country. Before the 1869 season, the Club's members made the unprecedented decision to field a team consisting entirely of professional ballplayers, hoping to compete with the top teams in the east (their only losses the season before came against clubs from New York, Philadelphia, and Washington).

Harry Wright set out to put together the best team money could buy, bringing in six new players—the roster consisted of just 10 players that year—including his younger brother, George. George Wright was considered one of the greatest players of the day, and he was more than happy to leave his career as an engraver to accept a contract for $1,400 to play shortstop for the Red Stockings.

Even before the season, expectations were high. The *New York Clipper* extolled the virtues of Harry Wright's collection of baseball talent, noting that: "Contestants for the championship will have to keep one eye trained toward Porkopolis."

The club from Porkopolis did not disappoint in the season opener. Though most expected a blowout victory, the Great Westerns kept the game close early, and it was 7-4 through three innings. In the fourth, the Red Stockings blew the game open by scoring 15 runs. In the end, George Wright, Andy Leonard, and 19-year-old Cal McVey had all homered, leading the Red Stockings to a 45-9 victory over the Great Westerns.

Despite opening in such a dominant fashion, not everyone was impressed. After another early-season contest, the *Enquirer* had this harsh review: "[The] playing on both sides was very poor. There was quite a large number of spectators present, but the enthusiasm of last summer was lacking."

There was plenty of enthusiasm in other cities as the Red Stockings began their eagerly anticipated month-long tour of the East Coast on May 31. On June 15, Cincinnati played the New York Mutuals, considered to be the best team in Gotham. The Mutuals featured star outfielder John Hatfield, who had left Cincinnati on unhappy terms just months before. The Red Stockings won in exciting fashion by an unimaginably low score of 4-2.

Cincinnati won all 20 games of the eastern tour and returned home to an exuberant city. By the end of the 1869 season, the Red Stockings had defeated all comers to finish with a perfect record of 57–0. George Wright cemented his status as perhaps the best player of the era by leading the team with a .633 batting average, 304 hits, and 49 home runs.[2]

George's big brother "only" batted .493 that season, but Harry's impact on the game was much more lasting.[3] As legendary baseball writer and historian Bill James said of Harry Wright, "Harry didn't play in the major leagues; he just invented them."

The same could be said of the Cincinnati Red Stockings. What they did on May 4, 1869, was integral to the evolution of the game that we know and love today, and it is memorialized every spring when the Reds open the season at home, in honor of Cincinnati's status as the birthplace of professional baseball.

2. If those stats look gaudy, it's because they are. But remember, in 1869, pitchers pitched underhand from 45 feet away, and none of the fielders wore gloves.

3. Though both of the Wright brothers would ultimately be elected to the National Baseball Hall of Fame. George was inducted in the second class, in 1937. Harry didn't join him in Cooperstown until 1953. Both were inducted into the Reds Hall of Fame in 2005.

5

BACK-TO-BACK NO-HITTERS

When he awoke on the morning of June 11, 1938, Johnny Vander Meer was about as unknown as a major league ballplayer could be. If the 23-year-old left-hander had developed any reputation in his season-plus with the Reds, it was for a live fastball and an inability to throw strikes with any regularity.

Five days later, Vander Meer was one of the biggest stars in the sporting world.

It was Knothole Day at Crosley Field, and the crowd of 10,311[1] included a sizable number of youth baseball players eager to watch their Reds take on the Boston Bees. Vander Meer took the mound sporting a 5–2 record. After a rough few weeks at the beginning of the season, Vander Meer had pitched three consecutive complete games, lowering his ERA to 2.77.

In the top of the first, Boston right fielder Gene Moore grounded out to Reds third baseman Lew Riggs, and Vander Meer was off to the races. He retired the first nine Bees in order before walking Moore to lead off the fourth. Vander Meer erased him with a double play, and through four innings, he had faced the minimum number of Boston batters.

As the game progressed, many of those in attendance were completely unaware that Cincinnati's pitcher had not yet allowed a single hit, since the scoreboard at Crosley Field didn't display the number of hits for each team.[2] In fact, Vander Meer himself didn't realize he had a no-hitter going until the seventh; as he took the mound, Boston manager Casey Stengel and coach George Kelly yelled to him from the visitor's dugout, kidding Vander Meer for not allowing the Bees to get any hits.

"My arm seemed to become stronger as the game went along," Vander Meer said later. "I had excellent control of my curve in the final four rounds, which made my fastball doubly effective. After I passed the eighth round without allowing a hit, I put everything I had on every pitch in the ninth."

1. The Reds average home crowd was just 9,361 that season.
2. Crosley Field didn't add the traditional scoreboard elements of "hits" and "errors" until the late 1940s.

INSIDE THE MOMENT

The game in Brooklyn was not broadcast on radio back in Cincinnati, so the local fans had no idea that history was being made by their Redlegs. At 11:42 PM, this announcement was made: "We may have a little surprise for you. Vandy has hung up a new record—another no-hit game."

Later, Reds radio announcer Red Barber would remember being awakened a number of times during the night by telephone calls from excited fans.

Vander Meer faced three pinch-hitters in the ninth, as Stengel used every weapon in his arsenal in an attempt to scratch out a hit. Bob Kahle began the inning by grounding out, then Harl Maggert struck out. When Ray Mueller ended things with an easy groundout to third, fans poured out of the Crosley Field stands and mobbed Vander Meer on the mound. His teammates lifted him onto their shoulders and carried him into the dugout. Hundreds of spectators milled in front of the dugout, yelling their approval.

For most players, pitching a gem like that would be the highlight of a career. Johnny Vander Meer was just getting started.

Nearly 40,000 fans squeezed into Brooklyn's Ebbets Field four days later. It was a night that would go down in baseball history, but not for the reason that most anticipated.

Before the game, fans enjoyed fireworks, along with a parade replete with marching bands and a color guard. Ohioan Jesse Owens, only a couple of years removed from winning four gold medals at the Berlin Olympics, laced on his track shoes and raced the Reds' Lee Gamble and Brooklyn's Ernie "Chief" Koy.[3] Even the recently retired Babe Ruth showed up. The festivities had nothing to do with Johnny Vander Meer, though. This was the first night baseball game in Brooklyn; in fact, it was the first major league night game anywhere outside of Cincinnati.

Vander Meer had personal reasons to be excited about the game. His parents were in attendance, the first time they had ever seen their son pitch in the big leagues. In addition, almost 500 friends and well-wishers (a quarter of the town) had made the 30-mile trek from Vander

---

3. Owens gave the players a 10-yard head start, but still won the race. He also delighted the crowd with exhibitions in the 100-yard hurdles and broad jump.

Meer's hometown of Midland Park, New Jersey, to present "The Dutch Master" with a wristwatch and to see him pitch. Friends and family were fortunate to be in attendance; more than 20,000 fans were turned away as the fire department ordered the general admission gates closed an hour before game time.

If Vander Meer had any nerves associated with all the hoopla, he never showed them once the game began, finally, at 9:20 PM. The Reds jumped out to an early 4–0 lead, and Johnny was mowing down Brooklyn hitters while barely breaking a sweat. Through eight innings, the Dodgers had only hit five balls out of the infield, and hadn't come close to a hit.[4]

With each successive inning, Brooklyn fans got louder and louder, as they realized they were witnessing something special, albeit from the visiting team. In the later innings, Reds manager Bill McKechnie ordered Bucky Walters to begin warming up. When the crowd saw Walters loosening in the bullpen, they booed lustily.

While the crowd was giving Walters a hard time, Vander Meer was trying to focus on the task at hand in the face of a throng of photographers, who harassed the man of the hour when he refused to pose for pictures during the top of the eighth. Ultimately, the umpires chased away the cameramen, and let Vander Meer get back to work.[5]

Indeed, there was still work to be done. Vander Meer emerged from the dugout to cheers in the bottom of the ninth, but he was clearly nervous. Brooklyn's leadoff hitter, left fielder Buddy Hassett, worked the count to three balls before grounding out weakly down the first-base line. With one away, however, Vander Meer proceeded to issue free passes to the next three Dodger hitters. The Reds had a 6–0 lead by this point, but a grand slam would make things too interesting.

McKechnie walked to the mound to talk to Vander Meer. The Cincinnati infielders surrounded the duo. The manager told his pitcher to take his time, relax, and not worry. McKechnie gave Vander Meer a couple of pats on his shoulder, then returned to the dugout.

Not particularly sophisticated strategic advice, perhaps, but it calmed the youngster's nerves. He induced a grounder to Riggs, and the third sacker threw quickly to catcher Ernie Lombardi to record the

---

4. Although Vander Meer did retain his customary wildness, walking eight hitters, five of them in the final three frames.
5. Photographers had the run of the field—at least foul territory—in those days.

Johnny Vander Meer warms up before the first night game ever played at Ebbets Field. (AP Photo)

force out at home. With two outs, Leo Durocher lifted a fly ball to deep right field that curved just foul. With two strikes, Vander Meer delivered a curveball that Lombardi thought had caught the edge of the plate, and when umpire Bill Stewart called it a ball, the Cincinnati dugout went ballistic. Vander Meer shrugged it off, and on the next pitch—a fastball—Durocher launched a fly ball to center field for the final out. Cincinnati's young hurler had accomplished what the newspapers called a "Vander Miracle"—back-to-back no-hitters.

Fans vaulted over the railings and rushed onto the field, with hundreds attempting to shake Vander Meer's hand. Teammates (with help from several New York policemen) escorted Vander Meer through the crowd and into the dugout where he was greeted by a "Nice going, kid" from Ruth. At the same time, autograph seekers converged upon Johnny's parents, who were seated behind the dugout.[6]

Back in the clubhouse, Vander Meer talked with reporters as team trainer Doc Rhode rubbed his now-famous left arm. "I was much faster tonight than last Saturday," he said. "My curveball also was breaking sharper. I realized after the fifth inning that I had a splendid chance to turn in another no-hitter, and after that just kept fogging 'em in. I felt a little tired in the final two heats, and it was certainly a relief to me when I turned around and saw Harry [Craft] circling under Durocher's fly."

Vander Meer had become an immediate sensation.[7] Overwhelmed by the attention, he finally made his way back to his parents' modest two-story home in New Jersey in the early morning hours. Unable to sleep, he tumbled out of bed at 5:00 AM and went fishing with his best friend, Orrie Van Dyke, Midland Park's police chief.

While John was fishing, his parents were once again subject to an onslaught of well-wishers, reporters, and photographers.[8] His father, Jacob, was customarily curt in his comments: "I'm proud of him. As long as he behaves himself, it's okay." Johnny's mother, Kathy, was more exuberant. "I'm the happiest woman in Midland Park," she said, "and maybe in the world too, but all I want to do is get away from you fellows. You make me nervous."

---

6. Which raises the question: precisely what type of person begs a player's parents for an autograph?
7. Over the next few days, Vander Meer received offers to endorse breakfast foods, clothes pins, and everything in between. He even received a $1,000 offer to appear on the Rudy Vallee radio program. Vander Meer turned Vallee down.
8. In the interest of ensuring the completeness of the historical record, we are compelled to note that Vander Meer caught four pickerel that day.

CINCINNATI REDS

The Reds didn't return to Cincinnati until July 1 (Vander Meer's streak was broken on the long road trip), but the fervor over his incredible feat had not diminished in the meantime. City officials organized a celebratory reception for the club at Union Terminal. There was a gigantic "Welcome Home" banner with the Reds logo, red and white bunting, music, and speeches by local dignitaries such as mayor James G. Stewart and team owner Powel Crosley. A throng of excited Reds fans crammed into every available space, even standing on the concrete walls surrounding the station plaza. They screamed and shouted for their Reds, and for their newest ace pitcher.

The celebration over Johnny Vander Meer's incredible achievement continues to this day. It remains one of the signature moments in baseball history.

6

BIRTH OF A DYNASTY: 1975 WORLD CHAMPS

The morning after Game 6's drama, the Red Sox, along with all of New England, were still walking on air.

Boston was abuzz (and hung over), but the Reds camp wasn't as down as Boston was up. "They were overly excited—and they should've been—for winning that game," Pete Rose remembered, "but that was their world championship."

Bill Lee was scheduled to start for the Red Sox, but he was still surly about being passed over for the Game 6 start that went to Luis Tiant instead. A control specialist with a wide selection of breaking balls, Lee (17–9, 3.95 ERA) provided a stark contrast to the Reds starter, hard-throwing Don Gullett.

Gullett was the Reds ace (15–4, 2.42), although he'd missed two months with a broken thumb. Still only 24 years old, Gullett was making his 15th career postseason start, and his third of this World Series. He hadn't pitched well in losing Game 1 at Boston, but had rebounded with 8⅔ innings of dominance in Game 5, as the Reds won 6–2.

Gullett himself had also been skipped for Game 6, even though the rain delays would've put him on his normal four days' rest. But in Gullett's case, the delay was due to his manager's faith in him. Sparky wanted Don Gullett on the mound for Game 7.

"I don't know about the fellow for the Red Sox," Sparky bragged pregame, "but sometime after this game, my boy's going to the Hall of Fame." The hype was typical Sparky. Lee's reaction was just as emblematic of his own "Spaceman" persona: "I don't care where Gullett's going, but after this game, *I'm* going to the Eliot Lounge."

Bernie Carbo started the Boston first with a double, high off the Green Monster in left center. He was left stranded at second, but Gullett was uncharacteristically wild from the beginning, missing high with his fastball over and over.

Meanwhile, Lee was cutting through the Reds lineup, including a memorable moment when he made Tony Pérez look foolish on one of the pitcher's trademark "Leephus" blooper pitches. The Reds were able to eke out a few hits, but couldn't get anything going.

Gullett's control problems got him into real trouble in the third. With one out, he walked Carbo, who moved to third on second baseman Denny Doyle's single to right. Carl Yastrzemski grounded the next pitch into right field, scoring Carbo and giving Boston a 1–0 lead. When Ken Griffey missed the cutoff man (for the second straight play), Boston had runners on second and third. With Carlton Fisk and Fred Lynn coming up, Gullett was in a jam.

Pedro Borbon and Jack Billingham jumped up in the Reds bullpen, as Sparky waved four fingers at Johnny Bench: "Put Fisk on." Sparky would take his chances with the left-handed Lynn, and set up the double play.

Power met power, and Gullett won the battle by striking out Lynn with a fastball on the outside corner. It was only a momentary success, however, as Gullett walked Rico Petrocelli and Dwight Evans to force in two more runs. He struck out Burleson to escape the inning, but not before nine men had come to the plate. Gullett had thrown 38 pitches, including four walks and three strikeouts.[1] More important, Boston led 3–0 after three innings.

Gullett worked out of trouble again in the bottom of the fourth. He gave up a leadoff single to Lee, and wild pitched him to second. But Gullett retired Carbo, Doyle, and Yastrzemski without the ball leaving the infield. Gullett's night was over—his spot was up fourth in the fifth inning.

Leading off the Reds half of the fifth, Dave Concepción beat out an infield single. That brought up Griffey, who hit a low, hard one-hopper that handcuffed Boston second baseman Denny Doyle. The hustling Concepción reached third on the error.

The good fortune didn't last long. Lee dug deep, striking out Gerónimo, and getting pinch-hitter Merv Rettenmund to bounce into a 6-4-3 double play. "Most teams would've quit," after such a backbreaker, Rose said. The 1975 Reds, of course, weren't like most teams.

Anderson called on Billingham, who'd gotten key outs in Game 6, and had the stamina to give the Reds a couple innings. Billingham got into—and out of—his own jam, loading the bases before getting Lee

---

1. After Yastrzemski's single, Gullett and the Red Sox went a full 11 minutes and five batters without putting the baseball into play. Not the best approach for Gullett, who had four Gold Glovers playing behind him.

to fly out. The Red Sox were threatening nearly every inning, and the Reds' championship hopes seemed to be dwindling.

With the Reds down 3-0 entering the sixth inning, Pérez approached Anderson, who was pacing and sneaking a cigarette in the tunnel just behind the dugout. Pérez told his manager not to worry, that someone would get on base, and then the Big Dog would hit a bomb.

Completely out of character, Sparky marched into the dugout and gave the team a pep talk during the game. "Look fellas, we've got some outs left. I don't want anyone to panic, don't go up there thinking home run—somebody get on base and Bench or Pérez will hit one out and we'll be back in it."

Rose did his part, grounding a sharp single to right field and raising his Series average to .346. After Morgan flew out, Bench hit a tailor-made double-play ball to short, but Pete Rose was Pete Rose. As always, he slid high and hard into second base, hoping to break up the double play. It worked. Doyle's relay sailed over Yaz's head and into the first-base stands. Rose was out on the force play, but Bench was awarded second on the overthrow, and the inning was still alive for Pérez.[2]

The Big Dog had taken Lee's blooper pitch earlier for a strike, but wasn't going to let that happen again. When Lee came back with that blooper pitch—a big, obvious one with no deception, Pérez was ready and waiting.[3]

As Lee quipped, Pérez "counted the seams of the ball as it floated up to the plate, checked to see if [AL President] Lee MacPhail's signature was on it, signed his own name to it, and then jumped all over it." Pérez obliterated it. The ball—assuming it was still in one piece—flew over the Green Monster, over the giant netting behind the Green Monster, and out onto Lansdowne Street. As broadcaster Marty Brennaman remembered

---

2. Rose insisted that he hadn't touched Doyle. "But he had to jump about 10 feet off the ground, and that's why he overthrew." It was Doyle's second error of the game. The Reds, always fundamentally strong, made just two errors for the entire Series.

3. In Johnny Bench's telling, the pitch was "just pure slop."

Pete Rose dives into third base in the ninth inning of Game 7 of the World Series at Fenway Park on October 23, 1975. (AP Photos)

years later, "Tony hit it about seven blocks. They still haven't found that baby yet."

Boston's lead was cut to 3–2. This was every bit a ballgame.

Billingham retired the Red Sox in order in the sixth. Lee came back out for the seventh to face the bottom of the Reds order. He retired Concepción, but walked Griffey. When a blister burst on Lee's throwing hand, Boston manager Darrell Johnson called for left-handed reliever Roger Moret, who got Gerónimo to pop out to shortstop. Sparky sent up Ed Armbrister to hit for Billingham. Griffey stole second easily, and Moret walked Armbrister (season batting average .185) to bring Rose to the plate. Rose lined a single to center, scoring Griffey and tying the game.

Neither team threatened again until the home eighth, when Dwight Evans walked against Reds reliever Clay Carroll. Burleson was next, and he was asked to bunt—something he'd done successfully 17 times during the season—but he failed here, falling behind 0–2. With the bunt off the table, Burleson swung away and hit into a double play.

Down to his final four outs, Johnson wasn't going to waste one of them by letting reliever Jim Willoughby bat. Instead, he called on Cecil Cooper, who'd hit well all year (.311/.355/.544) but was just 1-for-18 in the Series. Cooper fouled out on the first pitch.

The ninth inning of Game 7 of the World Series arrived with the game tied 3–3. Johnson called on rookie left-hander Jim Burton—who hadn't pitched in eight days—to face the left-handed stretch of the Reds lineup: Griffey, Gerónimo, and the pitcher's spot.[4]

A visibly uncomfortable Burton[5] walked Griffey on six pitches, and the Reds had the go-ahead run on base. Sparky called for the sacrifice, and Gerónimo laid down a hard bunt that hugged the third-base line. Third baseman Petrocelli slipped and fell as he picked it up. That eliminated any chance of getting Griffey at second, but Petrocelli made a nice throw from a seated position to retire Gerónimo.

The Reds sent the left-handed Dan Driessen up to pinch-hit. The 23-year-old South Carolinian hadn't done much against left-handed pitching (.130 in 23 at-bats), but he was Sparky's best option.[6] Driessen quickly grounded to second, advancing Griffey to third with two outs.

Up came the red-hot Rose (6 for his last 12), and out came Darrell Johnson. "Good," thought Morgan, as he stood in the on-deck circle. "They're going to walk him." Morgan had dreamed of this chance his whole life.

It wasn't an intentional walk, but Burton pitched Rose carefully—a series of breaking balls and fastballs out of the zone—and Rose did, in fact, work a walk. Morgan strode to the plate as the happiest man in Fenway Park. He was sure it was going to be just like in the backyard—Joe was going to get a hit to win the World Series.

With a 1–1 count, Morgan hit a liner down the left-field line, but it was foul by inches. Morgan fouled off another pitch, then settled in again. Burton threw his strikeout pitch, a nasty, hard-breaking slider headed for the outside corner. Morgan didn't make solid contact, but it was enough. The ball flared into center field for a bloop single. Griffey scored easily,

---

4.   Johnson didn't have many good options to replace Willoughby. Ace reliever Dick Drago had thrown three innings in Game 6, less than 24 hours earlier.

5.   This wasn't just supposition. Burton later told author Doug Hornig, "Warming up, my whole body went numb. It was surreal, like an out-of-body experience. I wasn't ready. I'd hardly pitched all the previous month. I was rusty. When I was warming up, I couldn't get loose. I could tell I didn't have anything."

6.   The other good hitter still on the bench was another left-hander, Terry Crowley, and Sparky wouldn't let him go near left-handed pitching. Of Crowley's 218 plate appearances in two seasons as a Red, 215 were against right-handers.

and by the time Rose reached third with a picture-perfect headfirst slide, the Fenway crowd had fallen silent.

Will McEnaney entered to protect the 4–3 lead in the bottom of the ninth. McEnaney was gathering his thoughts on the stairwell when Sparky approached to explain his plan. Deep in thought and scared to death, the rookie reliever replied in a completely out-of-character way: "Shut up, I know what I'm doing. Leave me alone," he barked. Sparky, choosing his battles as always, just said "Okay" and walked away.

Though terrified, McEnaney retired the Red Sox in order, clinching the Reds' first World Series win in 35 years on a soft Yastrzemski fly ball to Gerónimo in center.

Bench ran toward McEnaney and screamed: "What do we do?!" McEnaney knew. He thrust both arms into the air, then jumped onto his catcher, wrapping his legs around Bench's waist. Finally, six years after Sparky's hiring, four years after Morgan joined as the final puzzle piece, the Big Red Machine had its championship.[7] The Reds celebrated the long-awaited title on the Fenway infield. One person was missing— Sparky. Emotionally and physically drained, he trotted back toward the clubhouse and waited for his team. Away from the cameras, he wept.

7. Sparky later noted that Game 7 was a perfect microcosm of the Big Red Machine. They won with their strengths: speed, power, defense, and relief pitching.

7

CLINCHMAS: 2010 NL CENTRAL CHAMPS

In the 14 seasons after the Reds' 1995 NL Central division championship, Cincinnati had enjoyed only two winning campaigns. In fact, as the 2010 season got underway, Reds fans had suffered through nine consecutive years of losing. It was a franchise that mostly seemed adrift and rarely approached anything resembling competitiveness.

Most experts picked the Reds to finish fourth in a six-team NL Central. The Reds had a stable of talented young players who were beginning to make their mark, but most observers saw the club as at least a year away from seriously contending.

Early on, there was no reason to doubt that analysis. Cincinnati surrendered 17 runs in losing their first two games of the season and by May 2, they were under .500 and already five games out of first. A beaten-down fan base could be forgiven for thinking, "Here we go again."

But then, suddenly, these weren't the same old Reds. On May 3, reserve outfielder Laynce Nix beat the Mets with an 11th-inning walk-off home run. Two days later, shortstop Orlando Cabrera hit a walk-off homer of his own, this time in the 10th inning.

The Reds would go on to win nine of their next 11 games, vaulting into first place. The pennant race was on.

For most of the summer, the Reds and Cardinals duked it out at the top of the Central standings, neither pulling ahead by more than three games. In early August, St. Louis came to town and the clubs literally duked it out, engaging in one of the nastier on-field brawls that you're likely to see.[1] The Cardinals left Cincinnati with a three-game series sweep to retake first place. It was beginning to look like the upstart Reds had met their match.

---

1. The brawl was primed by Reds second baseman Brandon Phillips' comments before the series. His full statement contained a couple of phrases that—while arguably true—used colorful language that is unprintable here, but here's a portion: "I hate the Cardinals...I really hate the Cardinals. Compared to the Cardinals, I love the Chicago Cubs. Let me make this clear—I hate the Cardinals."

But again the baseball world was reminded: these weren't the same old Reds. Cincinnati won their next seven games, and 14 of their next 18. By September, the Reds were eight games ahead of the Cardinals, and a division title was firmly within sight.

A crowd of 30,151 converged on Great American Ball Park on a cool Tuesday night in late September to see if the Reds, needing just one more victory, could wrap up that title. It was a festive atmosphere long before the first pitch was thrown, as eager fans crammed into the plaza outside the park, lining up to buy one of the 7,786 walk-up tickets sold that day. When the Reds took the field at the start of the game, the crowd rose for the first standing ovation of the night.

It would not be the last.

The fans weren't the only ones keyed up for the evening's drama. The players, too, sensed that they were about to embark on something special.

"You try to pretend it is [just another day], but it's not," said manager Dusty Baker before the game. "This game is full of pretending. No, it's not the same as any other day. You strive to get to this point for so very long.

"You run this race and you're one step from the finish line. Anybody that's been in this situation, you're full of anticipation and desire to finish it. It's great that we were in a position to do this at home."

As Edinson Volquez kicked and released his first pitch of the night—a called strike to Houston leadoff hitter (and future Red) Jason Bourgeois—the Reds' ballpark operations staff jumped into action in the Cincinnati clubhouse. Five hundred feet of clear sheeting secured the players' lockers. Case upon case of champagne and beer were wheeled in. Next to the champagne were four large stacks of gray t-shirts, bearing the words "2010 Central Division CHAMPIONS."

Meanwhile, on the field, the Reds were trying to ensure that the celebratory gear wouldn't be packed away for another night. Speedy center fielder Drew Stubbs led off the bottom of the first with a walk, stole second, and later scored on an error. The Reds had grabbed an early 1–0 lead.

In the top of the second, Houston parlayed three singles and two bunts into a couple of runs. In the third, the Astros nearly ballooned their lead even further, when Carlos Lee hit a blast to deep center field. Stubbs turned quickly and sprinted to the fence.

"When it was hit, I honestly didn't think I had a chance," said Stubbs. "But it hung up long enough for me to get to the wall."

Once there, Stubbs timed his leap perfectly and, with his head higher than the top of the eight-foot center-field wall, grabbed the ball for out number two.

"That kept us in the game," Baker said. "It looked like Stubby had wings. Maybe somebody had wings for him."

After a shaky start, Volquez had settled down, allowing just two runs on seven hits through six innings. In the bottom half of the sixth, the Reds loaded the bases on singles from Cabrera and Joey Votto, and a Scott Rolen walk. Brandon Phillips collected an infield single on another weak grounder to third, plating the tying run. With an opportunity to break the game open, however, Jay Bruce grounded into an inning-ending double play.

As Bruce walked back toward the home dugout to retrieve his cap and glove, he silently hoped that he would get another opportunity before the game was over.

Both bullpens held up, and the game entered the ninth inning still tied at two. The buzz throughout the park had barely dulled all evening long, but emotions began to overflow as the Reds took the field for the ninth. Slowly, the crowd began to notice the door to the Cincinnati bullpen swinging open; they erupted when rookie phenom Aroldis Chapman emerged, trotting toward the pitcher's mound. Chapman had just arrived from AAA on August 31, and had bent the National League to the will of his blazing fastball. Houston never had a chance. Chapman, topping out at 103 mph, mowed down the Astros in order, with the GABP crowd screaming with delight on every pitch.

Bruce, the 23-year-old former minor league player of the year who, along with Votto,[2] was expected to lead the Reds back to prominence, stepped back into the batter's box to lead off the bottom of the ninth. The score was still 2–2, and Houston called on lefty Tim Byrdak to face the left-handed-hitting Bruce. The crowd was already on their feet, even before Byrdak looked in to get the sign.

---

2.   Joey Votto had his breakout season in 2010, winning the NL MVP award after hitting .324/.424/.600 with 37 home runs and 113 runs batted in.

Jay Bruce watches his walk-off homer clear the fence. (AP Photo/Al Behrman)

On Byrdak's very first pitch, a fastball on the inside half, Bruce lifted a high fly ball. As the ball soared majestically across the night sky, Bruce dropped his bat, raised his right arm, and lifted a single finger. The ball crashed off the black batter's eye beyond the center-field fence, and for the first time in 15 years, the Cincinnati Reds were champions of the National League Central division.

Bruce's teammates waited at home plate for the budding star to circle the bases, then mobbed him in celebration. The familiar GABP cry of "Bruuuuuuuce" rang out amidst the raucous cheering. As fireworks exploded overhead, the team donned the ubiquitous championship hats and t-shirts, continuing to hug anyone and everyone.

"You can't dream about hitting a walk-off to win the division," Bruce said. "It was unbelievable."

Joey Votto echoed that sentiment. "I'm so happy for him," Votto said. "To clinch a playoff spot with a home run in the ninth.... Are you kidding me? It couldn't have happened to a better guy."

Eventually, the players made their way into the clubhouse, where they cracked open the bubbly and began dousing each other. But outside, the fans weren't leaving. No one wanted to go home. The crowd kept cheering and kept chanting and kept celebrating. As if it had been a rock concert, they were begging for an encore, and the Reds obliged them.

One by one, the Cincinnati players began streaming back out onto the field, some wearing ski goggles, all of them soaked with champagne. They took a victory lap around the field, shaking hands with the delighted Reds faithful. It was a night that had been a long time coming, and no one wanted it to end.

While the Reds weren't yet used to winning championships, they were certainly accustomed to late-game heroics. The victory was one of a league-leading 45 come-from-behind wins for the young Reds.[3]

"How about that?" said Scott Rolen. "Why not? With this team, that seems to be the way."

Indeed it did, and September 28, 2010, would forever remain etched in the hearts and minds of Reds fans as "Clinchmas."

---

3. It was certainly a young club; 14 of the 25 players on the postseason roster were 27 years old or younger, including Votto, Bruce, Johnny Cueto, and Homer Bailey. But veterans like Scott Rolen, Ramon Hernandez, Jonny Gomes, and Bronson Arroyo all made key contributions, too.

8

JOHNNY BENCH SAYS GOOD-BYE

At precisely 6:11 PM on Saturday, September 17, 1983, a door opened in the right-field fence at Riverfront Stadium. As Johnny Lee Bench emerged, he looked up at the sellout crowd and at the first of seven standing ovations that he would receive before the evening was through. He slowly made his way toward a platform that had been constructed near second base, walking on a Cincinnati-red carpet that had been rolled out just for him.

Bench waved to the crowd. He tipped his cap, then looked up at the stage, where Reds broadcaster Marty Brennaman and local TV personality Bob Braun, both in tuxedos, waited and smiled. As the cheers of 53,790 grateful Reds fans rained down, Bench paused, as if overwhelmed, before climbing up to the platform.

Then he bowed to the fans. Four times, to each point of the compass—east, west, north, south—Bench bowed, thanking the fans who were themselves thanking Bench for 17 amazing seasons of baseball.

"If you wished all these things," Bench had said before the game, "you couldn't wish this good."

Even Bench couldn't have wished for what was to come next.

Johnny Bench had a history of making wishes, and seeing them come to life. When Bench was an 11-year-old pitcher and catcher for the Binger Bobcats, his teammates teased him because, when he wasn't practicing his throwing or his hitting, Bench practiced his autograph. Over and over and over, Bench would sign his autograph, in notebooks and school books. The other kids on the team thought that was hilarious. But Bench knew something they didn't.

Soon thereafter, sitting in the back seat of an Oldsmobile that carried him and two of his coaches—Hugh Haley and Del Carey—back to Bench's home town of Binger, Oklahoma, after another win, Bench let them in on the secret. "You know," he said, "I'm gonna be a big league ballplayer someday. And I'm going to invite you both there when I make it." Coach Haley just nodded. "Sure," he said.

CINCINNATI REDS

Six years later, after Bench hit .675 one season in high school (and pitched a no-hitter in American Legion ball), Haley drove Bench up to Oklahoma State University for a tryout. Oklahoma State said thanks, but no thanks. On the drive back to Binger, Bench was unfazed. All he wanted to do was play professional baseball, anyway.

Bench got that chance when the Reds picked him in the second round of the 1965 draft, the first amateur baseball draft in the game's history.[1] After some negotiation, the Reds made their final offer: a bonus in the neighborhood of $30,000 and a college scholarship that Bench could use whenever he wanted. Bench's father, Ted, rejected that offer immediately, but his son took him aside. "Dad, I was built to play ball." The son prevailed, and Johnny signed with the Reds that day.

Bench made his big league debut on August 29, 1967. Reds manager Dave Bristol got one look at the sturdy young catcher and said, famously: "I wish he was twins."

For the next 17 seasons, Bench terrorized pitchers and base runners in the National League. His career was the stuff of dreams, beginning with the 1968 Rookie of the Year Award. Bench would go on to win two NL MVP Awards (1970 and 1972) and earn selection to 14 All-Star Games. He led the league in RBI three times and home runs twice, en route to setting what was then the big league career record for homers by a catcher.

As good as he was at the plate, Bench was even better behind it, revolutionizing the catcher position. Big, athletic, and blessed with enormous hands, Bench popularized the one-handed catch-and-throw style that catchers use to this day, and had the strongest arm in baseball on top of that. Bench's unmatched defensive ability resulted in 10 Gold Glove awards.

In July of 1970, Bench's youth coaches from that long-ago trip in the Oldsmobile opened up their morning mail back in Binger. Each was surprised to find round-trip airline tickets and an invitation from Bench to attend the Major League Baseball All-Star Game in Cincinnati. When Haley and Carey arrived at Riverfront Stadium and took their blue field-level seats, they saw that President Richard Nixon was sitting a couple of rows in front of them.

1. Bernie Carbo, a high school third baseman from Michigan, was Cincinnati's first-round choice. Carbo would go on to play outfield in the majors for more than a decade, reaching the big leagues with the Reds in 1969.

When Bench decided he would retire after the 1983 season, the Reds immediately began planning for a celebration of his career. Tickets for Johnny Bench Night sold out quickly, and the Reds made 2,000 standing-room-only tickets available for purchase the day of the game. When the night arrived—and since Oktoberfest weekend was taking place at the same time—Cincinnati was abuzz. At a pregame press conference, Bench was astonished. "As I was driving down here today," he said, "I thought it was kind of a World Series atmosphere."

It was certainly as close to a World Series atmosphere as this version of the Reds—11 games under .500—was likely to get. The gates opened at 4:35, and an hour later, the St. Leon (Indiana) East Central High School band marched onto the field and began to play. Brennaman and Braun, as masters of ceremony, were supposed to get things underway at 6:10, but no one had accounted for the adoring throngs of Bench fans and their wild cheering.

Once Bench finally made it to the platform and the noise had died down somewhat, Sparky Anderson's recorded voice came over the stadium's public address system, complimenting his old catcher and sending regrets that he couldn't be there. Then former Reds radio announcer Al Michaels was introduced, and a recording of Michaels' famous call of Bench's 1972 NLCS home run was played.

After a congratulatory letter from President Ronald Reagan[2] was read and Hall of Fame catcher Bill Dickey made a surprise appearance, Bench was showered with gifts. There was a two-seat bass fishing boat, which his teammates carried onto the field like pallbearers. There was a new Ford Thunderbird convertible (white with a red number 5 on the side), a two-week golfing vacation to Scotland (complete with knickers to wear on the links), and a $25,000 check for the Johnny Bench Scholarship Fund.

Soon, it was Bench's turn to address the crowd, which prompted another standing ovation, this one lasting more than four minutes. The newspaper account noted that the "ovation rose and fell six times, reaching six separate peaks." Bench blew kisses to the crowd. A tear came to his eye.

Finally, the catcher spoke. "I'm here because I love you. I chose to stay in Cincinnati for one reason. I love the city, the fans, and I was

---

2. "The game is going to miss you, and so will I and all your fans," Reagan wrote.

fortunate to play for the Reds.... I've tried to be the best player I could be, and it was easier because you were in back of me. I am very lucky, honored, and grateful.... I thank you so much, my family thanks you...." Here, Bench stopped, and scanned the crowd. "And I'm going to try like hell to play good for you tonight."

It was another promise he would keep.

Most people expected that the actual game—last-place Reds against the third-place Houston Astros—would be anticlimactic. In fact, the game started late, because Bench still had to take a couple of laps around the stadium in the back of the new convertible, and his father had to throw out the ceremonial first pitch. Eventually, Bench strapped on the catcher's equipment and squatted behind the plate for what would be his 1,742nd and final game as a catcher in the big leagues. Cincinnati's starter, 22-year-old Jeff Russell, took the sign from Bench and delivered the first pitch, a ball to Houston second baseman Bill Doran.[3] The game was underway, and the fans settled into their seats, temporarily. Most assumed the night's excitement was over.

Batting cleanup, Bench walked in the first inning, but the Reds came up empty. Houston scratched across two runs in the top of the second and the Reds still trailed 2–0 when they came to bat in the third. Center fielder Paul Householder singled to left to lead off the inning. One out later, Bench came to the plate.

As the crowd was still rising to its feet, Bench swung and missed for strike one. Quickly, Astros starter Mike Madden delivered his next pitch. Just as quickly, Bench turned on it and hit a top-spinning line drive over the left-field wall, past a homemade banner reading "God Love Him." It was a home run, the 389th—and final—of Bench's career.

As he rounded first base, Bench showed uncharacteristic emotion, punching his right fist into the air, then lifting his index finger.[4] Riverfront Stadium erupted. Bench's homer, on Johnny Bench Night, had just tied the game at 2–2.

Bench singled in the fifth, but the Astros led 4–3 when he flew out leading off the seventh. Shortly thereafter, Reds manager Russ Nixon removed Bench from the game to yet another ovation. Dann Bilardello took over behind the plate, and the Reds finished the game meekly.

---

3. Bench and Russell formed an unlikely battery of the oldest and youngest members of the Reds roster.
4. "You've never seen me do that before in my career," said Bench. "That was for all the people who saw it and will go home and say they saw it for the rest of their lives."

No one in attendance was disappointed with the loss, however. It was a night for the ages.

After the game, a wild party in Bench's honor ensued at the Stouffer's hotel grand ballroom. Friends, teammates, and Reds employees all gathered to celebrate into the wee hours. Bench was one of the last to leave. He later said that he went home, had a big glass of milk and four pieces of pound cake, then collapsed into bed.

The next day, Bench arrived at the stadium just before game time; it was later than he had ever arrived for a game in his entire career, but Bench had gotten permission from Nixon to roll in later than usual. Bench watched the first pitch of the game from the dugout, then retreated into the clubhouse, where a rocking chair had replaced his customary director's chair. According to the papers, Bench spent the game resting his sore muscles after the beating they had taken when he caught the previous night's game.

Bench told a different story. "The sun was just too bright today," he said.

Indeed.

9

1940 WORLD CHAMPS

After decades of futility following the 1919 World Championship, the Reds had finally shown signs of life in the late 1930s. Warren Giles, the club's promising young general manager, hired well-respected manager "Deacon" Bill McKechnie for 1938. A kind, patient man—today, we'd call him a "players' manager"—McKechnie had already won pennants with the Pirates (1925) and Cardinals (1928) and was the incumbent NL manager of the year, having led a lousy Boston Braves team to a winning record in 1937.[1]

McKechnie's specialties were pitching and defense, and he brought them to a Reds team that already had a couple of good hitters in catcher Ernie Lombardi and right fielder Ival Goodman. Together, McKechnie and Giles added key pieces like middle infielder Lonny Frey and pitcher Bucky Walters.

A high school dropout signed from the Philadelphia sandlots, Walters had struggled for several years as a light-hitting third baseman for the Phillies. But on the mound with the Reds, he became the league's most dominating pitcher, as well as its best hitting and fielding pitcher.

The Giles-McKechnie Reds had a balanced veteran roster, and were described by writer Bill James as "a fun organization to be a part of...a team of likable, positive people who played together exceptionally well." In 1938, that group finally broke the .500 barrier, going 82–68, led by Lombardi, who was named NL MVP. In 1939, with the addition of veteran third baseman Billy Werber and an MVP season from Walters, the Reds won 97 games and the organization's first pennant in 21 years. Unfortunately, they were swept in the Series by Joe DiMaggio's Yankees.

Reds fans were stung, but not discouraged. It was easy to write off the loss to inexperience—and the invincibility of the Yankees—which meant that baseball fans in the Queen City had high expectations for 1940.

---

1.   The Braves were lousy in part because they did things like let the manager of the year walk away. McKechnie was elected to the Baseball Hall of Fame in 1962. His 744 wins managing the Reds still ranks second only to Sparky Anderson.

The core of the team would be back for another tour of duty. The team's undisputed star was Lombardi, who everyone expected to rebound after a weak 1939. Pitching aces Walters and Paul Derringer returned, as did the infield of Frank McCormick, Billy Myers, Frey, and Werber.[2]

After joining the club in 1939, Werber had dubbed the agile, slick-fielding group "the Jungle Cats," to build camaraderie and encourage hustle. Werber called himself "Tiger," shortstop Myers was "Jaguar," and second baseman Frey was "Leopard." First baseman McCormick, while graceful and the best defensive first baseman in baseball, didn't hustle enough to merit a nickname, in Werber's view.

After finally proving his worth and being admitted to the club as "Wildcat" (the 6'4", and 205-pound first sacker was initially led to believe he'd be the "Hippopotamus"), a giddy McCormick ran around the team hotel, proudly announcing the honor to every teammate and coach he saw.

The Reds took over first place in the National League on July 6, but the summer was far from calm. Lombardi battled injury for most of July, forcing the Reds to rely heavily on backup catcher Willard Hershberger. As he always did, Hershberger hit well in Lombardi's absence, but on July 31, Walters blew a three-run lead in the ninth inning and lost to the Giants. Hershberger, who had been behind the plate for the meltdown, blamed himself.

Always good-natured but distant from his teammates, Hershberger was an insomniac and a hypochondriac whose father had killed himself 12 years prior. Hershberger had been under a darkening cloud all summer. He remained distraught on the Reds' trip to Boston, his misery only deepening after the club dropped a doubleheader to the Bees.

After a walk-off loss in the second game, a weeping Hershberger told manager Bill McKechnie that he planned to kill himself. The two talked for several hours, and as they parted after dinner, McKechnie believed that Hershberger would be okay, as did reporters and teammates who encountered the catcher the following morning.

Hershberger never made it to the ballpark for the Saturday afternoon doubleheader. After promising teammates and the Reds

---

2.   Best friends on the Reds, Werber and Frey stayed in touch for decades. Both died in 2009. Werber was 100 and Frey was 99.

traveling secretary that he'd "be right out" to the park, Hershberger instead went into his Copley Plaza Hotel bathroom and slit his own throat.

* * *

As they do today, 1940s fans and writers debated just how much impact a manager has on his team's wins and losses. Also just like today, the truth is that the bulk of the manager's job happens before and after the game itself. The job is about managing *people*, not just deciding when to bunt, or when to change pitchers.

McKechnie was almost universally seen as an elite manager of people, even if he was sometimes criticized for his in-game tactics (too many sacrifice bunts and an overly conservative, "by the book" approach). In any event, the "Deacon" was probably one of the few managers, in any era, who could have guided a team through the shock and sadness that enveloped the Reds in the wake of this tragedy.

After receiving the terrible news, McKechnie gathered the Reds in his hotel suite, told them the details of his conversation with Hershberger the day before, and urged them to "win the pennant and vote Hershie's mother a full share of the World Series money."[3]

In Hershberger, the Reds lost not only a teammate and friend but perhaps the league's best backup catcher, a man who hit .316/.356/.381 in three seasons with the club.[4]

Not surprisingly, the team struggled, going 9–11 immediately after the tragedy, but they had built up enough of a lead that they were never seriously challenged for the pennant. But even with a 12-game margin late in the season, McKechnie wasn't able to sit back and relax.

On the season's final weekend, the Reds lost second baseman Frey to a freak injury—the metal lid of the dugout water cooler fell off and broke his toe.[5] Right around the same time, shortstop Myers, exhausted and apparently fed up with his wife's "harassment," went AWOL. Private detectives hired by the Reds tracked him down in Columbus, Ohio, and general manager Giles persuaded his shortstop to return. The Reds

---

3. The players' share of World Series revenue was a major financial incentive in those days. For 1940, the winner's shares were $5,803, while each member of the losing club took home $3,531 (the 2022 Series shares were $516,347 and $296,255). The players decide how to divide the money, awarding full and partial shares, as well as cash bonuses, to members of the team and organization.
4. Hershberger was an incredible contact hitter, striking out a mere 16 times in his entire career.
5. It's probably worth mentioning that the cooler wasn't kicked.

floated a cover story, explaining that Myers was attending to some personal business with the team's permission.

But the Reds' biggest question was also its biggest player, as the 230-lb[6] Lombardi had badly sprained his right ankle on September 15. Not only did the Reds lose the 1938 NL MVP and one of baseball's top right-handed hitters, but with Hershberger gone, the club didn't have a healthy catcher capable of performing at the major league level. Rookie Bill Baker had been a disaster at the plate (.217/.260/.261), and it was too late to trade for a replacement.

So McKechnie and the Reds coaching staff got creative. Very creative. A member of that staff, 40-year-old Jimmie Wilson, came out of retirement and strapped on the catcher's gear. Wilson had caught for 14 seasons in the majors, mostly as a backup, and had been the player-manager of the Phillies from 1934–38.[7]

While a respected baseball man, Wilson was far removed from the field. He'd made only a handful of pinch-hit appearances and caught three innings, combined, in 1938–39, and hadn't played at all in 1940. But Wilson's willingness to step in seemed to inspire his teammates, and the Reds went 12–3 when he played.

Wilson's aging body wasn't as easily motivated. He took a beating from the hard-throwing Reds staff, and pulled a muscle almost immediately upon joining the active roster. By season's end, Wilson was getting multiple hours of therapy and treatment every day, just to take the field.

This is how the Reds entered the 1940 World Series—battered and bruised, but playing well. (They'd gone 29–10 to close the season.) Awaiting them would be the American League–champion Detroit Tigers, who had edged Cleveland and the Yankees to win the pennant. The Reds (100–53) had a much better record than Detroit (90–64), but the teams were a near-perfect contrast.

While the Reds had allowed—by far—the fewest runs in either league, the Tigers had baseball's best offense, led by future Hall of Famers Hank Greenberg (.340, 41 HR, 150 RBI) and Charlie Gehringer (.313, 101 walks vs. 17 strikeouts), along with slugger Rudy York (.316, 33 HR, 134 RBI) and second-year center fielder Barney McCosky (.340, 19

---

6. At least.
7. As the Phillies manager, Wilson had been the man who convinced future Cincinnati ace Bucky Walters to move from third base to the mound.

triples). The Tigers had .300 hitters at five positions, and in Greenberg and York, the AL's top two home run hitters.

The Reds would rely on a great defense, along with the fact that Walters (22–10, 2.48) and Paul Derringer (20–12, 3.06) could start five of the seven games, if the Series went the distance.[8] Tiger manager Del Baker rationalized, not unreasonably, that his club could handle Cincinnati's studs, since they'd consistently hammered Bob Feller, the American League's leader in just about every pitching category.[9]

The Tigers had their own ace, in Louis Norman "Bobo" Newsom. A gregarious, if absent-minded[10] South Carolina farmboy, Newsom was a hard thrower and one of the last practitioners of the old-time windmill windup. He was coming off his best season, where he finished second to Feller in wins, ERA, and strikeouts, and was fourth in voting for the AL MVP.

In 1939, the Series had begun at Yankee Stadium, and the Reds were already down 0–2 by the time their train arrived back home. This year, the city wasn't going to miss an opportunity to enjoy the pageantry and excitement of the Series. Cincinnati hosted the first two games and in customary Queen City fashion, the city reveled in the attention, turning itself out in style for the politicians, baseball legends, and movie stars who poured into town to experience the biggest event in sports.

Hotels were jammed from Lexington, Kentucky, to Dayton, Ohio, with the downtown Cincinnati hotels boasting that they could handle even more guests—albeit on cots in the hallways. The Reds set up folding chairs in foul territory, and sold 3,000 standing-room-only tickets, swelling attendance to 31,793. Crosley Field also hosted 500 sportswriters and 62 Western Union telegraph operators, many in a special press box constructed on the stadium's roof.

Newsom and Derringer faced off in Game 1. A control specialist who relied on an ultra-high leg kick and deceptive windup, Derringer was the Reds second-best starter, but that doesn't tell the entire story. He was also probably the second-best pitcher in the National League.[11] But on

---

8. Across 1939–40, the Reds' two aces had combined to win 94 games, and complete a staggering 114 of their 144 starts.

9. Feller's overall ERA was 2.61. Against Detroit, it was 5.33. Remove Feller's eight games against the Tigers and his ERA would've dropped from 2.61 to 1.96.

10. Newsom was called "Bobo" because that's what he called himself—and almost everyone he met.

11. Bucky Walters was not only the Reds' ace, but the best pitcher in the NL and the league MVP. For his part, But from 1938–40, Derringer finished eighth, third, and fourth in NL MVP voting from voting from 1938–40.

INSIDE THE MOMENT

Despite his remarkable command of the strike zone, Derringer was known for a mirror-image inability to control his temper. He once reportedly knocked out a nurse after he woke up from surgery. A month after Derringer was traded to the Reds in 1933, he got into a pregame, on-field brawl with former Cardinals teammate Dizzy Dean—on Ladies Day at Crosley, of all days. The two had reportedly hated each other for years, perhaps dating to 1931, when the Cardinals general manager sent Dean to the minors to make room for Derringer—meaning that Derringer won a 1931 world champion ring, while Dean spent the summer sweating out 304 IP in the Texas League.

Derringer's worst incident came after a 1936 game in Philadelphia, when he was accused of drunkenly forcing his way into a hotel suite full of American Legion officials and New York dignitaries, then beating the man who tried to throw him out. In the early summer of 1939, the victim secured an $8,000 judgment against Derringer, and until he paid up, Derringer faced the threat of arrest in New York City. Eventually, Derringer and the Reds settled the claim and Derringer was able to start for the NL at the 1939 All-Star Game in New York City.

this day, things quickly fell apart for the Reds. Aided by two Cincinnati errors, the Tigers scored five runs in the second inning, sending Derringer to the showers. The Tigers never looked back, winning 7–2.

But as the Tigers celebrated, tragedy struck the Newsom family. Bobo's father suffered a heart attack in his Cincinnati hotel after the game, and he died a few hours later. While Newsom mourned, the Reds rebounded in Game 2. Walters tossed a complete-game three-hitter, for the Reds' first World Series victory since 1919.

The Series moved to Detroit for Game 3. The Reds' Jim Turner and Detroit's Tommy Bridges dueled for six innings, but the Tigers exploded for four straight hits to open the seventh frame, including homers by York and Pinkie Higgins. That knocked Turner out of the game and Detroit eventually won 7–4. The Tigers led the Series, two games to one.

Derringer returned for Game 4, while the Tigers went with Paul "Dizzy" Trout. Derringer was riding a personal four-game World Series losing streak dating back to his rookie season with the Cardinals in 1931, but on this night, he scattered five hits and two runs over nine innings, while the Reds offense came alive for a 5–2 Cincinnati win. Derringer finally had his World Series "W," but more importantly, the Reds had evened the Series and guaranteed that there would be at least one more game in Crosley Field.

Game 5 marked Newsom's return, while McKechnie countered with 23-year-old Junior Thompson. McKechnie wanted to spare the youngster the pressure of anticipating a World Series start, so he didn't tell Thompson (or anyone else) that he was starting until just before game time. Thompson's wife was so surprised that she passed out cold when the Briggs Stadium public address announcer proclaimed her husband as the starting pitcher.

The strategy may have backfired, as Thompson struggled—he gave up seven earned runs in 4⅓ innings—while Bobo was dominant. Pitching to honor his father's memory, Newsom shut out the Reds on three hits. The Series returned to Cincinnati, where the Reds would need to win both remaining games.

Though his back was against the wall, McKechnie had his chess pieces deployed precisely according to plan: Walters and Derringer for Games 6 and 7.

The first half of the plan came together like a McKechnie dream—Walters shut out the Tigers, allowing just five hits and two walks, while the infield defense turned three double plays. Walters himself displayed his full resume, hitting a home run and fielding his position well. Reds 4, Tigers 0.

It all came down to Game 7, with both managers bringing their remaining aces back: Derringer on two days' rest; Newsom on only one.[12]

Unlike the first six games, Game 7 was a tight, well-played contest from start to finish. The Tigers jumped out to a lead in the third, as catcher Billy Sullivan singled and was sacrificed to second by Newsom. After a popout and a walk, Gehringer hit a high hopper to Werber, who had trouble coming up with the ball, and then threw wide of McCormick at first. When Sullivan saw the throw get away, he broke for home and just beat Wilson's tag.

---

12. Newsom's durability wasn't a question, though. In the season's last week, he'd been the winning pitcher in both ends of a doubleheader.

CINCINNATI REDS

That left runners on second and third, but Derringer recovered and struck out Greenberg, keeping the Tigers lead at 1–0. Derringer calmed down and reverted to his normal form, allowing baserunners (five) but no more runs through the seventh.

Meanwhile, Newsom continued his Series-long domination, holding the Reds scoreless on four hits through six innings. But the incredible physical and emotional toll of the Series may have finally begun to wear him down. Bobo was about to pitch his 25th inning in seven days.

The first batter in the bottom of the seventh was Cincinnati cleanup hitter McCormick, who would be named 1940 NL MVP a few weeks later. He'd hit .309 during the season, with 127 RBI and a league-leading 44 doubles, but was batting only .200 in the Series. No matter: McCormick struck a line-drive double off the wall in left-center. Next, Jimmy Ripple pulled a fly ball down the right-field line, hitting the screen only a couple feet short of a home run.

Tigers right fielder Bruce Campbell played the rebound and fired the ball to shortstop Dick "Rowdy Richard" Bartell, who took the throw between second base and the mound just as McCormick was rounding third. McCormick had delayed leaving second base, waiting to see if Campbell would catch Ripple's drive, and would've been dead to rights at home if Bartell had just turned around. Bartell instead cut the ball off and tried (in vain) to tag Ripple sliding into second, letting McCormick score the game-tying run.[13]

That brought the old coach, Jimmie Wilson, to the plate. Wilson, whose aging, aching legs were the subject of daily newspaper coverage, had singled and stolen a base in the second inning.[14] Now, he was called on to bunt the go-ahead run over to third, which he did, bringing up second baseman Eddie Joost, who'd batted .216 on the season and .200 in the Series. But McKechnie had a major weapon in reserve: Ernie Lombardi. Before the game, McKechnie had said that he'd only use Lombardi if a base hit would mean the ball game. It did, so out limped the Schnoz.

---

13.   Bartell's teammates would've ordinarily been responsible for alerting him to the possible play at home. Either they didn't notice, or the screams of 26,854 Reds fans drowned them out.
14.   Wilson hit .353, and managed the Series' only stolen base. At the request of his wife, the Reds sent him second base from Crosley Field—the base Jimmy stole in Game 7—as a framed memento. It was the last game Wilson ever played; he was hired to manage the Cubs in 1941.

Tigers manager Baker wasn't interested in dramatics. He made the easy decision to walk Lombardi and take his chances with the light-hitting Myers.[15]

McKechnie sent Frey—who had led the NL in stolen bases—in to run for Lombardi. Frey was still struggling with that broken toe, but he was still infinitely faster than the hobbled Lombardi, who was infamously slow even when completely healthy.

With the World Series on the line, and the Crosley Field crowd on its feet, McKechnie called for the squeeze play. Ripple got a good jump from third, but Myers fouled the bunt attempt back. The Tigers then threw three straight pitchouts, trying to pick Ripple off third or, failing that, walk Myers to load the bases for Derringer. But with the count 3-1, Newsom came back with a fastball across the plate. Myers connected for a deep fly ball to deep right-center. McCosky ranged far into the gap to make the catch near the wall, but Ripple easily scored the go-ahead run. Derringer grounded to third for the final out, but as he took the field for the top of the eighth, he held a 2-1 lead.

Neither team scored in the eighth, so as the game headed to the ninth, Derringer and the Reds were three outs away from the championship. Not leaving anything to chance, McKechnie had Walters, as well as relief ace Joe Beggs, warming up in the bullpen.

The Tigers sent the bottom of their lineup to the plate, but it wasn't without a threat: third baseman Higgins came to the plate with a Series average of .348, including 3 doubles, a triple, and a home run. Derringer got him to ground out to third. Sullivan followed by grounding out to first. One out to go.

Earl Averill came out to pinch-hit for Newsom. After a Hall of Fame career with Cleveland, Averill was winding up his career as a reserve, hitting .280 in limited duty, but he grounded out to second to give the Reds their first championship since 1919.

The final out kicked off a massive celebration across the city. In the clubhouse, Warren Giles cried tears of joy. Outside the players' sanctuary, fans jammed the field, revelers filled the local bars to capacity, and the streets in the downtown business district were strewn with ticker-tape and confetti to a depth of several inches. Boys lit firecrackers, men

---

15. Myers' 1940 season line was .202/.283/.319, numbers the defensively-minded McKechnie would overlook for the best glove in the league at short.

shouted and threw paper, and one enterprising man exited a Fourth Street music shop beating a big bass drum. It all led to what the *Enquirer* described as a single, city-wide traffic jam.

Street sweepers took advantage of a brief dinner-hour (or happy hour) lull to make a dent in the mess, but were quickly overwhelmed as the celebration resumed after nightfall. Having gained momentum over eight-plus hours of merriment, the crowds turned rowdier, rocking trolley cars, setting fire to trash cans, and even tossing one youngster into the Tyler Davidson Fountain.

For the second time in franchise history, the Cincinnati Reds were World Series champions.

10

RAGAMUFFIN REDS:
1961
NATIONAL LEAGUE
CHAMPS

As the calendar turned to 1961, the Cincinnati Reds were a franchise in disarray. In the 20 seasons since their 1940 World Series championship, the club had largely languished in the second division, only once finishing within 12 games of first. During that span, every other National League franchise had appeared in at least one World Series.

The malaise surrounding the ballclub was evidenced at the Crosley Field turnstiles. Despite featuring two of the best young players in baseball—Frank Robinson and Vada Pinson—only 663,486 fans showed up to watch the Redlegs in 1960, the lowest attendance mark in either league.

Shortly after the 1960 season, general manager Gabe Paul departed to take a similar role with the expansion Houston franchise, after nearly a decade at the helm of the Redlegs. Owner Powel Crosley hired Detroit Tigers president Bill DeWitt, a disciple of legendary baseball executive Branch Rickey, to replace Paul.

DeWitt immediately set about remaking the roster. Out were the old guys, including three former All-Stars: shortstop Roy McMillan (30 years old), catcher Ed Bailey (30), and even Joe Nuxhall, who had made his debut as a teenager some 16 years before but had worn out his welcome in the Queen City (temporarily).[1]

In return, DeWitt brought an infusion of younger talent to join Robinson and Pinson on the major league roster. In exchange for McMillan, the Reds acquired 25-year-old hurler Joey Jay; Bailey was dealt for second baseman Don Blasingame (29). In a deal with the White Sox, Cincinnati snagged 27-year-old third baseman Gene Freese, who had hit 23 homers just two seasons before. DeWitt also handed big league roster spots to 22-year-old shortstop Leo Cardenas, pitcher Ken Hunt

---

1.   Nuxhall would return to the Reds in 1962, and he went on to become a beloved figure in Cincinnati sports, both as a player and a broadcaster. Fifteen of his 16 big league seasons as a player were spent in a Reds uniform. The only season he wasn't a Red: 1961. Nuxhall would never play in a World Series, but he did call five as a Reds announcer.

(22), catcher Johnny Edwards (23), and slugging first baseman Gordy Coleman (26).

Despite all the new talent, there was little reason for optimism among Reds fans. In February, Robinson—at age 25, already one of the biggest stars in the league—was arrested after he brandished a firearm in an altercation with the cook at a local diner. Robinson spent a night in jail, and a few weeks later he paid a $250 fine.

The following month, Crosley died of a heart attack. Local papers were filled with admiration for the man who was widely credited with keeping the Reds in Cincinnati during an era in which teams were constantly threatening to move to greener pastures.[2]

On the field, things weren't looking any better, as the Reds suffered through a lousy spring training. Near the end of training camp, manager Fred Hutchinson decided that he needed to rally the troops. He gathered his players and delivered an emotional, impassioned pep talk. Later, an anonymous player recalled: "It was the most inspiring sports speech I ever heard and I sat in on some good ones in high school and college, too."

For a short time, it even appeared to deliver results. The Reds won five of their first seven games, but then lost eight games in a row. It was a pattern they would repeat all season: a stretch of great play followed immediately by an extended losing streak.

Finding themselves in last place on April 30, the Reds went on a tear, winning nine straight, and 13 of their next 15. By May 30, Cincinnati had moved into a three-way tie for first, along with Los Angeles and San Francisco. The Giants would ultimately fade to a third-place finish, but the Reds and Dodgers were destined to battle for the NL's top spot for the rest of the season.

By the time the Dodgers came to Cincinnati for a four-game series beginning on July 7, the Reds had opened up a three-game lead. They extended that lead by winning three out of four, including a 14–3 shellacking in the series finale. In that game, Frank Robinson led the attack, reaching base six times and driving in seven runs with two homers, a double, and a single. In the sixth inning, LA right-hander Don Drysdale was ejected from the game after throwing at three consecutive

---

2. Six of baseball's 16 teams actually did move during this era (Dodgers, Giants, Braves, Athletics, Browns/ Orioles, and Senators/Twins).

Reds batters, hitting Robinson with his final pitch. Robinson got up, dusted himself off, and responded by hitting a home run and an RBI double in his next two at-bats.

In an era of intimidation via beanball, Robinson was largely exempt. Most club's scouting reports read the same way: "Don't hit Robinson." By 1965, Phillies manager Gene Mauch went so far as to fine any pitcher who deliberately threw at Robinson. This wasn't out of kindness; it was out of good sense. "Robinson is trouble enough any time," Mauch explained. "Get him riled and you've just got more trouble." But the Dodgers were still learning that lesson in 1961, and Robinson would teach them more than once.

The Reds were on a roll, and when they defeated the Cubs, 2-1, on July 15, they had opened up a six-game lead on the rest of the league. True to form, however, that lead was to be short-lived. Cincinnati lost their next six games, including two to the Dodgers by a combined score of 18–4. Exactly two weeks after building their biggest lead of the season, the Reds dropped to second place behind Los Angeles.

The teams continued to trade turns at the top of the league until mid-August, when the Dodgers looked like they were going to take control. The Reds lost two out of three in San Francisco, and as they traveled down the coast for a crucial three-game series in Los Angeles, the Dodgers held a 2½ game lead.

"Everybody is in good shape for a change," said Hutchinson. "Let's just play 'em and see how we make out."

Hutch may have expressed confidence, but the tension was evident. Dodger players were reportedly upset about an article written by Reds reliever Jim Brosnan in a national sports publication.[3] In the piece, Brosnan wrote that the Dodgers were unpopular with other teams in the league because they played "dirty baseball."

Several Dodgers responded by saying that Brosnan should stick to pitching and leave the writing to others. As events would transpire over the next couple of days, however, the Dodgers did very little to dispel Brosnan's accusations.

---

3.   Brosnan was a fine pitcher, but his writing had brought him some modicum of fame, as well. In 1959, Brosnan published *The Long Season*, a well-regarded insider account of the life of a professional baseball player. After the 1961 season, Brosnan published his account of the Reds' surprising run to the pennant in his second book, titled *Pennant Race*.

DO YOU BELIEVE IN MAGIC?

Peggy Guenther, a resident of the College Hill neighborhood in Cincinnati, took credit for the Reds' success in that memorable season. She claimed that she had a "magic fly swatter," which she would smack on the table whenever the Reds came to bat. She even tried it during the Pirates-Dodgers game that brought the Reds the pennant, and it seemed to work, she said.

"I'm going to beat the ---- out of that swatter during the World Series," she said. Unfortunately, the plastic swatter's powers were ineffective against the bats of Mickey Mantle and Roger Maris.

There was a festive atmosphere at Los Angeles Memorial Coliseum[4] for the first game of the series on Tuesday, August 15. More than 47,000 were in attendance, but they weren't all fans of the home team. More than 200 members of the Reds' Rooters Fan Club were there for the entire series, led by their founder Barney Rapp—a popular orchestra leader and jazz musician who had been credited with discovering such future stars as Doris Day and Rosemary Clooney. In addition to the Reds fans, Rapp brought a five-piece band to the stadium to help cheer on his beloved Reds.

L.A.'s brilliant left-hander Sandy Koufax—who had, at one time, been a freshman basketball (and baseball) player for the University of Cincinnati—was scheduled to start the first game. He would face hard-throwing Joey Jay.

Only 25, Jay had already been in the big leagues for seven seasons, languishing nearly unused on the bench for Milwaukee. He finally got a legitimate shot at age 23, but had already developed a reputation for reporting to camp out of shape. Milwaukee tired of him, and jumped at the chance to trade him to Cincinnati for a Gold Glove shortstop in McMillan.

Jay also jumped at the opportunity, dedicating himself to getting in shape. The results were evident immediately. By mid-season, Jay found himself on the National League All-Star team, and as he took the mound against the Dodgers, he sported a nifty 16–7 record to go along with a 3.21 ERA.

---

4. Dodger Stadium wouldn't open until 1962.

The Dodgers jumped out quickly against Jay, who walked LA leadoff hitter Maury Wills, then surrendered three consecutive singles. Before he had recorded an out, the score was 2–0 and the Dodgers had runners on the corners. Four pitches later, Jay had induced a double play and a popup, and escaped further damage.

There were no more fireworks until the fourth, when Koufax lined a Jay pitch into right field for an apparent single. Alertly, Frank Robinson charged the ball and threw it to first to retire Koufax, just your typical 9-3 force out.

"If someone did that to me, I would want to sit down and cry," Reds shortstop Eddie Kasko said. Koufax didn't sit down to cry, but later in the game, he would respond in the typical Dodger fashion.

In the fifth, Robinson doubled in two runs off Koufax to tie the game. One inning later, left fielder Wally Post homered, and Kasko singled in Gordy Coleman for another run. With the Reds leading 4–2, Koufax drilled Robinson with a fastball as he led off the seventh inning. That was the last batter Koufax would face, and Robinson would get the last laugh when he scored one out later on a double by pinch-hitter extraordinaire Jerry Lynch.[5]

Jay had held the Dodgers in check after the two first-inning runs, picking up his 17th win in a complete game effort. The win allowed Cincinnati to creep within one game of first place.

The teams were set to play a twi-night doubleheader the following day, with control of the National League pennant race on the line. The eyes of the baseball world focused on Los Angeles, as 72,140 fans crowded into the Coliseum. At the time, it was the largest crowd ever to see a baseball game. It remains the largest crowd ever to see the Reds play.

The raucous atmosphere was quieted substantially when the Reds jumped out in front in the top of the first inning of Game 1. Kasko led off with a single, then scored when Blasingame tripled. Pinson followed up with an RBI single to put the Reds up 2–0.

Then the Dodgers began headhunting again. L.A. starter Larry Sherry drilled Robinson with the first pitch, the third time Cincinnati's star right fielder had been plunked by Dodger pitching that season.

---

5. "Lynch in a Pinch" earned a reputation as one of the greatest pinch-hitters in franchise history. In 1961, Lynch had five pinch-hit home runs, an all-time Reds record. He also collected 19 pinch-hits; not only did that tie his franchise record (which he had set one year earlier), but it also led all National League pinch-hitters.

"I don't know whether Sherry's pitch was intentional or not, but I know it made Frank mad," said Hutchinson. "They don't scare him."

Making matters worse, Dodgers coach Leo Durocher began riding Robinson when he reached first base. From the home dugout, Durocher called him "gutless" and, curiously, yelled that Robinson couldn't have played 20 years before. Robinson was livid, and had to be calmed down by Reds first-base coach Dick Sisler.

As Jim Croce would later sing, you don't tug on Superman's cape. In the third inning, Pinson led off with a double to bring Robinson to the plate. The second pitch from Sherry was high and tight, and knocked Robinson to the ground. Robinson climbed back in the box and crushed Sherry's very next pitch for a long two-run homer that extended Cincinnati's lead to 6–0, which they held to win the opener.

"I've found that the best way to retaliate is with a base hit," Robinson said a few years later. "There's no sense in getting into a fight. You might wind up with an injury. Then you're out of the lineup. You just hurt your own team."

"They never learned their lesson," Reds pitcher Jim O'Toole said, "because every time they'd knock him down, he'd get up and hit the next pitch out of the park. He hated the Dodgers."

In the nightcap, the 24-year-old O'Toole—on his way to a 19–9 campaign with a 3.10 ERA, tossed a two-hit shutout, striking out seven Dodger hitters in an 8–0 Reds victory.

The dominant performance in Los Angeles was a microcosm of the elements that had made Cincinnati such a tough team all season long. Robinson and Pinson were brilliant, Lynch contributed a key pinch-hit, and Freese hit his 22nd home run of the season. On the pitching side of the ledger, Jay, O'Toole, and Bob Purkey (a complete-game shutout in the 6–0 win) held a tough Dodger lineup to just two runs in three games.

The series sweep put the Reds back atop the National League standings, where they would remain for the rest of the season.

Six weeks later, the Reds made it official, clinching a share of the National League pennant with a 6–3 win over the Cubs at Wrigley Field, on the strength of home runs by Robinson and Lynch. As the team flew back to Cincinnati, Reds fans watched the scoreboard: one more Dodger loss would give the Reds the pennant.

CINCINNATI REDS

Excited fans began gathering around Fountain Square, listening to the radio broadcast of the Dodgers doubleheader against Pittsburgh, some even packing supper. The crowd was estimated at 30,000—Reds radio broadcaster Waite Hoyt insisted that it was a bigger gathering than on V-J Day. Around 9:20 PM, the Reds team bus (coming straight from the airport) pulled into the dead center of the rally, sparking "pure pandemonium." Fans, screaming and cheering, pressed up against the bus, rocking it and preventing the players from exiting.

Beer bottles were thrown. Several people fainted. One unfortunate man was shoved through the window of the Maud Muller candy store at Fifth and Walnut.

Shortly before 10:00 PM, the moment everyone had been waiting for finally arrived: the Pirates finished off the Dodgers in the second game of the doubleheader, and the Cincinnati Reds were champions of the National League for 1961.

Reds players moved on to the nearby Netherland Hilton Hotel—Hutchinson had booked a ballroom—but the party outside kept rocking until well after midnight. A conga line formed, heading uptown. One enterprising young man dumped four bottles of liquid soap into the Tyler Davidson Fountain, and another jumped in to swim. Both were arrested for disorderly conduct.

Meanwhile, Rapp's band provided the music for the team's "wing-ding" of a party, as it was described later. Hutchinson was the master of ceremonies, giving his best effort at crooning popular Frank Sinatra songs, such as "My Blue Heaven."

"After all these years, this is wonderful," Brosnan said.

The Reds would ultimately lose to the powerful New York Yankees in the World Series, but it was a season to remember, nonetheless. The Reds had captured the pennant for the first time in over two decades, and set the franchise on a course that would inevitably result in the glorious Big Red Machine era. A big part of the story was the new guys, such as the diminutive Freese[6] and the burly Coleman, bookend corner infielders who each hit 26 homers, 27 doubles, and collected 87 RBI. After finally getting his big chance, Joey Jay responded with a 21–10 record.

---

6.   On the official roster, Freese was listed at 5'11", but that was an exaggeration, to say the least. "I lied on my bubblegum cards," he said. "I said five-foot-eleven just to make me feel bigger. Other guys lied about their age. I lied about my height."

More importantly, Frank Robinson rebounded from the embarrassment of the off-season arrest to hit .323/.404/.611 with 37 home runs and 124 RBI. He was named the National League's MVP, capturing 15 of a possible 16 first-place votes. The other first place vote went to Jay.

Though greater things lay ahead for the franchise, Cincinnati-area fans would not soon forget this lovable band of ballplayers that had become known as the "Ragamuffin Reds."

11

MR. PERFECT

Tom Browning was a little different. Always superstitious, he only wore red underwear on the days he was slated to pitch, and he didn't shave in between those starts. You'll probably remember some of the other more memorable moments in Browning's career, such as Game 2 of the 1990 World Series, when Browning left the stadium in full uniform to accompany his wife—who was going into labor—to the hospital. When it appeared that he might be needed to pitch, the Reds sent out an all-points bulletin over the radio for Browning to return to the ballpark.

A few years later, in July of 1993, Browning sneaked away again, this time from the visitor's bullpen at Wrigley Field. In the third inning, Browning disappeared and the next time he surfaced, he was on a rooftop across Sheffield Avenue, looking down on right field. In full uniform, he waved to the crowd and his teammates, and watched Kevin Mitchell hit a three-run homer that gave the Reds the lead. He was fined $500 for his shenanigans, which he paid happily.

But Browning wasn't just a novelty act. He won 20 games as a rookie, the only pitcher to accomplish that feat in the last 60-plus years. He made an All-Star team, and was a key pitcher on a World Series champion.

Plus, you may remember that he threw a perfect game.

As game time approached on September 16, 1988, things were dreary in every sense of the word. The Dodgers—who would go on to win the World Series—had just arrived in town, riding high with a seven-game lead in the NL West division with just 17 games to play. The Reds were mired in third place, 8.5 games back, and their playoff hopes were very slim indeed.

In addition, the weather had been nasty all day, with a steady drizzling rain. But it was a Friday night, and Cincinnati is a baseball town, so 16,591 hardy souls trudged through the turnstiles at Riverfront Stadium to watch a nearly-meaningless late-season tilt.

CINCINNATI REDS

Those Reds fans were greeted by a two-hour-and-17-minute rain delay. At 7:45 (the game's scheduled start time), the tarp remained on the field. Browning, the night's scheduled starter, sat in the dugout, watching the rain while his teammates were playing cards or relaxing in the clubhouse. Browning glanced across the field and saw LA's starter, Tim Belcher, hanging out in the visitor's dugout. With a wry grin, Browning yelled over, giving Belcher a little grief about the fact that the Dodger hurler had hit a home run off Browning the week before. Then Browning left the Cincinnati dugout, annoyed that the rain showed no signs of breaking up.

Over in the Dodgers clubhouse, players were beginning to get irritated too. Later, shortstop Alfredo Griffin would recall: "We weren't thrilled to have to play that game. You get lazy waiting around all that time. If you get in your mind that the game will [be rained out], then you don't have the same energy."

When, at 10:02 PM, Browning stepped onto the mound and finally threw the first pitch of the game—a ball to the leadoff hitter, Griffin— most of the ticket holders had given up and gone home. A small contingent of hardcore fans remained, and they saw Griffin lift a fly ball to Eric Davis in left-center field, the only play Davis would make all night long.

Once the game finally began, things moved quickly. Very quickly. Browning always worked fast, but this was something different. Through six innings, Browning had retired all 18 Dodger hitters on just 68 pitches. The only close play in that span came in the fifth. Leading off the inning, Los Angeles right fielder Mike Marshall smoked a ball into the hole between shortstop and third base. Cincinnati's rookie third baseman Chris Sabo pounced quickly, corralled the ball and made a strong throw across to Nick Esasky at first. Marshall was out by half a step.

While Browning was blowing through the Dodgers lineup, Tim Belcher was busy pitching a gem of his own. Davis had coaxed a walk from Belcher to lead off the second, but Belcher hadn't allowed any hits as he took the mound in the bottom of the sixth.

Reds leadoff hitter Barry Larkin finally broke up the no-hit bid with a two-out double into the right-field corner. Sabo followed by hitting a slow chopper to Dodger third baseman Jeff Hamilton. Hamilton came up throwing, but bounced the throw to first base. It skipped away from

Tom Browning tips his hat to the crowd at Riverfront Stadium after his perfect game against the Dodgers. (AP Photo/Mark Lyons)

first baseman Mickey Hatcher and Larkin scored easily, giving Cincinnati a slim 1–0 lead.

That was all the offensive support that Browning would need. The crafty left-hander was in a zone, and he actually credited Belcher for helping him stay focused. "He was pitching a hell of a game. That helped me maintain my intensity because it was so close," Browning said. "Any mistakes might have cost us this game."

Reds catcher Jeff Reed noticed: "He kept everything down; his breaking ball was really good. It seemed like anywhere I was, outside, inside, up, or down, the ball was always thrown right where I put the mitt." Slowly, it began to dawn on Reed that something special was happening. "In about the sixth inning...I started thinking that I don't want to mess this up. We all didn't want to mess it up for him."

The Dodgers, meanwhile, settled into their customary role as villain, unwilling to give Browning much credit at all. "He was a lucky [so and so]," said Hatcher. "Everything we hit was right at somebody."

Kirk Gibson—who would go on to win the MVP—blamed the umpires, and was still blaming them when interviewed 13 years later by author James Buckley. "It was a huge strike zone, ridiculous," Gibson said. "Not to take anything away from either pitcher, because it was a well-played game. We all argued, and you try to make adjustments, but when the plate gets too big, it's just hard to handle. But you've got to give them credit. The strike zone was established, and they utilized it."

The anger bubbled over for Gibson in the seventh inning, when he ended the frame by striking out. The final two strikes had been called by the umpire without a swing, and Gibson went nuts. The argument was short-lived; home plate umpire Jim Quick promptly ejected Gibson from the game.

Before the Reds took the field in the eighth inning, Reds manager Pete Rose pulled Reed aside. "Slow him down," Rose instructed. "He's getting excited; don't let him rush. Sometimes when he is going good, he throws a first-pitch fastball right down Broadway and gets hurt with a home run."

Reed tried his best, but it was difficult to slow Browning down. "Once I got to the eighth, I started feeling a little antsy," Browning said. "I was feeling the pressure and I had to make sure that I calmed myself."

INSIDE THE MOMENT

Reds right fielder Paul O'Neill would later play in two more perfect games as a member of the New York Yankees. O'Neill remains the only player ever to play for the winning club in that many perfect games.

The flip side of that coin is the Dodgers' Alfredo Griffin, who—three years later—would become the only player ever to play for the losing club in three perfect games.

Nerves or no nerves, Browning retired Marshall, John Shelby, and Hamilton in order. Through eight, the perfect game was still alive.

In the bottom half, Ron Oester lined a two-out pitch to center field for only the third Cincinnati hit of the evening, but the Reds failed to bring him around to score. So Browning walked purposefully to the mound for the ninth, clinging to a 1–0 lead, with history in his sights. The fans who had remained were on their feet and cheering as loud as they could manage.

The first hitter Browning faced was Dodgers catcher Rick Dempsey. "He'd been the only one who gave us trouble all night," said Reed. "He was a first-pitch fastball hitter and he had hit the ball hard his first two times up." So Reed called for a changeup, which Dempsey fouled off. Pitch two was a fastball, but Dempsey took it for ball one. Then Browning came back with a changeup that Dempsey drilled to the warning track in right field. Paul O'Neill gathered it in, and there was one away.

The next hitter was All-Star second baseman Steve Sax. On the first pitch, Sax grounded a ball sharply up the middle that looked for a moment like it might get through to the outfield to break up the perfect game. But Larkin ranged quickly to his left, fielded the ball cleanly, and threw across the diamond for the second out.

Dodgers manager Tommy Lasorda sent little-used Tracy Woodson to the plate to pinch-hit for Belcher. Lasorda had actually been in the stands for the most recent National League perfect game, when Sandy Koufax turned the trick almost exactly 23 years before, but he wasn't keen to see his first-place club on the losing end of history this time around.[1]

Woodson fouled off the first pitch, then took two straight balls before fouling the fourth pitch over the Dodgers' dugout. Amazingly, Browning had not reached a three-ball count on a single hitter all night, but with the count 2–2, Browning delivered "a forehead-high" fastball that should have run the count full.

But Woodson swung and Woodson missed, for strike three. Browning pumped his fist in front of the mound. On his 102nd pitch (and 72nd strike), Browning had completed baseball's 12th perfect game.[2]

Later, Browning recalled being tackled by second baseman Ron Oester and the rest of his teammates (and having his lip split in the process). "After that, it honestly felt like an out-of-body experience. It was like I was 15, 20 feet above the pile and looking down at it." Not a bad view for one of the most exciting moments in Reds history, the first perfect game in the 119-year history of the franchise.[3]

Moments later, Browning had another good view when his teammates lifted him to their shoulders and carried him off the field. Soon, he found himself being interviewed over the stadium loudspeakers by Reds broadcaster Joe Nuxhall, but everything was a blur. It wasn't until the next morning that he fully realized what he had done.

And what he had done was create a nickname for himself that would last for the rest of his life, at least in Cincinnati. Tom Browning was now "Mr. Perfect."

---

1.   The last no-hitter thrown against the Dodgers had been Don Larsen's perfect game in the 1956 World Series.
2.   The game lasted one hour and 51 minutes, which means that the rain delay lasted 36 minutes longer than the actual game.
3.   Asked after the game if he had ever seen a perfect game before, Kirk Gibson roared, "No, and I ain't seen one yet!"

12

NO WEAKNESSES: BARRY LARKIN

"Barry not only was one of the most talented and gifted players, but he was one of the most intelligent, on and off the field. He had great speed, but had the ability to slow down the game, so he made very few mistakes. Barry could do it all. He is the six-tool player all the scouts are looking for now, one with all the baseball skills plus intellect."

—Dusty Baker

The Larkin brothers were all-around athletes, but each had a specialty: Mike played football at Notre Dame, Byron is still Xavier basketball's all-time leading scorer, and you know where Barry ended up.

Barry Larkin's name first appeared in the hometown *Cincinnati Enquirer* in 1980 when, as a sophomore shortstop for Moeller High School, he went 3-for-4 with a home run to lead his team to the big-school sectional quarterfinals. He'd begun the season on the junior varsity squad, only joining the varsity (where older brother Mike was the left fielder) due to the mid-season illness of the starting shortstop.

Major league scouts quickly noticed the skinny kid's baseball tools: powerful arm, fast runner, quick hands, lively bat (he eventually set the Moeller school record for home runs), and a fluid grace that, to the trained eye, signaled big league potential. At least one scout was skeptical, though. "He doesn't have a great arm and he doesn't have outstanding speed," the scout said during Larkin's senior year. "Those two things will keep him from going in the first two rounds of the draft.... Right now, I'd estimate that he'll go in the fourth round."[1]

The scout was wrong. The Reds drafted Larkin in the second round, but his parents stressed education (they're both graduates of Xavier University in Louisiana), and Barry went to the University of Michigan.[2]

---

1. That Braves scout was Harold "Hep" Cronin, who was also a longtime high school basketball coach in the Cincinnati area, and the father of future University of Cincinnati and UCLA basketball coach Mick Cronin.

2. Larkin was actually recruited to play football at Michigan too, but when coach Bo Schembechler informed Larkin that he would be redshirting his freshman year, Larkin decided to focus strictly on baseball. Years later, Larkin remembered that Schembechler was upset about that decision. "He let me know it was the University of Michigan, and no one came to Michigan to just play baseball."

His star only rose in Ann Arbor, as he was twice named Big 10 player of the year, and made the 1984 U.S. Olympic team. In 1985, he was named to *The Sporting News'* college All-America Team, alongside future big league stars Barry Bonds, Will Clark, Rafael Palmeiro, and B.J. Surhoff.

In 1985, the Reds drafted him again, this time in the first round (number four overall), and he quickly signed. Despite being a number one pick, Larkin was slotted behind Kurt Stillwell on the Reds organizational depth chart. Stillwell, a brilliant glove man, was actually a year younger than Larkin, but had been drafted out of high school and was already in AAA when Larkin was drafted. Many observers expected that Larkin would eventually be forced to move to second or third base. Larkin had other plans: "I want to play shortstop for the Reds," he said.

When Stillwell started slow in 1986 (.176 in his first three months in the majors), he was sent down to join Larkin at AAA Denver. At that point the position switch nearly happened. Larkin played two games at second base ("It was an absolute disaster," he remembered) before Dave Concepción suffered a broken hand and Stillwell was called back to Cincinnati.

Meanwhile, Larkin was setting the American Association aflame in his first full season as a pro. He was the league's player of the month in July, and was hitting .329/.373/.525 for the year when the Reds could wait no longer. Called up on August 12, 1986, Larkin finally made it to Riverfront Stadium almost a full day later than expected...and without his luggage, so he was outfitted in a collection of equipment that would rival any Reds museum. Limited to pinch-hitting duty since he didn't have a glove, Larkin walked to the plate wearing Concepción's sliding shorts, Eric Davis' batting gloves, and using Pete Rose's spikes and bat. "Wearing everyone else's stuff made me feel like I was part of the team," he remembered a decade later.[3]

Larkin was spectacular from the start. As a 22-year-old in a major league pennant race, he hit (.283/.320/.403), ran (eight steals in eight tries), and played a steady, sometimes dazzling shortstop. He also had a big leaguer's confidence, as Rose remembered: "Barry came into my office one day and said, 'Pete, Kurt is a good player, but you may as well trade him. I'm going to be your shortstop here for 15 years.'" Larkin was

---

3.   Larkin also thought he'd snagged an incredible memento of his first game. Nope. Rose wanted his stuff back.

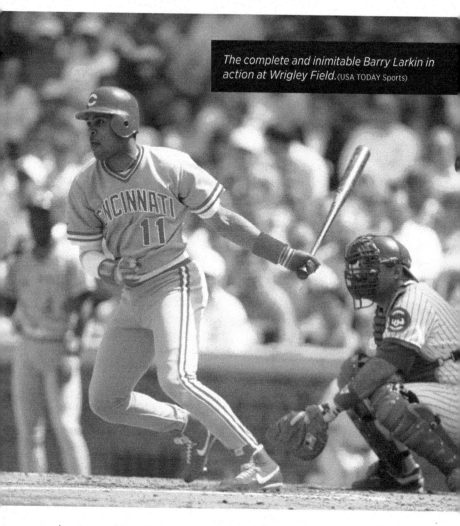

The complete and inimitable Barry Larkin in action at Wrigley Field. (USA TODAY Sports)

wrong about one thing—he would actually hold onto the Reds shortstop job for 18 years.

During those years, Larkin really *could* do everything you'd ask of a baseball player. He hit for average (.295 career) and for power (198 home runs), he could field and throw (three Gold Gloves and deserved more), and he had great speed (397 stolen bases at an 83 percent success rate). And yes, he was a profoundly intelligent ballplayer, who rarely made a mental mistake.

FAMILY TIES

The Larkin house was a competitive house. One day during Barry's first week in the majors, he stopped by his family's home. As was normally the case when the brothers got together, one thing led to another. Barry and Byron started a little baseball game...in their parents' room. They broke a chandelier and a window before Barry had to head to the ballpark.

Stephen Larkin, the youngest brother by eight years, had his high school sports career derailed by a heart condition, to the point that the family sued Archdiocese of Cincinnati in an unsuccessful attempt to let him play during his senior year at Moeller High School. Stephen was drafted by the Rangers out of the University of Texas and later traded to the Reds. In a 1996 spring training game, Stephen and fellow farmhand Aaron Boone joined their older brothers (Barry and Bret) as the starting infield. Two years later, Reds general manager Jim Bowden—always looking for a gimmick—promoted Stephen for the final game of the 1998 season, where he completed baseball's first all-brother infield.

Barry's son Shane preferred basketball to baseball, and starred for a Miami Hurricanes team that won the ACC and reached the Sweet 16 of the 2013 NCAA tournament. He was then drafted in the first round of the 2013 NBA draft. His cousin Austin (Mike's son) played football at Notre Dame, and later Purdue.

Though excellent in almost every facet of the game, Larkin arrived in the majors with one weakness, at least as he saw it. He only spoke English. Larkin looked at Tony Pérez and Dave Concepción—boyhood idols turned teammates—and saw one obvious step he needed to take to truly be their peer. So Larkin studied until he became a fluent Spanish speaker, building stronger relationships with his Latin teammates, and even gaining an edge on the field. "I was able to speak to the player in Spanish without the English-speaking guy understanding what I was saying. We were able to pick them off or do whatever it was to get the edge," Larkin said years later.

It seems ridiculous to say about a 12-time All-Star, but Larkin toiled in relative obscurity in Cincinnati. Early in his career, Larkin was overshadowed by Ozzie Smith's highlight film charm; later, by mold-breaking shortstops Derek Jeter, Alex Rodriguez, and Nomar Garciaparra.

CINCINNATI REDS

Maybe it was because no single strength stood out. "I consider myself an amoeba man," Larkin said in 1995. "I'll assume any shape to help the team. If the team needs someone to lead by example, I do that. If it needs someone to steal, I do that. If it needs someone to bunt or move a runner from second to third, I do that."

Or maybe Marty Brennaman was right. When Larkin was elected to the Baseball Hall of Fame in 2012, Marty said, "Maybe [Larkin] was overlooked by some people, as ridiculous as that might sound now, because he never patted himself on the back. He just went out and beat the other team every way he could, with speed, defense, at the plate with surprising power, and quiet leadership."

Enquirer columnist Paul Daugherty once wrote that "Larkin had to be seen to be believed," because his value far exceeded his admittedly impressive statistics. But that doesn't mean he was underappreciated by the numbers guys. If anything, the opposite is true. Writer Bill James, the spiritual father of "sabermetrics," rated Larkin the sixth best shortstop in history in his 2001 book. "Larkin is one of the 10 most *complete* players in baseball history," James wrote. "He's a .300 hitter, has power, has speed, excellent defense, and is a good percentage player. He ranks with DiMaggio, Mays, and a few others as the most well-rounded stars in baseball history."

Larkin was, in his own words, a chameleon, adapting his game to fit whatever role he was playing for the team at the time. He started 402 games as the leadoff hitter, 669 as the number two hitter, and 757 batting in the three hole. He started more than 20 games in every position in the batting order (except ninth, of course).

His 1995 MVP season (.394 OBP and 51 steals) was a template for a table-setter, hitting in front of Ron Gant (29 HR) and Reggie Sanders (28 HR). A year later, with Gant gone, Sanders hurt, and the Reds needing power, Larkin stepped up to hit 33 HR and slugged .567.

Larkin's numbers were remarkably consistent in all situations, whether at home or on the road, in the first inning or the eighth, in May or September, with runners on base or leading off an inning, Barry Larkin was basically the same hitter. He just had no weaknesses.

But he understood that while he was a great player, he wasn't a dominant one. Unlike Joe Morgan or Johnny Bench, who could just say, "This is what I'm going to do, and you're going to have to deal with it,"

Larkin understood that he could only achieve greatness in the context of his team. He often called himself "a complementary player," a line he was again reciting on the eve of his Hall of Fame induction. Eric Davis rightfully called him out. "You're in the Hall of Fame," Davis said. "There are no complementary players in the Hall of Fame."

Davis was right, but so was Larkin. Judged alone, Barry Larkin was a very, very good baseball player. But as a member of a team, Barry Larkin was one of the all-time greats.

13

1919 WORLD SERIES CHAMPS

Despite the grand tradition of baseball in the Queen City, the Reds had fallen on hard times by 1919. Cincinnati had not finished above third in more than 30 years, and the club hadn't sniffed a genuine pennant race since the World Series was created in 1903. The heady days of the original Red Stockings were but a distant memory to elderly baseball fans, who had learned to live with the automobile, the airplane, and motion pictures since their Reds had been in contention.

There was little reason to believe that the team's fortunes would change in 1919. The franchise was in disarray, essentially bankrupt after years of poor attendance.[1] Money woes almost prevented the Reds from being able to conduct spring training in warmer climes, but club president Garry Herrmann convinced some of the franchise's stockholders to pump in additional capital, keeping the team afloat until the season started.

But the managerial situation was up in the air. Baseball legend Christy Mathewson had managed the club for two and a half seasons, but he had enlisted in the United States Army in 1918 and was still serving in Europe. After the armistice in late 1918, Herrmann sent several urgent cablegrams to Mathewson about managing in 1919, but Matty never responded and the Reds were forced to hire Pat Moran, the New York Giants pitching coach who had managed the Phillies to the pennant in 1915.[2]

With a manager in place, the Reds headed down to sleepy Waxahachie, Texas, for what turned out to be a disastrous spring training. Star center fielder Edd Roush didn't show up, holding out for more money (as he usually did); also holding out were left fielder Sherry Magee and pitcher Jimmy Ring. Reliever Rube Bressler had only recently returned from the war and wasn't in camp.

While some key players weren't there, an unwelcome guest did make an appearance: monsoon season. Nearly every day it rained; the

1. For the preceding five seasons, average yearly attendance at Reds home games was just 201,516.
2. Mathewson was accidentally gassed during a training accident in France, irreparably damaging his lungs. Soon, he developed tuberculosis, which led to his untimely death in 1925 at the age of 45.

playing field was under water and unusable all spring. The Reds were forced to improvise; they used a nearby cow pasture, the local railroad yards, and an empty lot next to the Waxahachie bus depot to get in whatever practice they could. By the time the club made their way back to Cincinnati in mid-April, everyone was ready to begin the season, in spite of all the bad omens.

Almost as quickly as an Army plane dropped the Opening Day baseball onto the center field grass at Redland Field, Cincinnati's luck began to change. The Reds won nine of their first 10 games, and by May 4, they were in first place. All was right with the world.

On May 5, Cincinnati's workhorse starter Hod Eller went into the ninth inning of a game against the Cubs with a 6–0 lead. Eller proceeded to melt down, surrendering six runs in the final frame; the Reds ultimately lost 7–6 in 12 innings.[3]

The disaster showed Reds fans that things weren't going to be easy. A month later, Cincinnati was 20–16 and had fallen five games behind the first-place Giants.

Then, almost without warning, the Reds launched themselves into orbit. Starting in early June, Cincinnati won 60 of their next 78 games, one of the hottest streaks the franchise would ever see. As August drew to a close, the Reds were 81–34 and in first place, nine games in front of the Giants.

The key moment in the regular season took place in mid-August. The Reds and Giants had been engaged in a fierce battle all summer long, with the teams trading first place back and forth. Thanks to the heat of a pennant race, the rivalry with New York was becoming intense. After one mid-summer game, legendary Giants manager John McGraw responded to jeering Reds fans by yelling, "We beat you today and we'll be glad to get out of the home of the Huns!" (i.e., Germans). Coming less than six weeks after the signing of the Treaty of Versailles, which officially ended World War I, it was quite the slur. A Cincinnati policeman took exception and tried to slug McGraw.

The Reds had begun to open up a slight lead when the clubs met at the Polo Grounds in New York, where they would play doubleheaders on three consecutive days beginning on August 13. When the dust settled,

---

3. Eller shook off that nightmare quickly. In his next start, on May 11, he spun a no-hitter against the Cardinals. He'd go on to finish the season with a 19–9 record, 2.39 ERA, and 7 shutouts.

the Reds had won four of the six games, taking a commanding 6.5 game lead.[4] Cincinnati's first-ever National League pennant (in the NL's 44th season of play) was all but sewn up.

The Reds made things official on September 16 with a win over— who else?—the Giants. As the regular season drew to a close, the Chamber of Commerce celebrated with a parade throughout downtown Cincinnati. At the head of the parade were George Wright, Cal McVey, and "Live Oak" Taylor, the only surviving members of that historic 1869 Red Stockings club. The parade ended at the Hotel Gibson, where Reds players were treated to a testimonial dinner.

The excitement hadn't diminished at all by the time the American League champion Chicago White Sox arrived in town to start the World Series later that week. In contrast to Cincinnati, in the Series for the first time, the White Sox had been crowned champions just two years earlier. During the 1919 season, Chicago posted a record of 88–52, led by ace Eddie Cicotte, who won 29 games with a 1.82 ERA in 35 starts (9.5 WAR). Offensively, the Sox were paced by second baseman Eddie Collins (.319/.400/.405) and slugging right fielder "Shoeless" Joe Jackson (.351/.422/.506, 31 doubles, 14 triples).

The White Sox were considered the best team in the world, and conventional wisdom said that they would smash the Reds in the World Series. Cincinnati had reason for optimism, however. The Reds had put together a dominant 52–19 record at Redland Field, where Games 1 and 2 were scheduled to be played.

Plus, the Reds had their own stable of star players. Roush, a future Hall of Famer, won the National League's batting title with a .321 average; third-sacker Heinie Groh contributed a .392 OBP and a team-leading five home runs. Cincinnati didn't have any pitchers as brilliant as Cicotte, but top to bottom, the Reds had the better staff. Besides Eller, Moran could send out Dutch Ruether (19–6, 1.82 ERA), Slim Sallee (21–7, 2.06), and Jimmy Ring (10–9, 2.26).[5]

There is a very good argument to be made that Cincinnati was actually the better team. We'll never know, since eight White Sox

---

4.   The series finale was notable for the heroics of Reds right fielder Greasy Neale, who, in the ninth inning, stole second, third, and home. Neale's name and feat was back in the news over a century later, when Reds phenom Elly De La Cruz also stole his way around the bases (on just two pitches), on July 8, 2023.

5.   Cincinnati's starters were so good, in fact, that 28-year-old Dolf Luque couldn't crack the rotation. Luque was 10–3 with a 2.63 ERA in 1919, but he would go on to become one of the greatest pitchers in franchise history.

players—including Cicotte and Jackson—conspired with gamblers to throw the World Series.

No one outside the conspiracy knew about that as Game 1 approached, though, and Cincinnati was abuzz over its first-ever appearance on baseball's biggest stage. Interest in the Series extended far outside Cincinnati. Nearly 300 writers, from every corner of the country (and even five scribes from Cuba), reported back daily to their hometown papers. Western Union used more than 100,000 miles of wire to telegraph the action to 10,000 remote scoreboards in 250 cities all over North America. One of those scoreboards was set up in the Cincinnati Gym downtown, where Brendamour Sporting Goods invited baseball fans without tickets to the games to follow the action for free.[6]

There were plenty of ticket buyers, too. Scalpers reportedly commanded the astronomical price of $50 for two seats (face value for the best box seat tickets was only $6). The 30,511 lucky individuals who made it inside Redland Field were greeted by brand new American flags flown from the top of the press box and in center field. While everyone found their seats, John Philip Sousa led his band onto the field, where he conducted them in a performance of "The Stars and Stripes Forever."[7]

In attendance at Game 1 were comedian George M. Cohan, the famous writer Ring Lardner, both of the Cincinnati-area congressmen, and Ohio Senator Warren Harding (who would be elected President of the United States just 13 months later). Five former Reds managers were there, as well, including Christy Mathewson, finally back from Europe.

The surviving members of the 1869 team were back again. "I wish [more] of the old boys could be here to see this game," said George Wright, wistfully.

The game was everything Reds fans had hoped for, which was the Black Sox' idea. From the first inning, when Cicotte hit Reds leadoff hitter Morrie Rath in the back with a pitch—later reported to be a signal to gamblers that the fix was in—the Reds never trailed.

They scored five runs with two outs in the fourth inning, capped by a two-run triple off the bat of starting pitcher Dutch Ruether. Ruether actually hit a second triple later, and allowed only a single unearned run in a complete-game victory. The final score was 9–1.

---

6. Additional scoreboards were set up at the Emery Theater, the Sinton Hotel, and the Music Hall.
7. The 1919 Series also marked the first time "The Star-Spangled Banner" was played before each game. It didn't become a daily part of baseball's pregame ritual until WWII.

Everyone on the home side was jubilant afterward. Pat Moran waved to the crowd as he darted off the field. "You all helped," he yelled. "Helped a lot. And thank you!"

"Well, I'll say this," said old Cal McVey, who had been a raw 19-year-old on the original Red Stockings 50 years before. "I know the Reds, the good old Cincinnati Reds, can beat any baseball organization on this earth and I'll back 'em to win that celestial championship if there's any angels got the nerve to come down here and meet 'em."

A mass of people immediately began forming downtown. The crowd included a band of boys, led by a trumpeter and a kid with a washtub drum, who carried an effigy of Eddie Cicotte through the streets and into the lobbies of the bustling hotels.

Game 2 saw the Reds win 4–2 behind Slim Sallee's complete-game effort. In the seventh inning, an airplane dropped a stuffed dummy onto the field near the shortstop. Everyone was baffled, but the game resumed shortly and the culprit was never discovered.

The clubs traveled to Chicago's Comiskey Park for the next three games of the nine-game Series.[8] The White Sox narrowed it to 2–1 with a shutout win in Game 3, but the Reds returned the favor in both Game 4 and Game 5, shutting out the Sox 2–0 and 5–0.

The Series returned to Cincinnati for Games 6 and 7, but the ChiSox twice staved off elimination and disappointed Reds fans hungry to celebrate their first world championship.

With the Series standing at 4–3, 32,930 jammed into Comiskey Park for Game 8. Before the game, Reds manager Pat Moran received information that Hod Eller, his Game 8 starter, had been approached by gamblers. Upon hearing this, Moran confronted Eller, who admitted that he had been approached, but claimed that he had told the gamblers to go away and stay away. Moran warned his pitcher that he'd be keeping a close eye on him, but sent Eller out to start the game.

Eller's performance quickly removed any doubts about whether he was on the level, as he allowed only one run through the first seven innings. His pitches were jumping around so much that they were nearly unhittable, and Chicago manager Kid Gleason asked umpires to examine the ball on several occasions to see if Eller was up to any funny business.

---

8.   For the first time since 1903, the World Series was a best-of-nine affair. This change was made in an attempt to increase revenue; because of WWI, the 1919 season had been shortened by a couple of weeks.

CINCINNATI REDS

Among the group of on-duty Chicago police officers working the game, one rooted openly for the Reds: Detective Tony Mullane. Back in the 1880s and '90s, Mullane had been a star pitcher for the Reds, including a superb 31-win season for that second place 1887 club.[9] After his playing career was over, he spent 20-odd years with the Chicago P.D.

By the eighth inning, Cincinnati had built a 10–1 lead, and the Series seemed to be locked up. Roush was the hitting star, going 3-for-5 with two doubles and four RBI, plus "spectacular fielding" in center field. Left fielder Pat Duncan chipped in a double and a single to go along with three runs batted in.

The White Sox gave the Reds (and the gamblers) a bit of a scare, scoring four runs in the bottom of the eighth. But when Eller induced Joe Jackson to ground out to second an inning later, the victory was secured. The Cincinnati Reds were champions of the baseball world for the first time ever.

Kid Gleason praised Moran, but otherwise seemed baffled after the game. "The Reds beat the greatest ball team that ever went into a World's Series [sic]," he said.[10]

For his part, Moran gave credit to his players. "They played great baseball for me all summer," he said. "And they played the greatest baseball of all in this World's Series."

Indeed they did, and despite the controversy, that 1919 club is celebrated to this day as Cincinnati's first World Series champion.

---

9.   Mullane is a member of the Reds Hall of Fame, and one of the all-time characters to play for the organization. In the words of Bill James: "He was a great pitcher, and he was a spoiled, self-indulgent prima donna, a bit of a bully, a racist, and a pioneer who explored the depths of tactlessness and selfishness in contract negotiations."

10.   Over the years, evidence has surfaced that, early in the Series, the White Sox players who were in on the fix called the whole thing off after gamblers didn't pay up. Roush and his Cincinnati teammates always contended that the Reds would have beaten them anyway. Reflecting on the 1919 Series later in his life, Roush said: "I don't know whether the whole truth of what went on there with the White Sox will ever come out. Even today, nobody really knows exactly what took place. Whatever it was, though, it was a dirty, rotten shame."

14

BASEBALL GENIUS: JOE MORGAN

Joe Morgan was often called "a good little player." That second adjective burned him up. Yes, he was a short kid (and grew to only 5'5" and 140 pounds by the time he made the major leagues), but Joe never saw himself as little. And why did it matter, when he was picked first whenever the kids chose sides for a game?[1]

Morgan was born in Texas, but grew up in Oakland. The Morgan family wasn't well off, but Joe had what he needed, thanks to his father's quiet work ethic. "As a kid I thought I was rich, but I wasn't," Joe said. "Later, I found out it was because [my father] was working two or three jobs."

Although he excelled in youth ball and at Castlemont High School, that "little player" tag always held him back. He watched teammate Rudy May sign with the Twins, but Morgan wasn't on the radar of big league scouts. He headed off to Oakland City College, unable even to get an offer from a four-year school.

But after a year studying business and leading the team in average and stolen bases—not surprisingly, Morgan was the best player in the league—he finally attracted some attention. Eventually, in November 1962, Bill Wight signed Morgan to a contract with the Houston Colt .45s.[2]

Less than one year later, he was playing in the major leagues. And by Opening Day 1965, he was the starting second baseman for the newly renamed Houston Astros. He was a good player (no modifier) from the start, leading the National League in walks and finishing second in Rookie of the Year voting.

From the beginning, Morgan's biggest asset was his batting eye. Early in his minor league career, he'd learned a valuable lesson from manager Billy Goodman, who confronted Morgan for swinging at the first pitch. Goodman explained the theory he had adopted from

---

1. Eventually, he'd reclaim the phrase. "Good Little Player" was the title of the first section of his autobiography.
2. Joe's dad, after plying Wight with beer after beer, was able to negotiate the signing bonus from $2,000 to $3,000.

former teammate Ted Williams: swinging at the first pitch creates a disadvantage that may echo throughout the game.

Morgan learned that, even when he had a pitcher figured out early in the game, taking pitches would expose him to the pitcher's repertoire, which could pay dividends late in the game. It was simple, Morgan explained: "The more pitches you take, the more you see what he has. The more you see what he has, the more prepared you are."

In 1968, a season-ending knee injury proved to be "a blessing in disguise" for Morgan. "With time off, I had a chance to study. I made it a project to go to every single home game the Astros played. I took a seat directly behind the plate, and I literally went to school. I had no lesson plan, no curriculum that I mapped out for myself. I was intent only on learning by observing."

Morgan reaped the benefits of that self-study for the rest of his career. He started keeping a notebook of how every pitcher, catcher, and infielder played. He learned the nuances of every pitcher's pickoff move, their tells, and their blind spots. Always analytical, Morgan figured that hard work on reading pickoff moves would pay off particularly well, due to the unbalanced nature of the subject matter. "How many pitchers work hard at holding runners on? It stands to reason that I should be better than they are."

So Morgan entered the 1969 season with a unique self-administered "green light—red light" system for stealing bases. Most times, the pitcher's first move would tell him whether he could steal (green) or needed to head back to the bag (red). Not only did he get faster jumps, he could take bigger leads, confident that he could return to the bag in advance of any pickoff throw.[3]

When the knee injury healed and he was able to get back on the field, Morgan's confidence in his abilities began to soar. "My sense of who I was on the field was totally different. Far from feeling like I was a little guy up against it in cavernous new stadiums, I realized I was a player of the future, ideally suited to these new parks. When 1969 rolled around, I was a graduate of my own school."

Results? Morgan's stolen base total jumped from 29 in 1967 to 49 in 1969, and he even improved his success rate.

---

3.   Bigger leads make stolen bases easier, obviously. But Morgan's were so big that he could peek in and steal an unsuspecting catcher's signs *from first base*, then relay the information to the hitter.

CINCINNATI REDS

The new, improved Joe Morgan drew attention in Cincinnati. While the Reds won the 1970 NL pennant, it was already becoming evident that their roster wasn't at all suited to new Riverfront Stadium, with its wide power alleys and artificial turf. Late in the disappointing 1971 season, Reds general manager Bob Howsam began looking for ways to add speed, a left-handed bat, and a starting pitcher for the 1972 season.

Howsam set his sights on Morgan, who wanted out of Houston, badly. He didn't get along with manager Harry "the Hat" Walker—in truth, few black or Latino players did—and by October 1971, the Astros were ready to trade Morgan.

It took nearly two months, but Howsam finally closed the deal at the winter meetings in November. The Astros got power-hitting first baseman Lee May, Gold Glove second baseman Tommy Helms, and utility man Jimmy Stewart; the Reds got Morgan, third baseman Denis Menke, starting pitcher Jack Billingham, and outfielders Ed Armbrister and César Gerónimo.[4]

The trade was unpopular with many Reds fans, but Anderson knew how big the move was. "Boss," he told Howsam, "you just won us a pennant with that deal."[5]

The Reds welcomed Morgan warmly, and wisely. Sparky Anderson immediately began promoting Morgan as one of the game's elite players, a move that may have made some players nervous, but merely added motivational fuel for the already confident and competitive Morgan. Joe felt driven to live up to the hype.

Anderson also instructed clubhouse manager Bernie Stowe to put Morgan's locker next to Pete Rose's. He thought Morgan could take the leap from star to superstar, and correctly sensed that Morgan would see Rose as a measuring stick.

Sparky also acknowledged Morgan's intelligence right off the bat, greeting him with an unprecedented show of faith. "Joe, I'm going to let you manage Joe Morgan," Sparky said. Morgan could decide for himself when to steal, bunt, or swing away. There would be no signs, just trust. Sparky explained, "I will expect you to make the right decisions and I will

---

4.   Gerónimo was almost the deal-breaker. Howsam loved his glove, and believed that Gerónimo would eventually hit. Most observers, including Anderson, disagreed. To that point, Gerónimo's career average was .228. In nine seasons as a Red, he'd hit .261/.330/.371.

5.   Fan reaction was ridiculous and hyperbolic (May and Helms were both very popular), and *Enquirer* writer Bob Hertzel wasn't much better: "If the United States had traded Dwight Eisenhower to the Germans during World War II, it wouldn't have been much different than sending May and Helms to Houston."

never question your judgment unless you come to me and tell me you can't handle the pressure."

"It was an unheard-of thing," Morgan remembered. "No one else on the ballclub had this freedom. It was such a challenge and such an act of trust."

By late July 1972, everything was going according to plan. The Reds were now scoring runs with both power *and* speed, and they'd stretched their lead to seven games. *Sports Illustrated* declared Morgan to be the Reds'—and the National League's—Most Valuable Player.

Morgan's conscious evolution—his fulfillment as a player—is plain to see, in retrospect. The lost 1968 season led to 1969's stolen base explosion. And after spending the 1972 season watching fly balls carry over Riverfront's wall, Morgan was receptive to hitting coach Ted Kluszewski's suggestion that Morgan adopt a slight uppercut and hit more fly balls—a counterintuitive suggestion for the team's best base stealer and on-base man.

But like almost everything Joe Morgan tried, it worked beautifully. In 1973, Morgan hit 26 home runs, eclipsing his previous career high of 16. He also notched a career high with 35 doubles, seven more than his prior best.

Morgan was constantly seeking an edge, which meant he fit right in with the Reds. "The Reds had a kind of team intelligence I have never seen anywhere else," he said years later. "We were always looking for ways to gain that little extra, to help each other out." Where Morgan was sometimes the only Astro taking early hitting or fielding practice, all of the Reds Big Four stars, and most of the others, went in for extra work.

Morgan's search for an edge extended to the off-season, where his work went far beyond the usual exercise regimen, hitting drills, and video study. He challenged himself to master tennis (hand-eye coordination), dominoes (mental concentration and recall), and golf (pure competition).

Morgan's hyper-competitive, must-always-improve nature revealed itself in every activity. Fellow Alameda County native Willie Stargell told how Morgan kept the neighborhood domino expert up half the night, playing over and over again until he won. Another time, Morgan challenged Stargell, an Army Reservist and shooting sport enthusiast, to

Joe Morgan takes a lead off first base during a July 1975 game at Riverfront Stadium.
(Malcolm Emmons-USA TODAY Sports)

a skeet shooting match. Stargell won, but later learned that Morgan had been at the range all night before the match, practicing.

With constant work, Morgan's system for evaluating pickoff moves evolved into something he could barely explain. "I've advanced to the point where I see a pitcher's total body," he explained in 1976. "I don't focus on any part of it. I don't have to look specifically at his head or his shoulders or his legs, but I still see all of them in perfect focus. It all gets to be like a green light that says 'go' or a red light that says 'stop.'"

He was, in Sparky Anderson's estimation, the "smartest player I ever coached," and declared by *Sports Illustrated* to be "baseball's most complete player."

Morgan cherished that label (but was careful to distinguish it from "the best," which was a matter of opinion). "I'm blessed with the ability to do more things than other people can. I'm not the best power hitter in baseball, not the best hitter for average, not the best fielder, not the best base stealer. But when you put all those things together, no player in baseball can do any two of them better than Joe Morgan."

By 1976, Joe Morgan had earned the right to speak about himself in the third person. Even that was calculated, he said. "To be a star, to stay a star, I think you've got to have a certain air of arrogance about you, a cockiness, a swagger on the field that says, 'I can do this, and you can't stop me.'

"It's always been part of my makeup. Maybe it comes from being a little guy. I've always been a lot pushier than other people. Joe Morgan has never waited for things to happen. No, sir. Joe Morgan has always made things happen."

Joe Morgan liked making things happen. Being disruptive. "To me, my greatest moments are when I walk, steal second and third, then score on a sacrifice fly. We've produced a run without a time at bat. Think what it does to a pitcher's mind when he hasn't given up a hit but he's gotten one run behind." Just the thought of it made Morgan laugh with malicious delight.

An otherwise-forgettable July 1977 game displayed the breadth of Morgan's disruptive talents. He scored five runs without getting a single hit. He walked three times, stole two bases, and forced poor San Francisco infielders into two errors.

Morgan's day-in, day-out excellence in all facets of the game added up, as did the accolades. Morgan was an All-Star each of his eight seasons in a Reds uniform. He won the Gold Glove five straight years. He finished in the top 10 for MVP balloting five consecutive years, winning back-to-back trophies in 1975–76.

Battling injuries, Morgan's production fell off in 1978–79, and the Reds let him leave as a free agent after the 1979 season. He played out his career as a sort of homecoming tour, playing again for Houston, returning to the Bay Area to play for the Giants, spending another season with Rose and Pérez on the 1983 Phillies, and finally ending up with his hometown Athletics.

Meanwhile, very quietly, Morgan had been working on his education. His father, Leonard, had made it through three years of college, but quit to work and raise a family. Joe left Oakland City College after a year to sign with the Colt .45s, but promised his mother that he'd eventually finish school.

He went back to school after the 1972 World Series, and attended in the off-seasons through the 1970s (he often joined spring training a few days late while he finished exams). In 1990, 27 years after making the promise to his mother, Morgan graduated from California State University-Hayward. "I'm glad I didn't promise Mom a schedule," he remembered.

Just hours after his final game as a player in 1984, Morgan was on a plane to a business meeting. This wasn't a spur of the moment idea. He'd been planning for a life after baseball for years. While with the Reds, Morgan would spend the off-seasons working for the Bay Area's Budweiser distributor. While with the Phillies, he'd investigate business deals on his off days. Astros owner John J. McMullen hooked Morgan up with Coca-Cola execs.

"I wasn't interested in a little money," he wrote in his autobiography. "I had enough to retire on. But I was interested in a lot of money."

Eventually, Morgan owned Wendy's restaurant franchises—that flight right after retirement was to a two-week training at company headquarters—along with a Coors distributorship, a string of travel agencies, and a Honda dealership. Morgan the businessman made a lot of money—more than he ever did as a player.

While he was proud of leaving a legacy for his daughters, it wasn't only about the money. Morgan took pride in inspiring fellow players, and paving the path for other minorities in the business world.

For two decades prior to his death in 2020, Morgan helped preserve and promote the game's history as vice chairman of the Board of Directors of the National Baseball Hall of Fame. He was also involved in the Baseball Assistance Team (BAT), which provides confidential help to members of "the baseball family" who are suffering financial and medical hardships.

Joe Morgan may have been a little guy, but his tireless work ethic, keen intelligence, and uncanny ability to maximize his skills transformed him into one of the giants of his era and an integral cog in one of the most storied dynasties in baseball history.

15

THE MODERN SCIENCE OF HITTING: JOEY VOTTO

When Joey Votto was drafted in the second round out of a Toronto-area high school, his swing was much like you see today. He hadn't fully developed his approach to hitting yet, but he was well on his way. After all, Votto's homework was different from many high school kids. He toted around a copy of Ted Williams' *The Science of Hitting*, and (also unlike most high school boys) he had a Ted Williams poster on his wall.

Votto didn't just study books. He met with then-Reds minor league coach Leon Roberts shortly after he was drafted in 2002. Roberts had talked hitting with Williams several times and used that knowledge to help young Votto work out his ideal mental approach to hitting.

"I found out Joey Votto was a big Ted Williams enthusiast," Roberts said in 2014. "When I heard that, I started teaching him some of Ted Williams' concepts. I'd tell him, 'Here's what you're doing, here's what Ted did.' It helped him see what changes he needed to make."

As a minor leaguer, Votto paid for a subscription to MLB.TV, so he could conduct late night study of Barry Bonds, Todd Helton, and Manny Ramirez. Votto's voracious video study only expanded as he reached the majors.

Easily the most analytical, introspective Reds player of his era, Votto can casually drop the names of Sabermetric pioneers and second-level metrics.[1] He ranks high by almost any measure, but when you want a quick and dirty look at a hitter's performance, you can check OPS+. Between 1969 (baseball's second expansion year) and 2017, Votto ranked fourth with a 158 OPS+. The only men ahead of him: Barry Bonds, Mike Trout, and Mark McGwire.

That's greatness. Inarguably. Yet Votto still heard frequent criticism from some fans and members of the media, who argued that he got too many walks and not enough RBI.

---

1. Votto once told a Cincinnati sports radio audience that the most meaningful statistic is weighted runs created plus (wRC+).

"I don't care what people think of me," Votto responded. He told *ESPN the Magazine* in 2013, "I've stopped caring about runs and RBIs. I care more about how high a percentage of productive at-bats I can have, how consistently tough and competitive I can be for the opposing pitcher. That's my goal every single time I go up there."

On August 2, 2016, Votto delivered perhaps the purest execution of that goal—what writer August Fagerstrom called "the most Joey Votto game of all the Joey Votto games."

The game was a dramatic highlight of a lousy Reds season, so let's set the stage: It was an emotional night for Reds players and fans alike, as it was the Reds first game without longtime franchise mainstay Jay Bruce, who had been traded to the Mets a day earlier. The Reds pregame clubhouse was somber, as players processed the loss of their affable teammate.

The Reds recalled Scott Schebler from AAA to fill Bruce's right-field position, but didn't expect him to provide the same left-handed power—Bruce departed with 25 home runs and a league-leading 80 RBI—particularly on a night when the Cardinals were throwing their ace, Adam Wainwright. Votto probably wasn't looking forward to it, either. He entered the night with just a .163 career average against Wainwright.

Billy Hamilton led off the Reds first with a walk, then stole second. Ivan De Jesus, Jr. moved him to third with a groundout, bringing up Votto for the first time.

After a horrific start to his 2016 season (.213/.330/.404 through May), Votto first diagnosed the problem ("I was striking out a tremendous amount."—57 times in 52 games), then started "talking to" other greats who'd battled their way out of similar slumps.

But he didn't use the phone. Votto dug deep into old statistics online. "I looked back at Willie Mays in the early 1960s and Stan Musial in the 1950s and Derek Jeter in his early thirties. All of them had really poor starts," Votto told reporter Hal McCoy. "And they all exceeded their career numbers that year when it was all said and done."

"They didn't speak to me directly, but they spoke to me through their Baseball-Reference page, through their game logs and their game experience. And I'm grateful for that and hope that in the future I get to do that for a younger player."

Joey Votto watches his two-run home run leave Wrigley Field in an August 2023 game against the Cubs. (Paul Beaty/AP Images)

Communing with hitters past worked. For June and July, Votto hit .361/.505/.584, and for the two weeks immediately prior to this game, he'd hit an absurd .500/.619/.804. Votto was as locked in as anyone could be when Wainwright started him off with a high fastball.

Votto did the one thing he supposedly never did—swing at the first pitch, hitting a ground-rule double to left-center to knock in the game's first run (and extend his personal hitting streak to 16 games). While sometimes mischaracterized as *passive*, Votto was actually a very *selective* hitter. Like Ted Williams, Votto understood that the first rule of hitting is to get a good pitch *to hit*.

The game was tied 1–1 as Votto batted to lead off the fourth. Wainwright missed badly on the first two fastballs and with the count 2–0, he tried to get Votto to chase the curveball. Wainwright's curve was one of the best in the game, but Votto immediately recognized that this one wasn't going to be a strike and laid off. Just outside.

Votto had the green light with the count 3–0, and when Wainwright threw a fastball right down the middle, Votto smoked it to center field for a single. He was left stranded, but Reds catcher Tucker Barnhart gave the Reds the lead with a long home run in the bottom of the fifth.

Later that inning, Votto came to the plate with a runner on first and worked a walk, laying off several close pitches. It was Joey Votto, distilled to his purest form.

In the top of the seventh, Reds reliever Ross Ohlendorf gave up a leadoff home run to give St. Louis a 3–2 lead. Two batters later, Votto chased a foul popup near the Reds dugout, where he came into contact with a Reds fan seated in the front row, who was also going for the ball. Votto, irritated that the fan didn't clear the way for a possible out, gave him an icy stare and tugged at the Reds logo on the fan's shirt, as if to say, "Don't forget who you want to win this game."

It marked the latest step in Votto's summer-long, until-then-hilarious anti-fan trolling campaign. Votto seemed to take sinister delight in serving as the villain across the National League. In Los Angeles, he Godzilla-stomped a paper airplane that landed near first base. In Washington and Philadelphia, he teased fans begging for baseballs by (repeatedly) pretending to toss them a ball. After the Phillies game, he dryly told the media, "I have no problems with any of the Philly fans, except for the Philly fan kids. I can't stand kids here. Kids drive me crazy, Philly fans especially."

Then in San Francisco, he had curtly rejected a young Giants fan who asked for Votto's batting gloves as a souvenir. "You're sitting in the front row. You're elite," Votto said. "This isn't a 'Make A Wish' situation."

But this time was different. This was a Reds fan and Votto wasn't joking. Thankfully, after a few minutes to cool off, Votto realized that he'd gone a bit too far. He apologized, delivered a ball inscribed, "Thanks for being so understanding when I acted out of character," and posed for a quick picture with the fan between innings.[2]

In the meantime, Votto faced a new pitcher in the seventh, lefty Kevin Siegrist, against whom he had struggled during his career. As Votto settled into the batter's box, the national television announcers discussed how much Votto choked up on the bat, and how rare that is in today's game. What they didn't mention was *why* Votto choked up: It wasn't just about staying alive with two strikes. It was also the key to his strategy of defeating (and thereby discouraging) defensive shifts.

"The ability to spread the ball all over the field prevents shifting," he once told Eno Sarris of Fangraphs. "I'm still willing to hit the inside pitch to the middle of the field. The key is how close I can get that barrel to my body. Part of that is choking up. If I shorten my 34-inch bat to 31 inches by choking up, all of a sudden the barrel is three inches closer to my body."

And after getting ahead in the count 2–1, Votto drove an inside fastball up the middle for his third hit of the night.

Votto was known for his mastery of the strike zone, but how good was he? To this point in the game, he had seen 14 pitches. According to the computerized PITCHf/x tracking tool, 10 of the 14 were outside the strike zone. Votto took all 10. That means he saw just four pitches inside the zone. He swung—and got base hits—on three of them.

Votto's single was followed by an Adam Duvall home run (his 26th) and the Reds led 4–3.

The lead didn't last long. For the second time that night, and the team-record 22nd time[3] that season, a Reds reliever gave up a home run to the first batter he faced in an outing. This time it was Blake Wood, and

2. After the game, Votto said, "I felt like I was in the wrong completely there, so I was certainly regretful. He was forgiving and I would like to think all is good, and the [hitter] ended up striking out, anyway."
3. Remember, this was just August 2 and game 106 of 162.

the game was tied 4–4. Two batters later, Wood gave up another homer, and the Cardinals led 5–4.

The Reds loaded the bases with no outs in the eighth, and the Cardinals called on their 34-year-old "rookie" closer, Seung-hwan Oh,[4] who had held hitters to a .162 average in his first four months in the major leagues. Oh needed all of six pitches to get three outs, striking out Billy Hamilton and inducing Ivan DeJesus, Jr. to hit into a double play.

Cincinnati escaped its own bases-loaded jam in the top of the ninth, and the Reds still trailed 5–4 when Votto led off the bottom of the ninth against Oh. As he had in the first inning, Votto jumped on a first pitch fastball for a hard single to right. He was 4-for-4 and had reached base five times.

Duvall followed with his own single, moving Votto into scoring position. After Brandon Phillips popped out to short left, Schebler came up. He already had two singles to mark his return to the majors, and another one could be a game winner. With a 2–1 count, Oh grooved a fastball and Schebler quickly turned and crushed it. It was long enough— it cleared the right-field stands on the fly and then bounced out of the stadium entirely—the only question was whether it would stay fair. Schebler stood at the plate and watched it; on the mound, Oh contorted his body to get an angle. Reds catcher Tucker Barnhart ran from the dugout and was halfway to the plate before he realized how dumb he would look if the ball hooked foul.

On the radio, Marty Brennaman said, "If it's fair, the Reds win it.... It is a home run and this one belongs to the Reds!" Schebler eventually rounded the bases, tossed his helmet across the field, and leaped onto home plate into a mob of teammates.

Schebler was the hero of an emotional night, but there may be no better example of Votto's singular greatness—his mastery of the strike zone, his own refined mechanics, and the pitcher vs. hitter chess match.

---

4.   The 2016 season was Oh's first in MLB, but he had played 11 exceptional years as a reliever in the Korean and Japanese leagues, where he earned the fantastic nickname, "The Final Boss."

FORGOTTEN DRAMA: 1972 NLCS

16. FORGOTTEN DRAMA: 1972 NLCS

For the Big Red Machine, the 1970 World Series loss felt like a speedbump on the highway to immortality. They were loaded with young talent—Johnny Bench, Bobby Tolan, Bernie Carbo, Dave Concepción, Gary Nolan, Wayne Simpson, and Don Gullett—all under the age of 25. Despite the loss to Baltimore, Sparky Anderson and company were planning to dominate the '70s.

Those plans unraveled less than three months later, when Tolan tore his Achilles tendon playing in a January 1971 charity basketball game. Robbed of its primary sparkplug (Tolan stole 57 bases in 1970; Rose was second best with just 12), the Machine sputtered to a fourth place finish. The Reds' offensive output dropped from 775 runs scored to 586; their record fell from 102–60 to 79–83.

Stung by the setback, and educated by watching a full season of AstroTurf baseball at Riverfront Stadium, Reds general manager Bob Howsam knew that serious changes were needed. Without Tolan, the Big Red Machine had a one-dimensional offense and a plodding defense. Howsam fixed that by trading first baseman Lee May, second baseman Tommy Helms, and utilityman Jimmy Stewart to Houston for Joe Morgan, along with pitcher Jack Billingham, third baseman Denis Menke, and outfielders César Gerónimo and Ed Armbrister.

The season started inauspiciously. Or more accurately, it *didn't* start. On April 1, the Major League Baseball Players Association voted to strike. It was baseball's first labor stoppage. While it only lasted 13 days, the strike was an important skirmish in the decade-long war between players and owners.[1]

---

1.   This strike was particularly stupid and self-defeating for the owners. All the players wanted was to use excess money in their pension fund to increase current benefits—they were even willing to put the question to an arbitrator—but ownership chose this hill on which to crush a union that was steadily growing more powerful. The owners were dead wrong, and eventually agreed to what was essentially the union's opening offer.

THE BIG 50

National League play began on April 15, but it was almost like the Reds missed the bell. They started out 2–6 and were quickly five games out of first place. With the Reds at 8–13 on May 10, Sparky Anderson did something he rarely did—he called a team meeting. Whether that brief pep talk was the reason, the Reds ran off a nine-game winning streak, won 26 of their next 32, and were in first place by June 9. From May 12 through August 28, they went 68–32, and opened their lead to 8.5 games. They were never threatened after mid-July, cruising to the finish line and winning the division by 10.5 games.

Morgan was everything advertised, and more, thriving with Rose as a locker-mate and verbal sparring partner. He hit .292/.417/.435, stole 58 bases, and led the league in walks, runs, and OBP. Bench rebounded from a lousy 1971 season, hitting .270/.379/.541 with 40 HR and 125 RBI, and winning another Gold Glove. Rose was Rose, hitting .307/.382/.417 and scoring 107 runs. Bench won his second MVP, with Morgan finishing fourth in the voting.

Their opponent in the National League Championship Series would be the Pittsburgh Pirates. The teams were a near match in quality—Pittsburgh had won 96 games in defense of its 1971 World Series title; the Reds won 95. Though also playing in a modern AstroTurf stadium, the Pirates couldn't match the Reds newly-acquired speed and defense. But their "Pittsburgh Lumber Company" offense, led by Willie Stargell (.293/.373/.558, 33 HR), Richie Hebner (.300/.378/.508), and Roberto Clemente (.312/.356/.479), was certainly a match in terms of average and power. Seven of the Pirates' eight starters hit over .280, and every starter's OBP was above the league average.

Neither team had overwhelming pitching, though. The Pirates staff was led by Steve Blass, who had won 19 games and pitched 249.2 innings of 2.49 ERA baseball. For the Reds, Gary Nolan was the ace. He was on his way to one of the all-time great seasons through the end of July, starting 14–3 with a 1.71 ERA. Shoulder problems limited him to only five starts the rest of the way, and he finished 15–5 with a 1.99 ERA.[2] Billingham proved to be much more than a throw-in to the Morgan trade, leading the team in innings while putting up a league average ERA.

---

2. The Reds opposed surgery—they wanted Nolan back on the field quickly—and prescribed a variety of quack treatments, from having a tooth pulled (really), to using an electrified needle to kill a shoulder nerve. None of it helped.

BEST POSTSEASON PERFORMANCES BY A RED

Grimsley's start earned an 84 Game Score, which is a metric created by Bill James to judge how well a pitcher does in a single game. You start with 50 (an average outing), and add or subtract points based on the length of the outing, and the number of runs, hits, walks, and strikeouts.

The Reds all-time top five:
1. Hod Eller (89) — 1919 World Series Game 5
2. Trevor Bauer (87) — 2020 Wild Card Series Game 1 (Reds lost in 13 innings)
3. Ross Grimsley (84) — 1972 NLCS Game 4
4. José Rijo (81) — 1990 World Series Game 4
5. Homer Bailey (80) — 2012 NLDS Game 3 (Reds lost in 10 innings)

This was the year when Anderson's "Captain Hook" nickname came to the forefront. He'd adopted a simple rule for handling pitchers in the late innings—don't let the starter face the tying run with runners on base. His starters may not have liked it, but it worked. Tom Hall (124.1 IP, 2.61 ERA) and Pedro Borbon (122 IP, 3.17) proved to be a durable, effective left/right setup duo, and Clay Carroll (96 IP, 2.25 ERA, 37 saves) put up one of the Reds all-time great relief seasons.

The Reds had taken eight of 12 against the Pirates during the season, and were publicly cocky, but they entered the series tight. They couldn't forget the 1970 World Series, or the embarrassing 1971 season.

Game 1 of the best-of-five series didn't lighten that mental load. Nolan was busy battling his tooth/shoulder problem, so 21-year-old Don Gullett (3.94 ERA as a starter-reliever) took the mound for Game 1 against Blass. Morgan homered to stake the Reds to an early 1–0 lead, but the Pirates' bats woke up, and the Reds lost 5–1.

The tables turned in Game 2, as the Big Red Machine rumbled to life. The Reds started the game with single, single, double, double, double. Cincinnati was up 4–0 and Pittsburgh starter Bob Moose was in the showers before he recorded a single out. Morgan added another home run, and Hall pitched a masterful 4.1 innings (two hits, one run) in relief of Billingham. The final was 5–3, and the series was even as the teams headed to Cincinnati.[3]

Game 3 matched Nolan against Nelson Briles. Nolan lasted six painful, effective innings—the most Sparky could hope for—and handed over a 2–1 lead to Borbon, who promptly hit Richie Hebner in the foot, and gave up a single to catcher Manny Sanguillen. After a sacrifice bunt moved the go-ahead run into scoring position, Sparky called on Clay Carroll, then asked Carroll to intentionally walk Vic Davalillo to load the bases and set up the double play. Instead, Rennie Stennett, the Pirates 21-year-old utilityman, chopped a ball in front of the plate that bounded all the way over Tony Pérez's head, scoring Hebner, and tying the game.

Carroll escaped the inning without further damage, and returned for the eighth. With one out, he walked Stargell. Oliver followed with a double to the left-field corner, moving Gene Clines (pinch running for Stargell) to third. Another intentional walk set up the double play. This time, Carroll coaxed the ground ball, but it was hit too slowly to double up the hustling Sanguillen. Pittsburgh closer Dave Giusti came on for the five-out save, and the Reds were on the brink of elimination.

Ross Grimsley faced the Pirates' Dock Ellis in Game 4, and said that he'd never felt such pressure in his life. Grimsley had ways of dealing with pressure, though. During his rookie year, the man sometimes known as "Crazy Eyes" consulted with a witch and often took the field with his pockets weighted down with lucky pennies, rocks, and other good luck charms.

Whatever he carried to the mound that October afternoon, it worked. Grimsley gave up two hits, including a home run, to Clemente, but he no-hit the rest of the Pirates roster (and had two base hits himself). The Reds stole three bases, executed a pair of two-out squeeze bunts, and forced the Pirates into three errors. Final score: Reds 7, Pirates 1. Grimsley's final pitching line (9 IP, 2 H, 1 ER, 0 BB, 5 K) still holds up as the best performance by a Reds pitcher in an elimination game, and one of the greatest postseason starts in team history.

Game 5 brought a rematch of Game 1 starters, Gullett and Blass. Blass was again effective, but Gullett was knocked out in the fourth. Fortunately for the Reds, Borbon, Hall, and Carroll combined for six

---

3.   Hard to believe, but Game 2 wasn't televised nationally. NBC had the rights to both League Championship Series, as well as the NFL. The NL stubbornly started its game at 1:00 PM on Sunday anyway, and NBC chose to show football instead.

innings of two-hit, scoreless relief. The Reds entered the ninth down 3–2, just three outs from another disappointment. Pittsburgh had Giusti coming on to pitch. One of baseball's elite firemen, Giusti was having his finest season, giving the Pirates 74.2 innings of 1.93 ERA relief, and saving 22 games.

Johnny Bench led off the ninth for the Reds. Down a run, this was the ideal situation for the power-hitting Bench to swing for the fences. But Bench was smarter than that. He knew that Giusti's specialty was the palmball, which acted much like a split-finger fastball. The pitch was deceptive in trajectory and speed, punishing hitters who were anticipating a fastball.

Bench dreaded Giusti's palmball, but had a plan. "Before he went to the plate, he told me what he was going to do or, rather, what he was not going to do," Morgan wrote in his autobiography. "He had no thought of trying to pull Giusti, he said, he was going to take him to right field."

Bench did just that, staying back on a 1–2 palmball and lining a homer into the right-field stands—one of the most dramatic blasts in franchise history. The game was tied, and Tony Pérez came to the plate.

Pérez, long praised as the Big Red Machine's top clutch hitter, delivered again, singling to left. "Now we're gonna win," Bench thought from the dugout. Sparky sent 22-year-old George Foster out to pinch run. Third baseman Denis Menke singled, moving Foster into scoring position.

Pirates manager Bill Virdon pulled his closer and brought in Bob Moose. Moose may have been the Pirates number two starting pitcher, but he had made only one relief appearance all season, and he'd gotten shellacked by the Reds in Game 2, three days earlier.

The next hitter, Gerónimo hit a sacrifice fly to right, advancing Foster to third with only one out. But shortstop Darrel Chaney popped out to shortstop, greatly reducing the ways Foster might score from third.

Sparky sent up Hal McRae to pinch-hit for the pitcher. McRae was the Reds best pinch-hitter, with ten pinch-hits on the season and an overall .278/.295/.474 batting line. With the count even at 1–1, Moose overthrew a hard slider a foot and a half outside, uncorking one of the wildest wild pitches in postseason history. Sanguillen never had a chance. The ball spiked into the dirt and bounced 15 feet in the air, sailing all the way to the backstop. Time stood still for a moment, as McRae watched Sanguillen valiantly race toward the backstop, but McRae—and Foster, and everyone else in the ballpark—quickly realized that the run would score easily. McRae didn't even bother waving Foster home—he just started leaping high into the air, over and over. Foster was so tickled that he started celebrating before he even reached the plate. Bench climbed into the stands to kiss his mother.

For a bunch who'd already been to the World Series, it was still a transcendent moment. Morgan, who hadn't been on the 1970 club, said that "to date, it was the biggest thrill I had on a baseball field." Sparky went further, describing Game 5 years later as "my absolutely greatest thrill as a major league manager," even bigger than the 1975–76 World Series titles.

17

DAWN'S EARLY LIGHT: THE BRILLIANCE OF REDS ROOKIES

In the summer of 2023, the Reds unexpectedly found themselves the toast of the baseball world. A twelve-game winning streak powered by a brilliant crop of rookie stars vaulted them to the top of the division, bringing fans back to Great American Ball Park in droves. Elly De La Cruz—the top prospect in baseball—got most of the headlines, but the Reds had no fewer than seven rookies playing significant roles on the club. Among them: former first-rounder Matt McLain, the versatile Spencer Steer, and lefty Andrew Abbott, who became the first pitcher in baseball history to collect at least 60 strikeouts and an ERA under 2.00 in his first 10 career starts.

Leading the club was Jonathan India, a dynamic second baseman who had been named the National League's Rookie of the Year just two seasons prior. Though by 2023 he was considered a veteran at only 26 years old, India was also among the long line of Cincinnati players to make his mark on the league in his first season.

Drafted fifth overall in 2018, India was a slugging third baseman out of the University of Florida. His minor league results were mixed, but during spring training of 2021, India played well enough to force himself onto the Reds roster.

Pressed into duty at second base on Opening Day, India carved his name into history, becoming the first Cincinnati rookie position player to grace the field on the season's first game since Chris Sabo had the honor back in 1988. And if you're wondering when was the last time a second baseman made his debut for the Reds on Opening Day, we need to wind back the clock to Pete Rose in 1963.

India found himself brushing shoulders with heavyweights from Reds' history, but from the get-go, he was certain he belonged. He collected two hits on Opening Day, two more the next day, and ended up hitting safely in seven of his first eight outings. His long flowing hair and enthusiastic play on the diamond made him an instant hit among fans. By season's end, India had posted a line of .269/.376/.459 with 21 home runs and 69 RBIs in 150 games, leading the Reds in steals and runs scored. It was a brilliant debut, but not an uncommon one in franchise history.

* * *

Only three teams can boast more Rookie of the Year winners than the Reds. The first winner was one of the greatest players ever, Frank Robinson. Robbie, a 20-year-old kid who grew up in Oakland, won the award in 1956, the first chapter in a legendary career. That spring training, Robinson had faced a tall challenge, trying to crack a lineup packed with power hitters like Ted Kluszewski, Gus Bell, and Wally Post. But the Reds needed a left fielder, and they needed a right-handed slugger. Robinson fit the bill on both accounts.

Despite a good spring in which he hit .271 with four homers and 14 RBI in 27 games, Robinson felt certain he was destined to be sent back to minors. He was shagging flies before an early-April exhibition game in Chattanooga when general manager Gabe Paul called him over. Robinson prepared himself for disappointment, but was shocked when Paul told him he was being added to the roster. Robinson hit a homer in that game, and was in the Reds starting lineup on Opening Day.

Before an overflow crowd at Crosley Field, with spectators spilling into the outfield, Robinson delivered immediately. Hitting seventh in the order, Robinson turned around the first big league pitch he ever saw, a fastball from St. Louis' Vinegar Bend Mizell, and delivered a ground rule double off the center field wall, missing a homer by a couple of feet. By midseason, he was hitting .313 with 18 home runs and fans voted him in as a starter on the NL All-Star team.

A raw, uncompromised talent, Robinson dazzled fans and critics alike with his power and speed in leading the Reds to their first winning season in a dozen years. He finished with a .290 batting average, 38 home runs, and 83 RBI, and was a unanimous selection for Rookie of the Year. Robbie went on to be a 14-time All-Star, a two-time World Series champion, and the first (and still the only) player to win the Most Valuable Player award in both the National and American Leagues.

* * *

Seven years later, Pete Rose was the next Red to win rookie honors. Born and bred in Cincinnati, Rose's journey to becoming a Reds legend came when he signed for $5,000 out of Western Hills High. In his first full season of pro ball, Rose hit 30 triples and stole 30 bases, earning the nickname "Scooter."

That nickname was soon replaced, of course, when Rose earned the famous "Charlie Hustle" tag in his first big-league spring training. It wasn't a compliment—legendary Yankees pitcher Whitey Ford coined the name because he thought Rose's approach was phony—but it became Rose's brand.

The 22-year-old rookie burst onto the scene in 1963, not with the thunderclap of a power hitter, but the steady drumbeat of an indefatigable worker. His energy was contagious; his playing style relentless. He didn't just play baseball; he chased it, sought it, grappled with it, as if each game was his last. Mentored by Robinson, Rose batted .273 in his debut season, tallying 170 hits and 101 runs. Rose won the Rookie of the Year in a landslide (17 of 20 possible votes), and learned about the honor while he was waxing the kitchen floor, at boot camp for the National Guard.

* * *

Five years later, another baseball legend debuted with the Reds on his way to a spot in the inner circle of the National Baseball Hall of Fame. Hailing from Binger, Oklahoma, John Lee Bench arrived in Cincinnati as a 20-year-old brimming with potential. His blend of power and defensive brilliance made him an immediate standout. Bench's debut season was a showcase of this dynamic talent, signaling the arrival of a player who would redefine the role of the catcher.

Johnny Bench's first full season was 1968, a year known in baseball history as "The Year of the Pitcher." That didn't faze Bench, who had been featured on the cover of *Sports Illustrated* even before the season began. In his inaugural campaign, Bench hit .275 with 15 home runs, 40 doubles, and 82 RBIs, all while demonstrating game-changing, Gold-Glove-winning skill behind the plate. It was barely enough to take the ROY title, though. Bench finished a single vote ahead of Mets hurler Jerry Koosman, who had won 19 games with a 2.08 ERA [1]

---

1.   The irony is that Bench shouldn't have even been eligible for the award. A late-season call-up in 1967, Bench suffered a broken thumb on September 29, ending his season just four at bats short of exhausting his rookie status.

CINCINNATI REDS

The potential Bench demonstrated during that rookie season was a mere glimmer of the brilliance to come. He developed into perhaps the best catcher in baseball history, a key figure on the Big Red Machine teams that dominated the 1970s. Bench was a 14-time All-Star, 10-time Gold Glove winner, and two-time National League MVP. But the awards and statistics alone don't capture the true scope of Bench's impact. By the time he retired in 1983, Bench had cemented his place among the game's all-time greats.

* * *

Not every Reds Rookie of the Year Award winner was a superstar on the level of Robinson, Rose, and Bench. Tommy Helms, an unassuming infielder from North Carolina, emerged on the Major League scene in 1966 with a steadiness and consistency that belied his rookie status. Known for his defensive skill, Helms quickly became a reliable cornerstone of the Reds' infield.

A shortstop by trade, Helms was blocked by Leo Cardenas and Pete Rose in Cincinnati's middle infield. He shifted over to third base and, in the only season he ever played the position, won top rookie honors, hitting .284 with nine home runs and 49 RBIs. Moving over to second base the following year, Helms' rookie campaign served as the springboard for a solid big league career. He spent eight of his fourteen seasons with the Reds, earning two All-Star berths and a couple of Gold Glove Awards. Helms was inducted into the Reds Hall of Fame in 1979, but he is perhaps best remembered for being a piece of the trade that brought Joe Morgan from Houston to Cincinnati.

* * *

While some stars burn long and steady, others blaze brightly for a brief, unforgettable moment. A decade after Helms' debut, Pat Zachry became one of only three pitchers ever to secure top rookie honors while helping lead his team to a championship. Hailing from Texas, Zachry was 24 when he arrived in Cincinnati in April 1976, joining the defending World Series champs.

His first eight appearances were out of the bullpen, and he allowed only two earned runs in 20 ⅔ innings. In early May, Zachry was inserted into the starting rotation and he promptly won his first four starts, posting an ERA of 1.36 to go with two complete game victories. He would remain in the rotation for the rest of the season, finishing with a 14-7 record and a 2.74 ERA. His complete game victory over San Diego on September 21 clinched the NL West title, and Zachry would earn wins in both the NLCS and World Series, as the Reds swept through the playoffs.

Shortly after cashing his World Series bonus check (the colorful Zachry asked for the full $26,000 in singles), Zachry learned that he had been named co-Rookie of the Year with Padres hurler Butch Metzger. Zachry's tenure with the Reds was brief, however. The following season, he was involved in the trade that brought Tom Seaver to Cincinnati. Zachry was named an All-Star for the Mets in 1978, and while he never again achieved the same heights as his rookie season, he carved out a respectable 10-year career.

* * *

In the spring of 1988, Chris Sabo was not hopeful about his chances to make the Reds roster. "I think the utility job is taken (by Angel Salazar)," he said. "They think I can't play shortstop, but I can." Pete Rose was Reds manager at that time. "Anybody who can hit like him, field like him, run like him and looks like Spuds MacKenzie has a heck of a chance," Rose said. "He could go to Cincinnati with us."

A week later, Houston hurler Joaquin Andujar knocked Sabo back with a little chin music in a spring game. The 26-year-old Sabo responded by hitting three straight doubles. "I never have been, and I won't be intimidated," he said. Shortly thereafter, Rose announced that Sabo had made the big league roster as a utility guy after watching him play shortstop in a couple of B games. "Sabo plays shortstop real well," Rose said. "He is a lot like me. He looks unorthodox, but he catches the ball and throws it. He'll run through a wall for you and kill somebody to score a run."

And that's the story of Chris Sabo in a nutshell, the tale of an underdog who defied first impressions. It's a testament to the magic of baseball, where an unassuming rookie can rise to capture a city's imagination. Sabo, with his trademark goggles and tireless hustle—and a nickname, "Spuds," taken from the name of a dog in a beer commercial-- etched his name into Reds history.

When starting third baseman Buddy Bell sprained his left knee and was forced to open the season on the injured list, Sabo got his opportunity. In his second game, he tied the major league record for assists by a third sacker in a nine-inning game (11), and by the All-Star break, he was hitting .312/.352/.524 with ten homers and 28 stolen bases. He made the first of three All-Star games that summer, receiving the loudest ovation of any player before the contest at Riverfront Stadium. He tailed off a bit in the second half, but edged out Chicago's Mark Grace for rookie honors in the National League.

For the next six seasons, Sabo's distinctive style and relentless work ethic endeared him to the Cincinnati fan base. He was a crucial member of the team that won the 1990 World Series, hitting .563 with two home runs in the championship series (and providing one memorable speech at the parade afterward). In 2010, he was elected to the Reds Hall of Fame.

* * *

The 1999 Reds were a young, exciting team that surprised the baseball world on the way to a 96-win season thanks partly to one of the stingiest bullpens in baseball. Manager Jack McKeon expected to go with a closer by committee strategy, with Danny Graves and Gabe White tapped to finish out games. That was before Scott Williamson emerged.

A ninth-round draft choice in 1997 out of Oklahoma State, Williamson had been a non-roster invitee to 1999 spring training. Despite only 20 ⅔ innings experience at AAA, Williamson surprisingly made the Opening Day roster. After two rough outings in his first three big league appearances, Williamson took off into the stratosphere.

He picked up his first save in late April, tossing three innings of one-hit baseball to close out a one-run victory over Houston. McKeon realized quickly that he could use Williamson (a starter in the minors) for multiple innings, giving him a weapon many teams didn't have. Listed generously at six feet tall, the diminutive Williamson built up momentum on his pitches by crossing his front leg over his back leg as he drove into his pitching motion. This resulted in a 95 mph fastball[2] that gave National League hitters fits.

---

2. That was a pretty good heater in the late 1990s.

Teammates, coaches, and fans praised Williamson for his fearlessness, and the results showed. He was named to the All-Star team after going 7-4 with a 1.66 ERA and 11 saves in the first half. By season's end, he was the NL Rookie of the Year and a key figure in Cincinnati's incredible run to the brink of the playoffs.

In 2003, Williamson was traded to the Red Sox during one of Reds' ownership's regularly scheduled fire sales, and he won a World Series ring with Boston the following year. Unfortunately, injuries dogged him throughout his career, but his rookie performance will long be remembered by devoted readers of Reds history books.

18

1976: BACK-TO-BACK CHAMPS

The Cincinnati Reds were never more dominant than they were during the 1976 season. How dominant? The Reds went 102–60, winning the National League West by 10 games over the Dodgers. They scored 857 runs, nearly a hundred more than the Phillies. They had more singles, doubles, triples, and home runs than any other club. They stole 40 percent more bases than anyone else.[1]

The lineup was full of stars, top to bottom. If one didn't get you, the others would. "If they have one or two guys go into a slump, it's not a big problem," said Dodgers manager Walter Alston. Sparky Anderson knew it, too. "This isn't any three- or four-man team like most clubs, so how you gonna contain 'em? Sooner or later, these guys are gonna get you."

What's your criteria for a good player? It doesn't matter; the Reds were featured at or near the top of every statistical leaderboard.

Morgan (1st), Rose (3rd), and Foster (8th) ranked in the NL's top 10 in WAR. Griffey, Rose, and Morgan ranked 2nd, 4th, and 5th in batting average. Is on-base percentage your thing? Morgan, Rose, Griffey, and Gerónimo all finished in the top eight.

Runs scored? Rose, Morgan, and Griffey ranked 1st, 2nd, and 4th. Foster finished 4th in home runs; Morgan was 5th. In RBI, Foster led the league, Morgan finished 2nd, and Pérez 6th. Rose led in doubles. Morgan topped the league in slugging percentage.

Recognition and awards? Fans voted five Reds onto the NL All-Star team,[2] and Sparky (privileged to manage the team since the Reds were reigning NL champs) added two more as reserves.[3] Morgan won his second consecutive NL MVP. Foster finished 2nd in the balloting, Rose was 4th, and Griffey 8th. Pat Zachry was co-Rookie of the Year and had the league's fifth-best ERA. Morgan, Bench, Concepción, and Gerónimo won Gold Gloves. Rawly Eastwick was 5th in Cy Young voting, led the league in saves, and won the inaugural Rolaids Relief Man Award.

---

1. And with a 79 percent success rate, far better than anyone else.
2. Morgan (the overall top vote-getter), Foster, Bench, Rose, and Concepción.
3. Pérez and Griffey. Among the Reds' "Great Eight" starting lineup, only Gerónimo was missing.

CINCINNATI REDS

When the postseason started, Cincinnati showed no signs of slowing down; the Reds put on a dominating three-game show against the Phillies in the NLCS. Meanwhile, the Yankees were in a five-game dogfight with the Kansas City Royals. Filled with comebacks, controversy, and personal grudges, the ALCS ended with a New York walk-off home run to capture the AL pennant.

That night, the Yankees took advantage of being in "the city that doesn't sleep," partying until the wee hours after the physically and emotionally draining ALCS. Problem was, they had an early morning flight to Cincinnati. "We weren't in any shape to play the World Series," third baseman Graig Nettles later admitted.

That didn't stop Yankees manager Billy Martin from popping off, upon his arrival in Cincinnati. "We're gonna take the windshield wipers off the Machine," he said, before adding a key qualifier. "All I gotta do is sober up before the game tomorrow."

Don Gullett started Game 1 for the Reds, facing Doyle Alexander, who hadn't pitched in three weeks. Yankees manager Billy Martin thought Alexander's off-speed repertoire might fool the Reds heavy hitters.

After two quick outs in the Reds first, Morgan came to the plate. Hitless in the NLCS, Morgan turned things around immediately, crushing a 3-1 fastball from Alexander for a home run. Morgan raised a fist as he rounded first, then waved to his parents and wife in the stands.[4] "That's the beginning!" Sparky shouted on the Reds bench.

The Yankees tied it in the second, but in the third, the Reds flexed their muscle. With one out, Concepción lined a ball to left-center that skipped all the way to the wall. The scouting report said that New York's outfield arms were weak, and the Reds intended to test them. Concepción, who had seven triples on the season, never hesitated around second, and beat center fielder Mickey Rivers' feeble, off-target throw easily. Rose lifted a sacrifice fly and the Reds led 2-1.

That was all Gullett would need, but the Reds added a run in the sixth and two in the seventh. Cruising along with a 5-1 lead in the eighth inning, Gullett felt his ankle pop and left the game. Diagnosed

---

4.   "I came as close to hot-dogging it as I ever have," Morgan remembered in his autobiography.

October 21, 1976, the Bronx, New York: Johnny Bench is congratulated by third-base coach George Scherger after hitting one of his two home runs against the Yankees during Game 4 of the World Series. (Dick Raphael-USA TODAY Sports)

with a dislocated tendon, Gullet was placed in a cast. His season, and ultimately his outstanding Reds playing career, was over.[5]

For the first time in history, the Series combatants used the designated hitter. That, plus the short series, meant that not a single bench player made it into a game. The Great Eight played every inning of every game, and Dan Driessen took every at-bat as the Reds DH.

Leading off the second inning in Game 2, Driessen doubled to left-center off Yankee starter Jim "Catfish" Hunter. Foster singled him in, and the Reds led 1–0. Foster was then caught stealing, which hurt because Bench followed with a double. Gerónimo walked, and Concepción

---

5. Gullett was the only member of the Reds eligible for the newly instituted free agency. Just a month later, he signed a six-year, $2 million contract with the Yankees, breaking Sparky Anderson's loyal, traditionalist heart.

singled to score Bench and move Gerónimo to third (the Reds would *always* go first-to-third against the Yankee outfield arms). Concepción stole second and Rose walked to load the bases for Griffey, who hit a soft, short fly ball that Rivers caught running straight in. Again taking advantage of Rivers' arm, Gerónimo tagged up and scored easily. The Reds led 3–0.

Hunter shut the Reds down after that second inning outburst, while the Yankees were chiseling away at the Reds' lead, scoring one in the fourth and rallying in the seventh. With one run in, one out, and the tying run on third, Sparky called on Jack Billingham to relieve starter Fred Norman. Billingham got catcher Thurman Munson to ground out, but the tying run scored.

The game stayed tied into the bottom of the ninth. Hunter was still on the mound, and he quickly retired Concepción and Rose, then put Griffey in an 0-2 hole. Protecting the plate, Griffey chopped the ball to Fred Stanley at short. Griffey had 38 infield hits on the season, and might have beat this one out, but Stanley's throw went wide of first and into the Reds dugout.

The Yankees intentionally walked Morgan to get to Pérez, the man always touted as the Reds' best clutch hitter. "Big mistake," Morgan said to Munson as the Yanks completed the intentional pass. Pérez quickly proved him right, lining Hunter's first pitch into left field to score Griffey and put the Reds up two games to none. It was all according to formula: the Reds' speed pressured the defense into a mistake, and the big hitters turned the mistake into a run.

The Series moved to New York and the Reds turned tourist, gawking at newly remodeled Yankee Stadium and its monuments, the triple-decked grandstands, and the trademark facade. Zachry started Game 3 for the Reds; Dock Ellis for New York. An intense competitor, Ellis tried to single-handedly get the Yankees back in the Series. It didn't work. Overthrowing, he lost the sink on his sinker, and the Reds scored three runs in the second inning, then added another on Driessen's homer in the fourth.

The Reds were up 4–1 as Rivers led off the bottom of the fifth with a soft single to left. Playing with fire, Zachry walked Roy White to bring up Munson, the soon-to-be-crowned AL MVP. Munson hit a frozen rope to the right side, but Pérez, perfectly positioned, grabbed it and quickly threw to second to double off Rivers, a costly mistake by the Yankees' sparkplug. ("He took off, bless his heart," Sparky said after the game.) The Reds cruised to a 6–2 victory.

The Yankees—having been outscored 15–6 through the first three games—started Game 4 with a first inning run off Gary Nolan, giving them their first, and only, lead of the Series. It lasted all of two innings, because a three-run homer by Bench gave the Reds a 3–1 lead in the fourth. The Yanks cut it to 3–2 with an RBI single by Munson,[6] but would come no closer. Nolan and Will McEnaney would shut them out for the final 4⅔ innings, and Bench's second homer ended the drama in the ninth. The final score was 7–2, and the Reds were champions again.

The Reds' postgame celebration was different from the year before. Whether more professional or more mercenary, the 1976 version of the Big Red Machine was almost subdued in victory. They were thrilled, but composed. Only a few bothered to spray champagne. Rose and Morgan spent their time talking to the press—after first moving their custom suits and "$100 Gucci shoes" to a bubbly-free zone.

Rose missed the action and excitement of the 1975 Series. "This World Series was boring for me," said Rose. As *Sports Illustrated*'s Ron Fimrite put it, "the Yankees were no more of a challenge to [the Reds'] supremacy than a sandlot team from the Bronx."

Bench was named Series MVP, an honor that meant a lot to him. He'd struggled all year, and was finally able to carry the load in the Series, posting a Herculean .533/.533/1.133 batting line.

Another man was still impressed: Bob Howsam. The stoic Howsam's voice was cracking and he was near tears as he explained it: "Maybe when you're young—and I'm much older than our players—you don't realize how satisfying it is to know you're on top of your field—in anything. Right now is the most important period of my baseball life."

---

6.   Munson would add a fourth hit later, giving him a record-tying six consecutive hits. This tied a 42-year-old World Series record—a record that the Reds' Billy Hatcher would break in the 1990 Series.

19

JOHNNY BEISBOL

In March of 2004, Johnny Almaraz was busy.

Almaraz, the Reds' director of international scouting and player development, was working night and day to set up a baseball academy for the team in Boca Chica, a beach town on the southern coast of the Dominican Republic. At the same time, he was trying to get together a team for the Dominican Summer League, in addition to directing his network of international scouts who were scouring the globe seeking out baseball talent.

One of his friends, a local scout, kept pestering Almaraz to go take a look at a little right-handed pitcher from nearby San Pedro de Macoris. Almaraz had heard of the kid, knew he threw 90 to 91 mph, and he also knew that more than a dozen other big league organizations had already passed on him. Too small, they said. Too skinny.

Almaraz was too busy, but his interest was piqued by the glowing report from his scout. "One of my early mentors taught me that good pitchers, good players, come in all shapes and sizes," Almaraz said later.

Almaraz told his friend that the only way he could see the kid throw would be on the way to the airport the next day. "It has to be early and it has to be quick. I have a 10:00 o'clock flight," said Almaraz. "If you can get together a game at 7:00 in the morning tomorrow, I'll look at him."

The game was organized, and Almaraz showed up at the field the next morning. He jumped out of his car and hurried over. "Show me this next Pedro Martinez," he said. "Show him to me!"

Johnny Cueto, 18 years old, short and skinny, wearing the only pair of cleats and only glove that he owned, stepped onto the mound. He reached back and delivered a perfect strike. Over and over, his 91 mph fastball pounded the strike zone, and he mixed in a lethal slider, as well.

Before climbing back into his car and heading to the airport, Almaraz signed Cueto for $35,000.

Four years later, on a rainy afternoon in Cincinnati, Johnny Cueto stood on the mound at Great American Ball Park—his first time inside a major league stadium had been just days earlier. He slowly wound up, and delivered a perfect 96 mph fastball to Arizona's leadoff hitter, Chris Young. Strike one.

By the time he made his major league debut in 2008, Cueto had already demonstrated to everyone that his size was not going to prevent him from being a big-time prospect. Twice, Cueto had been named the Reds' minor league pitcher of the year, and he was barely 22 years old when he reached the big leagues.

Only 11,987 were in attendance that April afternoon, but what they witnessed was special. Cueto was perfect before surrendering a home run in the top of the sixth. That home run was the only time all game that a Diamondback hitter reached base against him. By the time he was removed, Cueto had pitched seven innings of one-run, one-hit baseball, striking out 10 Arizona batters and walking none.

How remarkable was that debut? Well, Cueto was the first pitcher in modern MLB history to strike out at least 10 with no walks in his debut game. He was also the first Reds pitcher in more than a century to record 10 strikeouts in his first appearance.

Special, indeed.

For the next couple of seasons, Cueto would go through the normal ups and downs that every young pitcher experiences. In 2011, at age 25, he turned the corner when he made a radical change to his windup, turning his chest toward second base before delivering to the plate. Observers compared him to Luis Tiant, the Cuban dynamo who Reds fans remembered well (if not fondly) from his work for Boston in the 1975 World Series.

The payoff was nearly immediate—Cueto's 2.31 ERA would've finished second in the NL if he'd pitched enough innings after returning from a nagging injury. In 2012, Cueto put it all together. As the unquestioned ace of an excellent pitching staff, Cueto finished the season with a 19–9 record and a 2.78 ERA, leading Cincinnati to a division title and 97 wins, the most for the franchise in more than a decade. He also started Game 1 of the playoffs, and one wonders how far the Reds might have gone if Cueto hadn't been injured on the eighth pitch of that game.

Two years later, Cueto cemented his place among the elite pitchers in the game. He won 20 games for the first time, with a 2.25 ERA and a league-leading 242 strikeouts (a total that placed him fourth on the all-time Reds single-season strikeout list). The season was a masterpiece, one of the best in club history. Cueto was only the third Reds pitcher since 1900 to lead the National League in both innings pitched and strikeouts in the same season, and the first since Bucky Walters turned the trick in 1939.[1] Even better, Cueto became one of only two Reds in history (Jim Maloney was the other) to strike out that many batters while winning 20 games. No Reds pitcher had started at least 33 games with an ERA as low as Cueto's since Dolf Luque in 1923.

It wasn't only a brilliant season in comparison to his fellow Redlegs. Cueto was only the sixth pitcher in all of baseball since divisional play began in 1969, 45 years earlier, to put together a season of at least 20 wins, 242 strikeouts, and an ERA under 2.30. The other names on that list read like a who's who of baseball's dominant starters of the last half-century: Bob Gibson, Steve Carlton, Tom Seaver, Dwight Gooden, and Clayton Kershaw.

By the time his Reds career ended in mid–2015, Johnny Cueto's name could be mentioned in the same breath as the very best starting pitchers in the history of this storied franchise. Only five pitchers since 1950 have bettered Cueto's total of 25.1 WAR as a Red: Jim Maloney, Gary Nolan, Joe Nuxhall, Mario Soto, and José Rijo, each of whom spent more time in a Cincinnati uniform than Cueto. Among starters who have pitched at least 1,000 innings for the Reds, Cueto has the third-best ERA+ of *all time* (126).

Cueto stands up well among other Reds pitchers by more traditional measures, too. His career strikeout total of 1,115 is eighth-best in club history. His career winning percentage (.594) is seventh-best. Cueto's Reds ERA of 3.21 is barely behind Reds legends like Tom Seaver, Jim Maloney, and Dolf Luque.

For Reds fans of a certain age, Cueto is likely the best pitcher they've ever seen in a red-and-white uniform. Certainly, he merits debate—alongside Rijo, Soto, Nolan, and Maloney—as the best Reds starter of the last 50 years. His career as a Red was brilliant, and over far too soon, unfortunately.

Cueto went on to bigger and better things, including a World Series championship in 2015, but he never stopped being the fun-loving guy that first emerged on the baseball scene in 2008. After each season,

---

1. Noodles Hahn was the other, in 1901.

CINCINNATI REDS

Cueto returns to the Dominican Republic, to his modest home not far from where he grew up, to the place where he was once considered too short and too skinny to be a big league pitcher. Every winter, Johnny Almaraz makes an effort to visit.

Cueto is still small in stature, at least compared to his peers. But back home in the Dominican Republic, and much further north in Cincinnati, Ohio, Cueto is a giant, one of the greatest pitchers in the history of baseball's oldest franchise.

20

THE NASTY BOYS

Norm Charlton was the college guy, a mild-mannered lefty with a fierce competitive streak simmering just below the surface. Rob Dibble was the combustible one, prone to outbursts every bit as spectacular as the fastballs that emerged from his million-dollar arm. Randy Myers was either a nut with a fondness for military gear or the consummate put-on artist—either way, he also happened to be one of the best relief pitchers in baseball.

Together, they were the Nasty Boys, and as the Reds and Pirates prepared to do battle in the 1990 National League Championship Series, Pittsburgh manager Jim Leyland knew that Cincinnati's bullpen was going to be standing between him and the World Series.

"There's no question why they call those guys the Nasty Boys," said Leyland. "They're aggressive pitchers. They're outstanding."

Red-white-and-blue bunting adorned the railings below the blue seats in Riverfront Stadium as nearly 53,000 fans streamed through the gates for Game 1 of the NLCS. It was the first playoff game in the Queen City in 11 years and when the Reds took the field, the applause was thunderous for the hometown nine.

Quickly, the Reds scored three runs in their half of the first inning, thanks to a walk, a single, and back-to-back doubles from Eric Davis and Paul O'Neill. The Pirates, however, chipped away at Reds starter José Rijo, ultimately tying the game at three apiece in the fourth inning.

After recording one out in the sixth, Rijo surrendered two singles, prompting Reds manager Lou Piniella to make the call to the bullpen. Enter Norm Charlton.

Charlton had graduated with a triple-major from Rice University, and thanks to his quiet nature, most assumed he was an eccentric brainy type. Not so, said his catcher, Joe Oliver.

"He's got the triple major," said Oliver, "but when he crosses the lines, he's about as focused or gets lost in the moment as anybody. We kind of called him an idiot when he crosses the white line, but he just plays with his hair on fire."

A perfect example of that "hair on fire" mentality came in June of that season. In the seventh inning of a nationally televised Sunday night game against the Dodgers, Charlton was on first base after being hit by a pitch. When Oliver doubled into the left-field corner, Charlton took off, running straight through the third-base coach's stop sign. Clad in his pitcher's warmup jacket, Charlton lowered his shoulder and smashed violently into catcher Mike Scioscia, and the ball dropped to the ground. Charlton was safe.

That play typified how the Reds wanted to be seen by their opponents: hard-nosed, hard-playing grinders who would never quit.[1]

Though he had been a member of the Nasty Boys bullpen trio all season long, Charlton was actually pressed into service as a starter just after the All-Star break. He started 16 games during the 1990 season, posting an earned run average of 2.60 in those games.

But Charlton was back in the bullpen for the playoffs, and found himself in a tight spot in his first appearance, with the game tied and Pirates on first and second. He immediately made things worse, walking a batter, but then induced Pittsburgh catcher Mike LaValliere to hit into an inning-ending double play.

The game was still tied in the following inning when former Red Gary Redus delivered an excuse-me bloop single into short right field off Charlton. Two batters later, Andy Van Slyke lifted a fly ball to Eric Davis in left field that looked like it would be the third out of the inning. Inexplicably, Davis—who had won three consecutive Gold Gloves— misjudged the ball, and it fell in for a double, scoring the go-ahead run. It wasn't scored an error, so an earned run was charged to Charlton, though you could hardly pin the blame on the lefty. Dibble pitched the ninth, striking out the side in order, but the Reds were down 1–0 in the NLCS.

That was the last earned run that any Nasty Boy would permit for the rest of the 1990 postseason.

Through six innings of Game 2, the Reds had scratched out a 2–1 edge, thanks to two run-scoring hits from O'Neill, who also made a brilliant throw from right field to gun down Pittsburgh's Andy Van Slyke at third base. The Reds had the Pirates right where they wanted them.

---

1. In that Dodgers game, Charlton risked life and limb to extend the Reds lead to 10–4.

"The strongest part of their club is what they can do from the seventh inning on," Phil Neikro, the Braves' pitching coach, had said earlier in the season. "I don't think I've ever seen a bullpen that strong."

A slim lead, seventh inning: time for the Rob Dibble experience.

Dibble was 6'4", 230 pounds and bursting with emotion and competitive fire. Drafted in the first round of the 1983 amateur draft, Dibble—who had been an all-state soccer and baseball player at his Connecticut high school—arrived with a chip on his shoulder. When he was just 19 years old, Cincinnati's big league pitching coach, Bill Fischer, told Dibble that he would never make it to the majors if he didn't change his mechanics.

Upset, Dibble set out to prove him wrong, but it was a long, slow slog through the minors until he finally made his major league debut in 1988. At one of those stops along the way, he met Charlton and the two became roommates (mostly because no one else on the club wanted to room with Dibble). They continued to room together until long after each was an established major leaguer.

Dibble's mechanics—arms raised behind his head, glove hand flailing, high leg kick—didn't change much, but his fastball kept improving. In 1989, Dibble's first full season with the Reds, he set an all-time major league record by striking out 12.8 batters per 9 innings.[2] In 1990, Dibble made his first All-Star team, the first setup man ever to earn such recognition. He consistently threw more than 100 miles per hour, according to the radar guns at the time, and he also had a penchant for throwing at hitters (or baserunners, or even fans in the center-field seats) when he felt the occasion demanded it. It all added up to an intimidating persona that made Dibble the most fearsome relief pitcher in all of baseball.[3]

"I don't care if you're right-handed, left-handed, cross-handed...or standing on your head," Leyland said. "If Rob Dibble is throwing strikes [at] 100 mph, it doesn't make a lot of difference."

Dibble sprinted to the Riverfront mound and stared in with his customary glassy eyes—another way he intimidated hitters—to get the sign from Oliver. The Pirates never had a chance. Dibble pitched an

---

2. As a measure of how much things have changed in the meantime, Dibble's 12.8 K/9 now ranks just 163rd (Min. 50 IP).

3. Marge Schott had a different view of Dibble. "Rob is like a baby," said Schott. "I'd like to just spank him. He's a good boy, but I'll smack his arm and tell him to shut up."

inning and a third of hitless baseball, striking out two. When he issued a one-out walk in the eighth, Piniella turned to his primary closer, Randy Myers. Myers went the rest of the way and didn't allow a hit, thanks to some outstanding defensive work from Barry Larkin, who made two brilliant plays at shortstop. When it was over, Myers had picked up a save and the Series was tied at one game apiece.

The teams moved to Pittsburgh's Three Rivers Stadium for Game 3. Reds center fielder Billy Hatcher hit a two-run home run in the second, and second baseman Mariano Duncan followed up with a three-run bomb of his own in the fifth to break a 2–2 tie. One inning later, the stage was set for the Nasty Boys to bring home yet another victory.

Dibble was the first of the trio to enter, replacing starter Danny Jackson with one out and a runner on second in the sixth. Nine pitches later, Dibble had struck out two Pirates hitters and the nascent rally was snuffed out.

Dibble retired the side in order in the seventh before making way for Charlton.[4] Pittsburgh left fielder Barry Bonds (the 1990 NL MVP) led off the inning with an infield single and later came around to score, thanks to a throwing error by Duncan, but Charlton didn't allow a single ball out of the infield in his one inning of work.

The Reds added another run in the top of the ninth, and with a 6–3 lead, Randy Myers made his second appearance of the Series.

Myers had been acquired by Cincinnati in a controversial December 1989 trade that sent popular Reds closer John Franco to the Mets. Myers' antics created an immediate impression on his new teammates. One day during spring training, he went out to a retention pond behind the right-field wall at Cincinnati's facility in Plant City, Florida. The pond was full of water moccasins, and Myers terminated a few, picked them up with a shovel, and returned to the clubhouse. When they saw Myers and his snakes, his teammates scattered quickly.

While he may have made his teammates nervous, the clubhouse was Myers' sanctuary and it was where he got himself in the right frame of mind to go out and finish off games. Some days, he would sit on the floor and read the newspaper with his legs spread, slicing salami and cheese with a machete and eating it. In his locker at Riverfront, Myers

---

4. On the night, Dibble retired all five batters he faced (including three strikeouts) on 15 pitches, 12 of them strikes. That's dominance.

kept two defused hand grenades, two Bowie knives, and a handful of toy plastic soldiers. Under his uniform, Myers wore camouflage.

All these hijinks were irrelevant once the game started because, as it turned out, Myers was an excellent pitcher. In the two seasons prior to the trade, Myers posted a 3.07 ERA with 50 saves for the Mets. Upon joining the Reds, he fell in immediately with his new bullpen mates. Myers is occasionally given credit for naming the trio when, as the legend goes, he walked past Dibble and Charlton throwing on the side during spring training in 1990 and said, "Man, those guys are nasty."[5]

Myers didn't mess around with the Pirates in Game 3, striking out the side on 11 pitches to secure the win and a 2–1 Series lead for the Reds. It was the 15th time that season that all three Nasty Boys appeared in the same game, and it provided more evidence of how important the bullpen triumvirate had become to the team.

"When we're ahead in the late innings," said Todd Benzinger, "you can feel the tension start to grow on the other team's bench. You know they feel their backs are to the wall."

Game 4 saw the Reds take a commanding 3–1 lead in the NLCS with a 5–3 win. O'Neill hit another home run and Chris Sabo broke a 2–2 tie with a two-run homer in the seventh.

It took one of the greatest defensive plays in Reds history to secure the victory, however. In the top of the eighth, Pirates shortstop Jay Bell led off with a home run off starter José Rijo to bring Pittsburgh within one run, at 4–3. Myers entered and retired Andy Van Slyke. Next up, Bobby Bonilla ripped a ball to deep center field. Billy Hatcher leaped against the wall but couldn't make the catch, and he fell to the ground as the ball caromed back toward the infield. Bonilla put his head down and rounded second, nearly assured of a triple.

But out of nowhere Davis, the left fielder, materialized with the baseball in his hand. "It was like Captain Kirk on *Star Trek*," said Reds outfielder Glenn Braggs. "'Beam me up, Scotty.' All of a sudden, he was just there."

On the crack of the bat, Davis had begun sprinting to back up Hatcher, so when the ball bounced off the fence, he was in perfect position. Davis fielded it facing the wall, turned and uncorked a perfect

---

5. Like "The Big Red Machine," there are several alternative stories as to the origins of the "Nasty Boys" nickname. Some credit Myers. Others say that it came from a Janet Jackson song of the same name. Another story is that Nasty Boys was taken from the title of a cop show with that name that was then airing on NBC.

throw to Sabo at third, gunning down Bonilla. As the umpire yelled "out," Bonilla, confused, looked up at his third-base coach and asked: "Who threw that?"

"I was proud of that play," Davis said later. "I believe it's the best play I ever made."

Nasty Boy roles were somewhat reversed in this game, as Myers had entered in the eighth inning to face the left-handed heart of the Pirates lineup. Now he would hand the ball to Dibble to close things out.

As he was warming up in the bullpen, Pirates fans heaped abuse on Dibble. "The people with the green weenies were really giving us the razz," Dibble said.[6] "But their Field of Dreams is collapsing around them. When they throw stuff like that, it just fires you up. I was just happy to get a chance to go in there and show them what we were made of."

Dibble retired the Pirates in order in the ninth, picking up his first postseason save in the process. In the Series so far, Dibble had faced 16 batters, struck out 10 of them, and had not allowed a single hit.

Pittsburgh won Game 5, so the Series shifted back to Cincinnati for Game 6. More than 56,000 fans packed Riverfront for a chance to watch the Reds win their first National League pennant since 1976. As a nod to the Big Red Machine, Johnny Bench threw out the first pitch before the game.

Danny Jackson started and allowed only one run through six innings. With the score tied 1–1, Jackson walked Bonilla and Bonds to start the seventh. Lou Piniella approached the mound, glanced down at Charlton and Dibble warming in the bullpen, and lifted his left arm. He wanted Charlton.

"I was very surprised," said Charlton. "We were both warming up in the bullpen. I said, 'Rob, this is you, right here. They've got three righties coming up.' When they said left-hander, I thought, no, they messed up."

But Piniella was playing chess with Leyland in the other dugout. "Carmelo Martinez was the first guy up, and I know he hasn't bunted much," said Piniella. "A left-hander can field a bunt and throw to third quicker. And if I brought in Rob Dibble, they'd bring in Sid Bream, which I didn't want."

---

6. The "Green Weenie" was a green, hot-dog-shaped plastic rattle that Bucs fans waved at opponents. It was created by Pirates broadcaster Bob Prince and team trainer Danny Whelan in the 1960s.

The gambit worked brilliantly, as Martinez popped a bunt to Sabo at third for the first out. Charlton then collected two fly ball outs, and the inning was over. Charlton had thrown just five pitches to collect all three outs and squash the Pittsburgh rally.

The story of the game turned out to be the contributions of a group of bench players. With the score still tied in the bottom of the seventh, Ron Oester came to the plate for his first at-bat of the game. Oester, the longest-tenured Red, had been the starting second baseman for the club during most of the 1980s, but had been relegated to the bench after Mariano Duncan joined the Reds midway through the '89 season. Oester had entered the game earlier as part of a double switch and now led off the inning with a line-drive single to right. One batter later, Hatcher singled and the Reds had a rally going.

Next up was O'Neill, who was hitting .471 in the Series. Piniella surprised everyone by lifting O'Neill in favor of pinch-hitter extraordinaire Luis Quinones (.361 as a pinch-hitter during the regular season).[7] The switch-hitting Quinones responded by singling to right field, scoring Oester, and giving the Reds a 2–1 lead. As the diminutive Quinones clapped his hands and ran to first, everyone throughout Redleg Nation breathed a sigh of relief.

"When I was standing on first base," Quinones said, "the only thing in my mind was that we're in the World Series. With the bullpen we have, I knew we'd shut them down."

With the lead now 2–1, Piniella made another double switch, bringing in Randy Myers to pitch and Glenn Braggs to play right field. Myers retired the Pirates quickly in the eighth, and with the Reds clinging to a slim one-run lead in the ninth inning, it was Braggs' turn to play the hero.

With one out, Myers walked Bonds, bringing Carmelo Martinez to the plate. Martinez worked the count full, then lifted a long fly ball to right. Braggs went back on the ball, timed his leap perfectly, and reached over the fence to rob Martinez of a home run that would have given the Pirates the lead.

Myers collected himself and struck out Pittsburgh catcher Don Slaught for the third out. Larkin celebrated with a backflip and a cartwheel; the Reds were National League champions.

---

7.   O'Neill, who would go on to star for the New York Yankees, would later say that not getting the chance to hit in that spot was "one of the four or five most disappointing things that happened in my career."

Charlton was credited with the win in Game 6, and Myers and Dibble were named co-MVPs of the NLCS—the only time a reliever has ever won the award—after saving all four games for the Reds. Myers was quick to deflect the attention.

"I consider it a bullpen MVP," he said. "Dibble and I are co-closers, but we're a group down there and that's what made us so good."

"Tonight's game was like so many this season, especially when we struggled a bit in the second half," said Piniella. "Every time you looked up, we seemed to be in a one-run game in the ninth inning, and our guys nearly always found the strength and desire to win."

There were lots of heroes in the Reds' wire-to-wire march to the National League pennant, but the Nasty Boys got most of the headlines, and for good reason. The trio combined to pitch 15⅔ innings, allowing just one earned run and striking out 20 Pittsburgh hitters.

After the game, Dibble was asked how the Nasty Boys would stack up against the big bats of the Oakland Athletics lineup in the World Series.

"I'm not worried about them," Dibble said. "I'll let them worry about us."

In that World Series, the Nasty Boys would continue to dominate, combining for 8⅔ innings of scoreless baseball as the Reds swept the A's. It was a magical season for a magical team, and especially for a rare crew of outstanding relief pitchers.

"That was a very unified bullpen," Dibble said later. "We knew how good we were, and it was fun to actually torture hitters on other teams. It was a blast, I never had so much fun. It wasn't just baseball; it was like you were in Little League again."

21

HAPPY FATHER'S DAY, JUNIOR

Ken Griffey Jr. is a Hall of Famer, a baseball legend, and an American cultural icon. He made his first All-Star team at age 20, won an MVP award and 10 Gold Gloves, and was named to the MLB All-Century team at the tender age of 29. He's seventh on the all-time home run list, among such names as Willie Mays and Babe Ruth.

But in the beginning, in Cincinnati, he was just "Li'l Kenny."

His dad was the original Ken Griffey, a standout player for the Big Red Machine in the 1970s. Back then, Junior was one of a group of players' kids who ran through the tunnels of Riverfront Stadium, taking swings in the batting cages, and generally wreaking havoc. There was Li'l Kenny, as manager Sparky Anderson called him, and his brother Craig, plus Petey Rose, Pedro Borbon Jr., Lee May Jr., and Eduardo Pérez, among others.[1]

Sparky encouraged his players to bring their children to the ballpark, but he had a couple of rules. Kids were welcome in the clubhouse before games, and after games that the Reds had won. Not during the game.

Li'l Kenny and Eduardo—his father was Tony Pérez—were intimidated by Sparky. That didn't stop them from, on several occasions, sneaking into Anderson's office during a Reds game and swiping red pop from the manager's well-stocked mini-fridge.

Meanwhile, on the field, Junior's dad was hitting balls into the gap and speeding around the bases for the fearsome Reds. Sometimes lost in the glare of Junior's brilliant career is the fact that Ken Griffey Sr. was a great player in his own right.

Senior was a three-time All-Star and a member of two World Series champions with the Reds.[2] In the second of those championship seasons, 1976, Griffey led the club with a .336 average; he narrowly lost out to Bill Madlock for the National League batting crown on the

---

1.   Five sons of Big Red Machine players grew up to be first-round draft picks themselves: Ken Griffey Jr., Eduardo Pérez, Lee May Jr., Ed Sprague Jr., and Brian McRae (son of Hal McRae).
2.   Senior actually has three World Series rings. In 1990, he spent most of the season with the Reds before being released in August (whereupon he joined his son in Seattle's outfield). His Reds teammates were upset, as most considered him the leader of that team, so they voted Griffey a full share of the playoff money...and another ring for his collection.

Ken Griffey Jr. gets a big hug from his father, Ken Griffey Sr., after Junior hit home run No. 500. (AP Photo/Tom Gannam)

season's final day. Griffey's .401 on-base percentage was third in the National League, trailing only teammates Joe Morgan and Pete Rose. Griffey was a genuine star who collected 2,143 hits in a 19-year big league career, and was inducted into the Reds Hall of Fame in 2004.

From the beginning, Junior tried to emulate his dad, but it was clear that Junior was a different type of player. While Senior once had 38 infield hits in one season, Junior was known for the high, majestic bombs that he would hammer to all parts of the stadium—even as far back as his days at Cincinnati's Moeller High School.

Once, as a teenager, Junior took batting practice on the field at Riverfront as Ken Sr. and his old teammate Tony Pérez looked on. Pérez was astounded. He turned to Senior, eyes wide. "Don't let anybody ever change that swing," he said. "That's a big league swing right now."

Memorably, Senior finished his big league career playing in the same Seattle outfield as his son.[3] "A lot of times I'd look over to center field," said Ken Sr., "and this is no lie, I still see the hat too big for his head, a baggy uniform, and he's got number 30 across his chest and back. That's a father-son game I was remembering when he was just a little kid and I was with the Reds.... Relationships between fathers and sons are unique and different in certain ways."

Junior pulled on that No. 30 uniform—his father's old number—in a real Reds uniform in 2000, when he was traded from Seattle to his hometown Reds. By June of 2004, Junior was on the chase for his 500th career home run.

The countdown began with home run No. 495 on June 1. He hit number 499 on June 13 and as the media began shadowing his every move, Junior was forced to reflect on how he got there. Ken Sr. was never far from his thoughts.

"My dad hit 152 [home runs] and that's the person I wanted to be like," Junior said. "My hero growing up. That's the person who taught me how to play and is still telling me how to play."

A week later, Junior still hadn't been able to hit No. 500. His extended family—including his father—had come to Cincinnati to see the big moment, and Junior was getting anxious. His teammates, however, were not.

---

3.   And most memorably, father and son hit back-to-back home runs for the Mariners on September 14, 1990.

"I promise you, he's going to hit number 500 before he retires," said Reds slugger Adam Dunn, noting the crowd of reporters asking the same questions about Junior every single day. "Call me crazy. But I say he's going to do it."

With Junior unable to connect for the big blast in Cincinnati, his family was forced to follow the Reds on their road trip to St. Louis, but that ended up being the perfect way to conclude the chase for 500.

In fact, it could hardly have ended any other way. Junior was just waiting for Father's Day.

Yes, Father's Day, June 20, 2004, a bright, sunny day at St. Louis' Busch Stadium. Seated next to the Reds dugout were Ken Sr. and Junior's children, Trey, Taryn, and Tevin, ranging in ages from two to 10.

Before the game, Senior had offered his son some advice: forget about it. "Pick out a pitch you can hit," he told Junior. "Still get your base hits, and one is going to fly out."

Junior got another pregame visit, this one from Cardinals Hall of Famer Stan Musial. Musial had been born in the same town, Donora, Pennsylvania, as both Griffey men, 49 years to the day before Ken Jr. But he had another link to the Griffeys, as well. One of Musial's teammates on the Donora High baseball team was Buddy Griffey. Yep, Ken Sr.'s father, Junior's grandfather.

Musial wished Junior good luck, then laughed. "And hurry up and get this over with."

In his first two at-bats, Junior lifted high fly balls to center field. In the sixth, however, with the Reds leading 5–0, the moment arrived.

Cardinals starter Matt Morris was still on the mound, and he wasn't particularly eager to be a footnote to Griffey's historic moment. "I stayed away with breaking balls," said Morris, "until on a 2-2 count, I tried to slip a fastball by him.

"I guess people have been doing that 500 times, and it didn't work."

Junior turned on the inside fastball and hit a mammoth blast into the right-field stands. Cardinals right fielder Reggie Sanders didn't even chase after it.

"I didn't move," said Sanders, who had been a star for the Reds in the mid-90s. "It was a no-doubter."

Junior stood to watch the ball fly away, just for a moment, before dropping his bat and beginning his slow trot around the bases. The crowd of 45,620 stood and cheered enthusiastically, even though they were saluting an opponent.

As Griffey stepped on home plate, Dunn greeted him with a fist bump and a pat on the helmet. The rest of the team had also emerged from the dugout, and they took turns embracing Junior and offering congratulations. Reds captain Barry Larkin was one of the first players there.

"I just told him, 'About time,'" Larkin said. "That's all."

Then came the moment that put a lump in everyone's throat. Junior climbed over the camera well next to the Reds dugout, leaned over a railing and hugged a smiling Senior.

"Happy Father's Day, Dad," he said. "I love you."

After collecting hugs from own children, Junior stepped back onto the field. He lifted his helmet to the crowd, and they roared even louder.

Not only had Junior knocked down the door to the 500 Club, but the home run was also his 2,143rd career hit—the exact number of hits collected by Ken Sr. in his major league career. Talk about a Father's Day tribute.

"It was a nice Father's Day present," Griffey Sr. said after the game, "but it's an easy way to get out of giving me something."

Junior laughed at that. "I always buy you Old Spice and underwear!" he joked.

It was a special day for two special Reds Hall of Famers who just happened to be father and son.

22

DUAL NO-HITTERS

This game was described at the time as "the strangest, the most unheard-of, the most unique occurrence that ever starred a game whose commonest feats are unusual." Amazingly, a century later, that purple prose sounds reasonable in describing what happened on May 2, 1917, a cold, wet Wednesday afternoon at Weeghman Park (now Wrigley Field).

The fact that it was a pitcher's duel wasn't a surprise. Not only was the Chicago weather gloomy, but the Reds were missing two starting outfielders, Tommy Griffith (hitting .500 while battling tonsillitis through the season's first three weeks) and Edd Roush (.429), and the club was riding a 25-inning scoreless streak. But the biggest factor was the day's starting pitchers: Jim "Hippo" Vaughn for the Cubs and Fred Toney for the Reds.

Vaughn, a big lefty (though, at 215 pounds, perhaps not big enough to deserve his nickname), was one of the NL's best pitchers, employed by one of its worst teams. In 1917, he'd go on to post a 23–10 record for a Cubs team that went 50–67 in games he didn't start. His 6.8 WAR ranked sixth among all NL players.[1]

While his overall career didn't reach Vaughn's level, Toney was a very solid pitcher in his own right. In his three-plus seasons with the Reds (1915–18), Toney threw 999 innings with a 123 ERA+. An exceptionally strong right-hander from Tennessee, Toney was one month into his career year. For the 1917 season, his 4.3 WAR would rank seventh among NL pitchers, and he would place in the top 10 in most pitching categories.

As might be imagined from a double no-hitter, there isn't much game action to describe. Both pitchers easily worked their way through the opposing lineup three times. Toney allowed only two baserunners, walking Cubs center fielder Cy Williams twice. Vaughn was even better. He struck out 10 to Toney's three, and faced the minimum 27 batters

---

1.   Vaughn's next two seasons were even better; he went 22–10 with a 1.74 ERA (8.3 WAR) in 1918 and 21–14 with a 1.79 ERA (7.4 WAR) in 1919.

THE GREATEST ATHLETE OF THE 20TH CENTURY?

Jim Thorpe, voted the best athlete of the 20th century, won gold medals in the decathlon and pentathlon at the 1912 Olympics, was an All-American college football player, and is a member of the Pro Football Hall of Fame. He was stripped of those gold medals in 1913, because he played in some minor league baseball games in 1909 and '10, thus making him a "professional athlete" and ineligible for the Olympics.

The upside of the scandal was that it made Thorpe the most attractive free agent in baseball history, despite having never played above the Eastern Carolina League. He signed with the New York Giants, but had little in the way of big league playing time or success, hitting .195/.215/.271 in 121 plate appearances over three seasons.

Thorpe had been loaned to the Reds from the New York Giants about a week earlier. Giants manager/president John McGraw may have been running out of patience trying to develop Thorpe into a major league hitter, and in any event couldn't spare much playing time on his pennant-winning roster. At the same time, the Reds were now managed by McGraw's best friend, Christy Mathewson, who needed an outfielder after the injuries to Roush and Griffith. The friends worked out a deal that sent Thorpe to Cincinnati for the regular waiver price of $1,500, but with a gentleman's agreement that the Giants could recall him when the Reds no longer needed him. Four months later, with McGraw seeking depth for the pennant race, Thorpe went back to New York.

through nine innings. He walked two Reds and another reached via error, but they were erased by two double plays and a caught stealing. A shallow fly ball by Reds center fielder "Greasy" Neale in the first inning was, according to Vaughn, the only ball the Reds hit out of the infield until the 10th.

Toney, who once pitched a 17-inning no-hitter in the minor leagues, said that he didn't even have his good stuff until the seventh inning, and didn't realize he was throwing a no-hitter until the ninth.

Both pitchers retired the side in order in the ninth inning, completing their regulation no-hitters. They'd made baseball history, but hadn't yet decided the day's game.

With one out in the top of the 10th, Reds shortstop Larry Kopf finally broke through with the game's first hit, a liner to right field past lunging

Cubs first baseman Fred Merkle. Neale then flew out to Williams in center field for the second out.

Then Cincinnati's cleanup hitter, Hal Chase, hit a hard fly ball ("Not a line drive," Vaughn said) that was uncharacteristically booted by Williams, who was "about the best fly catcher in the league," according to *The Sporting News*.

Running with two outs, Kopf took third on the error. That brought Jim Thorpe to the plate. Yes, *the* Jim Thorpe was a Red.

Thorpe nubbed one in front of the plate. Vaughn came off the mound to grab it, and had to make an instant decision: should he try to get Thorpe—literally one of the world's fastest men—at first, or flip the ball to catcher Art Wilson and hope Wilson could tag Kopf out at the plate?

Vaughn chose Door No. 2. Accounts from the next day's newspapers say that Vaughn's rushed scoop-toss hit Wilson's shoulder at the same time Kopf crashed into him, sending the ball rolling away as the go-ahead run scored. Chase, for reasons known only to Chase, tried to score on the play from second, and was tagged out by Wilson.

That ended the Reds half of the 10th and gave Toney the chance to complete his no-hitter. He was feeling "fit and determined" as he struck out Larry Doyle to start the Cubs' 10th. Then Merkle hit what Toney described as "a terrific wallop that looked like a fat home run," but was run down short of the wall by Reds left fielder Manuel Cueto. Toney proceeded to strike out Williams to end the day.

Baseball Magazine's F.C. Lane described the day as a "matching of strength [that] has never been equaled and probably never will be equaled as long as the game endures." A hundred years and more than 190,000 games later, it hasn't.

23

THE BIG RED MACHINE ROLLS ON: 1976 NLCS

The 1975–76 off-season had been thrilling, but draining for the Reds. They were not just the world champions, they were a potential dynasty, and the stars of the highest-rated sporting event in television history.

To complicate things further, the 1976 season was delayed about a week by an owners' lockout of spring training camps.[1] After spending all winter riding the banquet and interview circuit, the Reds weren't able to start spring training until March 20. But a short spring actually provided a competitive advantage to the Reds, whose lineup was carved into stone, and whose starting pitchers had less need to build up their endurance; manager Sparky Anderson would be coming with the hook in the sixth or seventh inning, anyway.

Everyone expected the Reds to repeat, and Sparky needed to find a way to motivate his troops. He wasn't sure how he'd do it—this experience was new to him, too.

The truth was that, by 1976, the Reds were a unique team of self-motivated, veteran superstars—the rarest of athletes who actually could "turn it on" when they needed to. "I don't see any problems," Joe Morgan said that off-season. "We don't have the kind of guys who would let each other get complacent."

No, the Machine didn't *grind* day-to-day like Sparky may have liked, but whenever the Dodgers began to close the gap in the standings, the Reds would rip off a streak of essentially perfect baseball, sweeping a series against a contender. As Sparky said, "The Reds of 1976 operated on pride." They didn't take over first place until Memorial Day, but they ended up 102–60, a full 10 games ahead of Los Angeles. They were the best baseball team Sparky, and most anyone else, ever saw.

Sparky liked to rest his regulars, and give periodic playing time to the bench guys. But when the "Great Eight" suited up together,

---

1. The biggest sticking point in negotiations was how many years a player would need to play before becoming eligible for free agency. Worried about losing all the goodwill gained in the 1975 postseason, commissioner Bowie Kuhn ordered the camps opened while negotiations continued.

they truly were unstoppable: the Reds were 34–8 in games when the trademark Big Red Machine lineup took the field.

Remarkable for such a veteran team, almost everyone improved on their 1975 numbers. George Foster jumped to 29 home runs and 121 RBI, and even stole 17 bases in 20 tries. Ken Griffey's batting average leaped from .305 to .336—he lost the batting title to Bill Madlock on the season's final day. Even César Gerónimo hit .307/.382/.414. Only Johnny Bench, still suffering from a 1975 shoulder injury, struggled, hitting just .234/.348/.394.

So many weapons. So many options. "Early in the game, if we saw that the opposing pitcher was going to have a good night, we'd go to our speed game," Sparky said years later. "If they wanted to let us stay in power mode, we'd stay in power mode."

On the mound, Pat Zachry boosted the rotation (14–7, 2.74 ERA) and shared the National League Rookie of the Year Award. Don Gullett and Fred Norman battled injuries, but were effective when they did pitch. In all, *seven* different Reds pitchers won 11 or more games.

"No one talks about our pitching," Griffey remembered, "but I thought it was the best in the league."

The Reds even dominated defensively. The entire "up the middle" defense (Bench, Morgan, Concepción, and Gerónimo) won Gold Gloves, and the Reds led the majors in fielding percentage.

Cincinnati's NLCS opponents were the Philadelphia Phillies, on paper at least, a strong opponent. The Phillies had won 101 games, and could throw three excellent veteran starters at the Reds, in Steve Carlton, Jim Kaat, and Jim Lonborg.

Led by Mike Schmidt (.262/.376/.524, 73 extra base hits, and a Gold Glove), Greg Luzinski (.304/.369/.478), and a resurgent Dick Allen (15 HR and 49 RBI in 85 games), the Phillies were the only offense that could compare themselves to the Reds without embarrassment. The Phils ranked second in almost every offensive category. Their problem was that they were playing the team that ranked No. 1 in those same categories.

The lead up to the Series was a little odd, though. Phillies manager Danny Ozark publicly compared Sparky Anderson to Adolf Hitler. Even stranger, he did it in a way that Sparky was able to embrace.

"Sparky Anderson reminds me of a paper hanger during WWII," Ozark said. "That paper hanger wanted to dominate the world, too."[2]

True to form, Sparky took it as a compliment. "My father really was a paper hanger," he said, "and with the prices they're getting today, maybe I should be one."

Controversy averted. The writers were disappointed, but Sparky had been doing this long enough to know how to avoid a distraction on the eve of the playoffs.

For Game 1, Sparky went with lefty Gullett (11–3, 3.00 ERA). Gullett was a battle-tested veteran (eight postseason starts over the prior four seasons), but he'd missed two months in three separate injury stints.

Sparky actually had more faith in Zachry at this point, but Reds super-scout Ray Shore argued for Gullett, with some canny logic: the Phillies would definitely be pitching Carlton in Game 1, and neither Reds pitcher could really be expected to match him. Why not save the Reds' ace for Game 2? Plus, Carlton's personal catcher was always Tim McCarver—both batted from the left side. Gullett would have a platoon advantage against them. Shore's last point: Gullett was pitching for a free agent contract.[3]

Gullett didn't hurt his case, allowing only two hits and a run in eight innings. The Reds took advantage of an ineffective Carlton and a nervous Phillies defense. Right fielder Ollie Brown misplayed two singles into triples, and shortstop Larry Bowa let two balls pass right under his glove—scored as base hits, but obvious miscues nonetheless. McCarver was helpless against the Reds' speed—four stolen bases, including one by Bench.

Things were working even better than Ray Shore had hoped. Carlton was out of the way, and the Reds had Zachry ready for Game 2. The Phillies threw Lonborg. In the second inning, the Phillies scored a run on three straight singles; a Luzinski solo homer in the fifth made it 2–0.

Meanwhile, Lonborg was no-hitting the Reds through five innings, retiring 14 straight hitters after an early walk. Dave Concepción walked to start the sixth, and the wheels quickly came off. After Pete Rose

---

2. A "paper hanger" is a person who installs wallpaper. It's unclear whether Hitler ever actually worked at that job, but it was a tag that stuck with him from the late 1930s. It was intended to be pejorative, suggesting an unskilled, unsophisticated laborer.

3. The long-negotiated collective bargaining agreement was finally signed in July, making all players currently playing without a signed contract free agents after the '76 World Series. This meant Don Gullett was probably playing his final season in a Reds uniform.

and Griffey singled, the lead was cut to one run, and the Reds had men on second and third with only one out.[4] Just moments after losing a no-hitter, Lonborg's night was over.

Gene Garber entered and intentionally walked Morgan to load the bases. First baseman Allen then made a back-breaking error on a Pérez line drive, and the Reds led 3-2. They would tack on three more to make it another blowout. As Bench later put it, the Phillies were "punctured."

Game 3 finally provided a bit of drama. Gary Nolan faced Kaat, and both were sharp. Philadelphia scored a run on back-to-back doubles by Schmidt and Luzinski, and added two more off reliever Manny Sarmiento in the seventh.

Kaat had shut the Reds out through six innings, but the Machine exploded in the bottom of the seventh, scoring four runs to take the lead.[5] As Tom Seaver, commenting for NBC put it, "This Cincinnati ballclub, they just sit back there and they know they're gonna get going sometime."

The Riverfront Stadium crowd smelled victory. Sparky didn't mess around—he went right to Eastwick, his closer. Unfortunately, Eastwick gave up two runs in the eighth, and another in the ninth.

The Reds entered the bottom of the ninth down 6-4. There was no panic in the dugout, though. Foster (1-for-11 so far in the Series) led off against big right-hander Ron Reed, and quickly fell behind 1-2. With his next delivery, Reed left a running fastball out over the plate and Foster crushed it—an estimated 480 feet into the seats in left-center.

Bench came to the plate next, and everyone in the ballpark, including Ron Reed, was thinking about Bench's dramatic ninth inning, game-tying home run in Game 5 of the 1972 NLCS (Chapter 16), and his walk-off blast against Seaver in Game 1 of the 1973 NLCS (Chapter 36). Could Bench do it again? Yes he could! Another no-doubter and the game was tied.

The Phillies melted, right there on the turf. The game was over, it was just a matter of filling in the details. Garber took over for Reed and surrendered a hit to Concepción. Tom Underwood came on to face Gerónimo. Sparky didn't want to take any chances with a double play, so he called for the bunt. Underwood, walking into Big Red Mayhem in

---

4.   Griffey had advanced to second when Phillies center fielder Garry Maddox threw to the wrong base.
5.   The go-ahead run scored when César Gerónimo hit a soft liner that Phillies left fielder Bobby Tolan—just subbed in for defensive purposes—misplayed into a triple.

his first postseason appearance, couldn't accept the gift of an out. He walked Gerónimo on four pitches, putting the pennant-winning run in scoring position.

Sparky tried again, sending Ed Armbrister in to pinch-bunt in the pitcher's spot. Underwood finally managed a strike, and Armbrister bunted the runners over. The Phillies intentionally walked Rose to set up the double play, but with Griffey—38 infield hits on the season—coming to the plate, that would be a tall order. Griffey hit a slow chopper to the right side. Tolan, now playing first base, charged it and quickly determined that his only chance was forcing Concepción at home. But as he rushed, Tolan couldn't come up with the ball, and the winning run crossed the plate.

As diagnosed by writer Roger Angell, the Phillies had fallen victim to Reds Fever, a debilitating anxiety that struck otherwise-solid baseball teams, convincing them that their only hope of winning was to be beyond perfect. The disease afflicted its victims with flashbacks of improbable comebacks in playoffs past—Bench's 1972 NLCS homer, Tony Pérez's World Series bomb off Bill Lee—until a feeling of utter doom caused the very collapse they dreaded. In the case of the 1976 Phillies, the disease was fatal. Next victim: The New York Yankees.

24

MARTY AND JOE

Early in 1974, Marty Brennaman traveled up I-75 from Cincinnati to meet the Reds off-season media caravan in Dayton. A 31-year-old Virginian, Brennaman had been doing play-by-play for ABA basketball and minor league baseball games when he was hired by the Cincinnati Reds to join their radio booth.

One of his first duties in Dayton was to have publicity stills taken.. As he opened the door to the local photo studio, he saw Joe Nuxhall sitting there. After a fine career as a Reds player, Nuxhall had joined the Reds' broadcast team in 1967 and he was eager to meet his latest young broadcast partner—his fifth different partner in eight years.

Marty thrust out a hand in Joe's direction. "I have your baseball card," Marty said.

And thus, a legendary partnership was born.

"From that moment on, we developed a one-of-a-kind relationship," Marty said. Their bond would be cemented a month later, when the pair began broadcasting games from spring training in Florida.

Brennaman was taking the place of the very popular Al Michaels, who had moved on to the San Francisco Giants' radio booth. Marty would later admit that he was feeling the pressure. The first spring game came and went without incident; he and Nuxhall seemed to work well together, and Brennaman gained confidence. The second game was at Al Lopez Field in Tampa. As they went on the air, Brennaman opened the broadcast by welcoming listeners to "Al Michaels Field." He recognized his Freudian slip immediately and, looking to his right, he could see Nuxhall convulsing with laughter—the old left-hander nearly fell out of his chair.

Brennaman quickly went to a commercial break. "I was embarrassed almost to tears," he said. "And [Joe] shows me no mercy."

Nuxhall, still laughing, slapped Brennaman on the back. "I'll be damned. We haven't even gotten to the regular season yet and I've got material for the banquet circuit next fall!"

A few weeks later, in the first inning of Marty and Joe's first regular season game (Opening Day 1974), Brennaman called Hank Aaron's record-tying 714th career home run. At the next commercial break, Nuxhall turned to his young partner.

"What the hell do you do for an encore after that?" he asked.

In fact, there were many encores over the next 31 years, as Marty and Joe were witnesses to many of the greatest moments in Reds history. Three World Series championships, Tom Browning's perfect game, Johnny Bench's dramatic farewell to the game, Ken Griffey Jr.'s 500th career home run.

One of the biggest highlights of Marty and Joe's broadcast careers also served as a perfect example of their different, but perfectly complementary styles. It came when Pete Rose collected his 4,192nd career hit, breaking Ty Cobb's record. In the foreground, a listener hears Marty launch into the biggest call of his career. But the dominant sound comes from Nuxhall in the background, yelling at the baseball to land safely in front of left fielder Carmelo Martinez: "Get down, get down, get down!!!"

That was just Joe, the regular guy from nearby Hamilton, Ohio, who never stopped openly rooting for his favorite team. He was always down-to-earth, drawing listeners in with his slow-paced folksy manner. Sometimes he made mistakes, sometimes he mispronounced names. Often, he would go silent between pitches, causing fans to check the radio to make sure it was still plugged in. Joe's was an unconventional style—if you can even call it a "style"—but Nuxhall had been an immediate hit with listeners.

"Nuxie" was a hit with his partner, too. "He was great to me," said Brennaman, "which meant a whole lot. He taught me how to treat the fans from day one, how you have to be on 24/7, how to extend the respect and attention fans deserved."

If Nuxhall was the most popular man in Cincinnati—and he was, according to Marty—then Brennaman was the smooth professional who made the partnership work.

After the Reds hired Brennaman, from a group of 220 applicants, he was described in the *Cincinnati Enquirer* as an on-air "cheerleader," or in his own words, an "unmitigated homer." It didn't take long for Brennaman to alter that style. One day, after he remarked, "We had a great win yesterday," Brennaman was challenged by Reds pitcher Jack Billingham.

"[Billingham] said 'How many hits did you have? What is this 'we' business?'"

"He was 100 percent correct," Marty realized. "For me to say 'we' was completely wrong."

Almost immediately, Brennaman became known for—and proud of—his blunt assessments of the action on the field. It would become a hallmark of his style for the rest of his career.

His dedication to "telling it like it is" sometimes drew criticism, both from the front office and from a certain segment of Reds fans. In the early 1980s, Reds general manager Dick Wagner grew weary of Brennaman's constant critiques of a team that paled in comparison with the Big Red Machine teams of preceding years. Wagner added a third person—Dick Carlson—to the radio booth for a short time. "That was Wagner's way of warning me," said Brennaman. Undeterred, he continued criticizing the club on the air. In 1983, after Wagner refused to give Marty a contract extension, the broadcaster felt sure that he would be fired at season's end. Instead, Wagner was fired, and Marty lasted another 36 years.

The complaints, though, were always outshined by the fact that no broadcaster anywhere, with the possible exception of the legendary Vin Scully, could describe the action on the field with as much vivid precision as Marty.

"His voice is excellent, he's smooth, he's right on the ball with the action in the game," Nuxhall said. "If you sit there listening to him at the stadium, you can follow the ball with him. That's one of his biggest assets."

It's hard to overestimate their popularity in "Reds Country," the sprawling, six-state territory throughout which Marty and Joe's broadcasts reached. Listeners delighted as the duo talked about Marty's tomato plants, their golf games, Elvis, or whatever else might come to mind on any particular night. Some of their most memorable moments occurred during rain delays, when they would take calls from listeners on the "banana phone." Marty and Joe were the soundtrack of summer to generations in the Queen City and far beyond.

"I think our success has to do with two things," Brennaman once said. "First, we genuinely like each other. Second, we talk about stuff outside of baseball that people can relate to. We make fun of ourselves and we don't take ourselves too seriously. I don't know if our act would fly outside of Cincinnati."

That act included each man's trademark phrases. After every Reds win, Marty intoned his signature "...and this one belongs to the Reds!" Early in the 1974 season, the Reds won a game with a hit in the bottom of the ninth, and the words just tumbled out of his mouth. "I thought, 'That ain't half bad,'" said Marty. "In fact, it's the best thing I've ever come up with. In those days, with the way the team was going, I used it a lot."

Nuxhall customarily signed off at the end of a broadcast with his own trademark: "This is the ol' left-hander, rounding third and heading for home." A couple of weeks into his first year as a radio broadcaster, one of the Reds coaches, Whitey Wietelmann, approached Nuxhall and informed him that he needed a "sign-off."

"He gave me the line," Nuxhall remembered. "I did it for a few weeks, then I thought it sounded corny, so I quit. I started getting all kinds of letters, so I went back to it." The catchphrase became so popular that it was ultimately emblazoned across the outside of Great American Ballpark.

Over the course of a partnership that saw Marty and Joe work more than 5,500 games in the same booth, they became cultural icons in Cincinnati. They appeared in radio and television commercials together, and especially after the Big Red Machine era, were often more popular than any Reds player. At the end of the 2004 season, however, the longtime partnership came to an end with Nuxhall's retirement after more than 60 years with the Reds as a player and broadcaster.

Instead of Nuxhall's customary postgame "Star of the Game" show, the friends sat and reminisced on the air about the previous three decades. In an emotional farewell, both men tried to fight off tears.

"You look at all this and it's been 31 years," said Nuxhall, "and we've had some great times together. You look back on the '70s ballclubs, then the '90 ballclub, which no one was expecting that much out of, go wire to wire and sweep the Oakland A's. What a great time we've had."

"I've been lucky because I was here through the most fruitful period of this club's history, and of course sitting side-by-side with you for 31 years," agreed Marty.

As the broadcast began to wind down, the emotions bubbled over.

"Well, Marty, again, thank you," said Nuxhall.

"No, thank you, Joe. Thank you. Thank you."

"It's been the best."

"I guarantee you," said Brennaman, "there's been nobody that's worked together in this business that ever derived this much fun out of broadcasting a ballclub's games as we have had over the last 31 years. I mean, it's impossible. And this is a business where you're working together every day for six months. If you don't like the guy you're working with, this job can be absolutely hell on earth. And thank God two left-handers came together in February of 1974 and were off and running from that point."

"It's been great."

Reds fans who were lucky enough to listen to Marty and Joe over the years would agree. It was great.

25

PETE ROSE: 3,000 & 44

At the time, 1978 was the most tumultuous year of Pete Rose's career. Later years would certainly surpass it in the drama department, but at the time, it was like nothing the Queen City's hometown star had ever experienced. Rose was setting records and raising his own high bar for publicity, but all with an undercurrent of existential dread—everyone knew (even if they didn't want to admit it) that this might be the end of Pete Rose's extraordinary career as a Cincinnati Red.

Free agency had arrived in baseball, and on the heels of back-to-back World Series titles, Rose was the game's biggest star, and still a top talent. He and the Reds had engaged in a nasty, public, and protracted salary dispute during spring training in 1977. At loggerheads and terrified of Rose's grassroots popularity, the Reds took the bold (and self-defeating) step of purchasing a full-page, 1,500-word ad in the local papers to make their case against Rose.

"They're trying to force me out of Cincinnati," Rose said.

The situation was resolved shortly after spring training, when Rose arrived in Cincinnati. The press mob at the airport ignored his teammates in a rush to ask Rose about his contract issue. He liked being the center of attention, but only when the subject was baseball. Rose quickly signed a two-year contract running through 1978, but his relationship with the front office was irreparably damaged, and the specter of Rose's upcoming free agency loomed over the 1978 season.

Rose entered the campaign needing just 34 hits to reach 3,000. Always supremely aware of his statistics, Rose looked at the schedule and picked out the exact day he expected to reach the milestone: May 7, during a doubleheader against Montreal. "If the hit comes any later than May 7," he reasoned, "I'll be batting around .250 when I get it, and I don't want that to happen."

The 37-year-old Rose shrugged off speculation that he might someday reach 4,000 hits. "No, I don't think that's possible." But he thought he might have another 800 hits left in him, giving him a good shot at Stan Musial's National League record of 3,631 hits. "I'd like that," Rose said.[1]

Rose short-changed himself on the number of career hits he'd accumulate, but hit number 3,000 *did* come against the Expos, just a couple days earlier than predicted. On May 5, Rose lined a Steve Rogers pitch into left field to become the 13th member of baseball's 3,000 Hit Club. In a preview of events to come seven years later, Rose's teammates rushed from the dugout to mob him at first base. Photographers swarmed the field, and the Riverfront Stadium crowd gave a lengthy standing ovation. Longtime teammate and friend Tony Pérez (by then the Montreal first baseman) was there to share the moment.

Reds fans might've been forgiven if they thought they'd just seen the highlight of Rose's 1978 season. Forgiven, but wrong.

Rose had two hits on June 14, two more on June 15, and didn't look back. By the All-Star break, the streak was at 25 games. On July 15, he broke the Reds' modern team record with a hit in his 28th straight game with a hit.

One big scare came in Philadelphia, on July 19. With the streak at 31, Rose went hitless in his first three trips to the plate. In the eighth, with the Reds protecting a one-run lead, reliever Tug McGraw walked Rose, drawing the familiar Philadelphia boos from the 45,608 in attendance. The streak looked over.

But then Ken Griffey singled, Joe Morgan walked, and George Foster hit a grand slam. Johnny Bench got an otherwise-meaningless single, assuring that Rose *should* get one more turn at bat in the ninth.[2]

Rose came to the plate with two outs in the ninth, to another large ovation from the road crowd. He bunted Ron Reed's first pitch down the third-base line. Mike Schmidt wasn't able to make the barehanded play, and the streak extended to 32.

"Normally, I wouldn't bunt with a five-run lead, but it took me 16 years to get to 31 in a row," Rose rationalized. "If Schmidt gives me the bunt, I'll take it."

---

1.   Rose had a special connection to that 3,631 number. Musial's final hit, on Stan Musial Day at St. Louis' original Busch Stadium in 1963, was a hard single past the Reds rookie second baseman—a kid named Pete Rose. Pete retrieved the historic baseball and delivered it, along with a handshake, to Musial.
2.   "Don't get picked off," Rose hollered at pinch runner Rick Auerbach. Rose was looking at the lineup card, too.

Rose was bearing down on the modern National League record of 37 games, a streak set by Tommy Holmes with the 1945 Boston Braves. A gracious gentleman who was then working in the Mets front office, Holmes reveled in his return to the spotlight ("Heck, until two weeks ago nobody knew I was alive."). Coincidentally, the Reds were playing the Mets at Shea Stadium when Rose tied Holmes with a seventh-inning single off former Red Pat Zachry.

Mets fans gave Rose a three-minute standing ovation, forgetting that just five seasons earlier, during the 1973 NLCS, they wanted to kill him. He was visibly moved by the change of heart, and by Holmes' kindness. "I just hope I can show as much class, if I get this record, as Tommy Holmes has shown," Rose said afterward.

The next day, Rose lined a sixth-inning single to break the record. Holmes jumped out of his box seat and raced to embrace Rose at first base. As they had with hit No. 3,000, photographers were permitted to swarm the field as Mets fans repeated their lengthy ovation. After the game, there was another packed press conference.

Rose enjoyed every moment as the ringmaster of a national media circus. "Pressure? What pressure?" he asked reporters. "This isn't pressure, it's fun."

The big target, of course, was Joe DiMaggio's 56-game hitting streak from 1941. But first, Rose had to pass Ty Cobb (40 games) and George Sisler (41), along with two 19th-century streaks: Bill Dahlen's 42-game streak from 1894, and Wee Willie Keeler's 44-game streak from 1897. (Officially, baseball didn't recognize any pre-1900 hitting records, because foul balls didn't count as strikes at the time. But Rose, knowledgeable and obsessive, wanted to pass Keeler. "He's got the National League record and even though people say it was before 1900, I'd like for people to say that I have the record before and after 1900.")

Crowds poured into ballparks around the league to catch the Pete Rose show. The two-game series in Philadelphia drew 89,000—25 percent higher than their average crowd. In Montreal, Expos attendance surged 43 percent. In New York, the Mets drew 86 percent more fans than usual.[3]

---

3. Based on the ticket prices of the time, each of these clubs was pocketing around $100,000 in extra revenue—just about the average MLB salary in 1978.

Rose passed Cobb, Sisler, and Dahlen at home, and then headed to Atlanta in hopes of passing Keeler. For the series opener, 45,007 came to Atlanta-Fulton County Stadium, the largest crowd of the season, and almost four times the Braves season average of 12,739, to that point.

The Braves started Phil Niekro, the ageless knuckleballer who Rose had faced more often than any other pitcher in his long career. Enjoying the "World Series atmosphere" in Atlanta, Niekro walked Rose the first time up. (Like McGraw, Niekro heard boos from his own fans.) In the third, Rose lined out to shortstop. Finally, in the sixth, Rose grounded a single to tie Keeler for the all-time National League record.

Twenty-four-year-old rookie Larry McWilliams started for the Braves the next day. Rose hated facing rookies, or any unfamiliar pitcher, and this was just McWilliams' fourth major league start. He'd gone 2-0 with a 2.12 ERA. Perhaps more relevant to our story, opposing hitters were batting just .242 against him.

Rose led off the game, of course. After a long battle, he coaxed a walk, moved to third on Ken Griffey's double, and scored on a groundout.

Next time up in the second, Rose hit a scorching liner right back at McWilliams. "That ball was absolutely tattooed," Marty Brennaman told his radio audience, "and McWilliams, with reflex action, threw his glove off to his right and picked it off."

Rose, who never made it out of the batter's box, actually stood and applauded McWilliams, then tipped his cap. "I don't know how he caught it, I really don't," Rose said afterward. "Two inches either way and it's a base hit."

In the fifth, Rose grounded to shortstop. Meanwhile, the Braves were pounding the Reds. After five innings, the score was 8–4 in Atlanta's favor.

Rose batted next in the seventh, this time facing Atlanta's relief ace Gene Garber, a side-arming righty whose best pitch was his changeup. Garber entered the game with a 1.62 ERA and a .203 opponents' batting average.

First base was occupied, in the form of Dave Collins. On a 2-2 count, Collins broke for second. Rose smoked a line drive, but it went right at third baseman Bob Horner. "Ah, Jesus!" shouted Joe Nuxhall into the microphone. Rose was out and Collins was doubled off first.

CINCINNATI REDS

Up 12 runs in the ninth, Atlanta manager Bobby Cox left Garber in for a third inning of work. He struck out the first two Reds, leaving Rose with one last chance to extend the streak. Six times previously, Rose's streak had come down to his final at-bat. This time, Rose was met with a vociferous standing ovation from the Atlanta fans. "Pete! Pete! Pete!" they chanted.

On the first pitch, Rose tried to push a bunt past Garber. It rolled foul down the third-base line. Garber then missed twice in a row, to fall behind 2-1. A walk would end the streak, too. Rose was visibly frustrated, and the Braves crowd was audibly so. The fifth pitch was a strike, and Rose fouled it off.

With 31,159 on their feet, Garber visited the rosin bag, then took the sign. He shook off catcher Joe Nolan's sign, and delivered a changeup on the outside corner. Rose was fooled and could only wave weakly at the pitch. The streak was over.

Garber impulsively leaped with both arms in the air, like he'd just clinched the World Series. He quickly checked himself—his team was still in fifth place, after all—but it was hard to fault the man for being caught up in the moment.[4]

Rose, still stinging from the streak's end, didn't appreciate it. "I was a little surprised that, in a game that was 16–4, he pitched me like it was the seventh game of the World Series," Rose said.

There was rich irony, of course, in Pete Rose criticizing another player for giving 100 percent in an ostensibly meaningless situation. Rose, the man who steamrolled Ray Fosse in an All-Star exhibition. Rose, who had made his name sprinting to first on walks in spring training. Rose, whose greed for base hits never let him give up even a single at-bat. Rose, who had just tried to bunt for a hit in that same "meaningless" at-bat against Garber. Yes, Pete Rose was begging for quarter from a relief pitcher.

Rose later expressed regret about criticizing the Braves pitchers. Garber was understanding and gracious. "It was an emotional time for Rose," he said.

---

4. Your authors were both small children in 1978, but devoted Reds fans even then. One, in particular, was an obsessive Pete Rose fan, hiding under the covers long after his bedtime, to hear Marty and Joe announce another Rose hit. But on that August Tuesday night, the boy's heart was broken wide open as his hero failed four times to get a hit. And much, much worse, the boy shared the name of the tale's most diabolical villain. A summer's worth of buildup, gone in an instant. So the five-year-old boy, inconsolable, crept into his parents' room at 10:30 PM. Barely coherent through his sobs, he finally got his message across: There was only one thing to be done. He must be allowed to change his last name to anything but Garber.

Postgame comments aside, it was a great time for Rose, and for baseball. The Atlanta fans stuck around after the game, chanting Pete's name and demanding a postgame curtain call from a man who had just gone 0-for-4. A crowd-pleaser even in defeat and disappointment, Rose gave the fans, in Atlanta and across baseball, just what they wanted.

26

CRAZY, CRAZY, CRAZY

"In every baseball game I see something I've never seen before." That was Roger Craig, who spent the better part of five decades in professional baseball, as a player, pitching coach, and manager. Craig was just parroting an old baseball cliché, one that's repeated a hundred times a summer. On Tuesday, July 22, 1986, the 23,707 present at Riverfront Stadium could honestly say it—again and again and again.

It started as an ordinary weeknight game between the struggling Reds and the juggernaut Mets. When it finally ended, five hours after the first pitch, fans were able to check a number of oddities off their baseball bucket lists:

- Forty-two players appearing in a single game? Check.
- Two teams combining to go 1 for 25 with runners in scoring position? Check.
- Batter kicking a dropped third strike 75 feet up the first-base line (and reaching base safely)? Check.
- Bench-clearing brawl (with real punches!)? Check.
- Four players ejected? Check. (And it could've been more!)
- Pitcher playing right field? Check.
- Pitcher playing left field? Check.
- Pitcher moving from right field to left field, then back to the mound? Check.
- Game played under protest...by both teams? Check.
- Game-tying rally culminating in a dropped fly ball by a three-time Gold Glover? Check.

It was a transition year for the Reds. Pete Rose was still the player-manager, but with Cobb's record broken, Rose was finally ceding playing time to younger players in what would be his final season as a player. The same was true for Tony Pérez.[1] Dave Concepción, now 38, had gotten

---

1. Pérez was struggling in his final season, entering the game hitting only .213. But in the second inning, he singled to left for career hit number 2,700, drawing a very appreciative ovation from the Riverfront crowd.

hurt two weeks before, and would never regain the starting shortstop role (Barry Larkin debuted in mid-August, and kept the job for the next 18 years). The lineup was anchored by Dave Parker, Buddy Bell, and Bo Diaz, all in their mid-thirties.

But the real attraction was the club's wealth of young talent: 24-year-old Eric Davis (ended the year with a .901 OPS and 80 steals), 22-year-old Kal Daniels (.917 OPS and 15 steals in 74 games), and 21-year-old first-round draft pick Kurt Stillwell had just arrived. Top prospects Larkin and Paul O'Neill were soon to come.

The Reds entered the night in fourth place, two games under .500 and 5.5 games out of first. But things were looking up—they were riding an 11–4 stretch since the fourth of July. They'd eventually finish in second place, the second of four consecutive runner-up seasons under Rose. The 1986 Mets, of course, were on their way to the history books—a 108–54 record and a World Series title over the Red Sox.

Rookie Scott Terry took the mound for the Reds, having moved from the bullpen to fill in for an injured Chris Welsh. The Mets starter, Bob Ojeda—who entered the night with an 11–2 record and a MLB-best 2.13 ERA—was on a real hot streak, allowing only one earned run in his last four starts (0.28 ERA).

The night started quietly enough. Neither Terry nor Ojeda were sharp, each allowing—but stranding—a lot of baserunners and each departing after five innings with the Reds ahead 3–1 on homers by Parker and Bell. The Reds bullpen tossed three scoreless innings, and Cincinnati headed to the ninth with the advantage.

Big right-hander Ron Robinson had pitched a scoreless eighth, and Rose elected to send him back out to face the bottom of the Mets order. Rose did bolster his defense, bringing Eddie Milner off the bench to play center, and moving Max Venable to left.

Mets manager Davey Johnson led off the top of the ninth with a pinch-hitter—the switch-hitting Howard Johnson. Robinson struck him out, but catcher Bo Diaz dropped the ball, and Johnson—hustling to first base—inadvertently kicked the baseball up the first-base line. Robinson picked up the ball but his throw hit Johnson in the back. "Safe" was the call. Several Reds (including Dave Parker, in from right field) argued the call for several minutes, but the umpiring crew stuck to their decision.[2]

Marty Brennaman told the TV audience, "I have never, ever seen that before."

Get used to sentences like that.

Robinson induced a double play, and the Reds were only an out away from the win. Immediately, Robinson got himself back into trouble by issuing another walk to Len Dykstra.

Tim Teufel came to the plate representing the tying run. Robinson got ahead of the Mets second baseman, a ball and two strikes, and the Riverfront crowd rose to their feet in anticipation. Teufel battled back to a full count, then hit a long fly ball to left-center that bounced over the wall for a ground-rule double. For a moment, that seemed like a big break for the Reds, as the play forced Dykstra to stop at third.

That was enough for Rose. With runners on second and third, he called on John Franco to get the game's final out. Franco would face veteran first baseman Keith Hernandez. With a 2-2 count, Hernandez lifted a fly ball to deep right field. Parker got a bad read on the ball but hustled back to the edge of the warning track and settled under it. Brennaman began his traditional call: "And this one belongs to the—nooooooo, he dropped the ball!" Two Mets scored to tie the game at 3-3.

Franco survived the inning without further damage, but the Reds were unable to score in the bottom of the ninth, so the game went to extra innings. The Mets had runners on second and third with only one out in the tenth, but Franco struck out Johnson and Dykstra to escape again.

In the bottom of the 10th, Davey Johnson brought on his fifth pitcher of the night, left-hander Jesse Orosco. With one out, Rose called himself off the bench to pinch-hit for only the second time all season. Batting right-handed, Rose promptly singled to center field for career hit number 4,247. As soon as he reached first, Pete signaled for "time," and called on Eric Davis to pinch run.

Davis was nursing an injured hand, or he certainly would've hit against Orosco. As it was, Davis was the perfect weapon for a tie game—to that point in the season, he was 45 for 50 in steal attempts.

---

2. Reds coach Billy DeMars was ejected somewhere in the debate, reportedly for the only time in his 23-year big league playing and coaching career.

Davis took his lead as he always did—one foot on the AstroTurf, hands resting on his knees. On Orosco's second pitch, Davis easily stole second. Two pitches later, he broke for third. Milner swung and missed for strike three but Davis stole the base easily. Davis, who almost always used a pop-up slide, made contact with third baseman Ray Knight who was leaning across third base to apply the tag.

Umpire Eric Gregg called Davis safe, but Knight continued to lay claim to the airspace over third base, putting both his hands on Davis and, depending on your allegiance, either tried to steady himself or shove the baserunner off the bag.[3]

Davis turned around, put his forearms on Knight's chest, and began shoving Knight backward. Gregg quickly grabbed Davis from behind, which gave Knight the opportunity to throw an undefended right cross. Gregg spun Davis out of the fray, but the fight was on. Milner locked up with Orosco, Gary Carter dragged Davis to the ground, and big Dave Parker was throwing Mets around two at a time.

Things seemed under control for a moment, until Round 2 broke out between Mets rookie Kevin Mitchell and the Reds' John Denny, two of the tougher, crazier competitors on the field.[4] Denny was well-known as a martial-arts practitioner, and Mitchell wasn't long removed from the hard neighborhoods of San Diego. Tom Browning and Mario Soto, scrappy guys in their own right, also piled on Mitchell.

Sixteen minutes later, Davis, Soto, Knight, and Mitchell were ejected.[5] The Mets announced that they were playing the game under protest, inexplicably contending that they were short-changed in the ejection department, since they lost two starters and the Reds lost two men from their bench.[6]

Browning, after crawling out from the bottom of the pile, became the new baserunner at third base. But the real circus was happening on the Mets lineup card, where there were now two open positions but only one remaining bench player—backup catcher Ed Hearn. Brennaman later described his lineup card as "hieroglyphics." (The teams' roster difficulties were exacerbated by the fact that, for a few years in the mid-80s, MLB

---

3.   The authors agree that Knight was clearly attempting to shove Davis off the third base bag.
4.   Randy Myers, then with the Mets, had pitched earlier and was presumably in the showers.
5.   Mitchell was only in the game because Darryl Strawberry had been ejected for arguing balls and strikes in the sixth inning.
6.   Under the official MLB rules, this protest would be filed under "whining." Only errors in the interpretation of the rules can be the object of a protest.

teams were permitted to play with 24 men—and they almost all did, each saving the $60,000 minimum salary.)

To make room for Hearn, Carter moved to third base, for the first time in more than a decade. Right-hander Roger McDowell came in to pitch, and Orosco moved from the mound to right field. As McDowell warmed up, Orosco could be seen conferring with Dykstra and Mookie Wilson, presumably asking for a crash course in playing the outfield. With this ragtag defense behind him, McDowell got Reds shortstop Wade Rowden to ground out to second, ending the rally.

Marty noted at the time that this was a game that neither the players nor the fans would soon forget, adding, "I've seen a lot of baseball in 12-plus years, and I've seen things tonight I never dreamed I'd see in a big league game."

That big league game continued, with Reds reliever Carl Willis working into and out of trouble, and the Mets using both McDowell <u>and</u> Orosco on the mound. The former faced the right-handers; the latter faced the lefties, with Wilson shuttling between left and right field, depending on the hitter. This oddity drew a formal protest from Rose, since Orosco was given the customary eight warmup pitches upon returning to the mound.[7]

By the top of the 14th, Tuesday had turned into Wednesday,[8] and Carl Willis was entering his fourth inning on the mound—two innings had been his longest outing to that point in the year. Hearn led off with a double, and Willis then walked Orosco, who was trying to lay down a sacrifice bunt. With the tying run on second, Rose called on Ted Power to face McDowell, who struck out trying to bunt. That brought up Howard Johnson, who blasted a hanging curveball into the green seats in right field for a three-run homer.

All the air had escaped the balloon. Reds fans suddenly remembered that it was past their bedtime. As they filed out, McDowell returned for his third formal inning of pitching (divided into two portions), and sent the Reds down in order to end it with a whimper.

Davey Johnson was still bewildered after the game. "That was a funny ballgame. I'll say that. I think I got brain damage after it was over.... That's the strangest game I've ever been involved in."

7. This one had no better luck. Reds bench coach George Scherger spent the better part of two innings poring through rulebooks, looking for precedent for the warmup pitch issue, but at least according to the official scorer, the umpires handled things correctly.
8. In case you had any doubt, there was a full moon in Cincinnati that night.

27

1970
NATIONAL
LEAGUE CHAMPS

Bob Howsam had taken over the Reds in January 1967, and immediately began reshaping the organization in his own image—hard-working, ruthlessly efficient, and single-minded in pursuit of success. Howsam was patient in adding young talent, but quick to replace misfits and malcontents. He began steadily building the foundation for success.

On-field though, the results weren't yet there. The Reds finished in fourth place in 1967 and '68, and despite several key acquisitions in 1969, finished a disappointing third in the NL West. Howsam decided it was time for a change, and fired manager Dave Bristol.[1]

The next day, the Reds announced their new manager, a fellow named Sparky. Anderson made two phone calls after accepting the Reds job. The first was to invite old friend George Scherger to be the Reds bench coach. The second was to Pete Rose—Sparky wanted to name Rose the Reds' official captain. This was a calculated move. Anderson already understood that in Cincinnati, Pete Rose made a much better "face of the franchise" than some obscure minor league manager would. Rose took to the job from the start, volunteering to serve as a scapegoat or punching bag for Anderson, if the manager needed to prove a point to the ballclub.

Future Hall of Famers Johnny Bench and Tony Pérez quickly clued Sparky in to the type of team he'd been given. The Reds shot out of the gate, starting 10–3, then 20–6, then 30–11. Anderson was greeted with the type of streak that most managers never see in a career—the Reds went 70–30 in his first 100 games. "It was enough to spoil a manager forever," he wrote years later.

In those first 100 games, the 22-year-old Bench had 33 home runs and 95 RBI—on pace for 55 and 158. But even Bench said that it was Pérez who drove the Reds, especially early on. In the same time frame,

---

1.   Howsam had inherited Bristol, who was just 33 when he was promoted to manage the Reds at mid-season 1966.

the then-third baseman hit .341/.431/.640, with 30 home runs and 94 RBI.

It wasn't just his numbers, though. "Tony cast a net over the entire team with his attitude," Bench said. "He was always up, always had a sense of humor."

Pérez and first baseman Lee May came up with a simple motto: "Stay with 'em." Had a bad at-bat? "Stay with 'em." Tough loss? "Stay with 'em." There was always another at-bat, or another game, another chance for your teammates to pick you up.

The Reds weren't just about hitting, though. Longtime Reds ace Jim Maloney[2] went down with an unfortunate Achilles tendon injury in April, but the rest of the young staff was excellent. New addition Jim McGlothlin went 11–4 in the first half, with a 2.79 ERA. Twenty-two-year-old Gary Nolan continued to blossom into a star, but the big revelation was 21-year-old rookie Wayne Simpson. Simpson, Cincinnati's first pick in the 1967 amateur draft, was 13–1 at the All-Star break, and was already drawing comparisons to the great Bob Gibson. Both were tall (and seemed taller than they were), hyper-competitive, and unafraid to pitch inside.[3]

Construction on new Riverfront Stadium was nearing completion in mid-summer, so the Reds played their final game at Crosley Field on June 24. They sent the old park out on a high note, when Bench and May hit back-to back eighth-inning homers off Juan Marichal to give the Reds the lead. The fans stuck around for an impromptu party, as they watched the grounds crew dig up home plate and Cincinnati mayor Eugene P. Ruehlmann load it in a helicopter for the two-mile flight to Riverfront.

The Reds headed out on a short road trip to Houston, and returned on June 30, hoping to put some dents in that home plate. The opener was a disappointment—51,500 saw the Braves pummel the Reds 8–2—but Riverfront's real debut was two weeks later, when Cincinnati hosted the 1970 major league All-Star Game.

Bench and Pérez were voted into the starting lineup, while Rose, Simpson, and left-hander Jim Merritt were added as reserves. Rose provided the memories, though.

---

2. Maloney ranked among the league's elite pitchers. From 1961 to '69, Maloney was sixth in the NL in ERA+; fourth in wins; and fifth in strikeouts. The only names ahead of him are Hall of Famers: Sandy Koufax, Bob Gibson, Juan Marichal, Jim Bunning, Don Drysdale, and Ferguson Jenkins.
3. The Pirates' Al Oliver also compared Simpson to Steve Carlton and Tom Seaver, thus completing the "Dominant NL Pitcher" bingo card.

Entering for Hank Aaron in the fifth, Rose watched his NL teammates rally from three runs down to tie the game in the bottom of the ninth. Things remained tied at 4–4 when Rose singled with two outs in the bottom of the 12th. Dodgers third baseman Billy Grabarkewitz followed with a single of his own, putting Rose in scoring position as the tying run. Cubs outfielder Jim Hickman then lined a single to center, and Rose rounded third with a full head of steam. The throw came in to Cleveland catcher Ray Fosse, who was straddling the baseline, two steps up from home plate. "The right play is to block the plate," Fosse said a few years later. "I was the Cleveland catcher, not the San Diego Chicken."[4]

Rose really had no choice if he wanted to score—he lowered his shoulder into Fosse's chest, arriving at the same time as the baseball. Fosse went flying, and Rose touched the plate as he rolled past, winning the game for the National League and creating one of the indelible moments in All-Star Game history.

The Reds were riding high at the end of July, with a 12 game lead over the Dodgers.[5] But a series of disasters struck the pitching staff, starting with Simpson. On July 31, the rookie's dominant season disappeared with "a sudden pop" in his right shoulder. Simpson suffered through two more abortive starts (shot up with painkillers to numb the pain in his shoulder), but his season was effectively over. Simpson finished 14–3 with a 3.02 ERA. His .824 winning percentage was tops in the league; his ERA ranked second to Seaver.

(Along with Jim Maloney, Don Gullett, and Gary Nolan, Simpson is another tragic example of how the Reds once ignorantly abused young pitchers' arms. From the start of the 1969 season through his injury in July 1970, Simpson threw 489 innings—and that's not counting spring training games. As writer Earl Lawson noted, "The Reds' brass seemingly had forgotten he was also only 21 years old.")

McGlothlin was next, missing substantial time in August after taking a line drive off his temple. Then Merritt went down. After winning his 20th game on August 26, he was looking at a potential Cy Young Award. Instead, he had developed elbow tendinitis, and struggled through just three starts in September, giving up eight earned runs in seven innings.

---

4. As he aged, Fosse's story evolved. When he told it in 2012, he implied that Rose had cheap-shotted him. "I was waiting up the line for the throw from (center fielder) Amos Otis, not there to block anybody," Fosse said.
5. The Reds broke their single-season attendance record...on August 1.

Sparky Anderson confronts an umpire during an April 1970 game at Crosley Field. (Malcolm Emmons-USA TODAY Sports)

So the Reds limped into the postseason (just 32–30 after their splendid start) with a flagging offense and battered pitching staff. They faced a good, but not yet great Pittsburgh Pirates team in the NLCS. Roberto Clemente continued his late-career resurgence, hitting .352/.407/.556 at age 35. But otherwise, the Pirates were a mix of not-quite-there (Al Oliver, Richie Hebner) and past their prime (pitcher Bob Veale, Bill Mazeroski). Even slugger Willie Stargell had a relatively weak year, managing only 52 extra-base hits.[6]

The Reds swept the NLCS, despite scoring just nine runs in the three games—their beat-up pitching staff held the Pirates to only three runs. Nolan opened with a complete game shutout, and Merritt and Tony Cloninger added short, but effective starts.

The World Series would match the season's two strongest teams, as the 108–54 Baltimore Orioles also swept their league championship series, and were looking to atone for their upset loss to the "Miracle Mets" in the 1969 Series.

In contrast to Cincinnati's tattered staff, Baltimore featured three 20-game winners, in Jim Palmer, Mike Cuellar, and Dave McNally. Those three handcuffed Reds hitters, while Brooks Robinson hit .429 and turned in a half dozen of the greatest plays you'll ever see from a third baseman.

In a sense, the Reds had been playing with house money. Howsam and Anderson had expected them to be good, but not this good, this soon. Before the NLCS, Sparky told Scherger that he'd consider the season a success, even if the Reds lost to the Pirates. It was the last time Sparky thought small. After losing the World Series, he realized that "getting there isn't anything; winning is everything, the only thing." From that point on, both Sparky and his players understood exactly what it would take to win it all.

---

6.   In 1971, Stargell rebounded with 48 *home runs* plus 26 doubles.

28

PIONEERS: CHUCK HARMON AND NINO ESCALERA

"Nino Escalera and Charlie Harmon made their National League debuts as pinch-hitters in the seventh inning. Nino's was successful as he belted a single to center. Harmon popped out."

That's how the *Enquirer* covered the integration of the Cincinnati Reds. The color barrier, at least in Cincinnati, vanished with barely a whimper.

The Reds were the second-to-last National League team to integrate; only the Phillies waited longer. By 1954, the question was not if the Reds would integrate. It was *when*. Jackie Robinson's 1947 debut wasn't just the arrival of a trailblazer; it was the introduction of a superstar. By 1954, Robinson had won an MVP, a Rookie of the Year Award, a batting title, two stolen base crowns, and had appeared in five straight All-Star games.

And Robinson was the just the tip of the iceberg. In the seven years following Robinson's integration of the National League, black players won six Rookie of the Year Awards and three MVPs, and black stars led Brooklyn and the New York Giants to five NL pennants.

Their impact wasn't just on the field. Robinson and the others drew black fans to major league ballparks like never before, boosting attendance around baseball—27,164 fans crowded into Crosley field on a Tuesday night in May 1947 to watch Robinson's Cincinnati debut.[1] Cincinnati became a destination for black fans from the south, who boarded special excursion trains to watch and cheer for Robinson's Dodgers.

The influx of talent changed the face of the game, and any team that delayed in integrating was doing so for non-baseball reasons. Unfortunately, Cincinnati, in the immediate post-WWII years, had some of those. Cincinnati was the southernmost of major-league cities; located just across the river from Kentucky, the Queen City has always had a bit of a southern flavor. Among black baseball players in the postwar years,

---

1. In a season where the Reds averaged only 11,688 at home.

the city had a bad reputation. One famous story has Cincinnati fans mercilessly heckling Robinson before his first game in Cincinnati, only to have Louisville-born shortstop Pee Wee Reese walk over and put his arm around Robinson, silencing the racist crowd. That story, perpetuated by the movie *42* and even commemorated in a statue outside the ballpark of the minor league Brooklyn Cyclones, is likely myth, but its sheer persistence says something about Cincinnati's reputation at the time.[2] Robinson *did* receive death threats there in 1952, and a year later, influential black sportswriter Wendell Smith ranked the Reds as the National League's second most prejudiced team.

In 1948, Reds general manager Warren Giles spoke approvingly about integration, but never got around to actually signing a black player. His Reds did look closely at Dodgers farmhand Sam Jethroe in 1949, who was available because Duke Snider had center field locked up in Brooklyn. Ultimately, however, the Reds declined to match the Braves' $100,000 offer for Jethroe's contract.

The Reds offered the usual song-and-dance: "When we find a Negro player who'll help the club, we'll sign him." That was little more than lip service; they clearly weren't looking as hard as the Dodgers and Giants, who managed to find and sign stars like Roy Campanella, Don Newcombe, Monte Irvin, and Willie Mays.

Midway through the 1951 season, the Reds finally decided to integrate their organization, but by starting with the minor leagues. A few weeks after the plan was announced, Giles was hired as National League president and assistant Gabe Paul took over as GM. Paul quickly hired black scouts—luring Elwood Parsons away from the Dodgers and adding Alvah Caliman—and signed five black players in the 1951–52 off-season, the first of whom was Charles Byron "Chuck" Harmon, who had starred in both baseball and basketball at the University of Toledo.

Paul inadvertently dug a pothole in his path toward integration by hiring Hall of Fame player Rogers Hornsby as manager midway through the 1952 season. Hornsby was an uncompromising, abusive tyrant who was universally hated by almost everyone who ever played for him. He was also an unrepentant racist. Writer Wendell Smith called Hornsby "one of the most bigoted men in baseball," while Cincinnati writer

---

2. For the record, the *Enquirer* coverage from the date in question contains a single line about Robinson: "Jackie Robinson was applauded every time he came to the plate."

Earl Lawson described him as "one of the most prejudiced, uncouth, thoughtless individuals I've ever met."

"He hated the black players. He was terrible," former front office staffer John Murdough told authors John Erardi and Greg Rhodes for their book *Opening Day*. Hornsby nixed a February 1953 trade that would've brought Dodger farmhand (and Negro League veteran) Jim Pendleton to the Reds.

Hornsby aside, Gabe Paul's Reds were fully committed to black talent by 1953. In addition to Harmon, they'd acquired Puerto Rican utilityman Saturnino "Nino" Escalera during the '52 season. In '53, they also traded for minor league pitcher Brooks Lawrence,[3] signed Cuban shortstop Chico Terry, and gave a $3,500 contract to a 17-year-old third baseman from Oakland named Frank Robinson.

A photo of Escalera appeared in the *Enquirer* during spring training 1953, noting that he had a chance to make the Opening Day roster. (There was no mention of the fact that he'd be breaking the Reds color line in doing so.) While praised by Hornsby, Escalera didn't make the club and was sent to the Reds' Tulsa affiliate, along with Harmon.

Years later, Harmon told baseball historian Jules Tygiel about an ugly, but somehow flattering incident from that season, when the duo was "burning up" the Texas League (Escalera hit .305/.389/.451, with 47 extra-base hits; Harmon hit .311/.353/.466, with 49 extra-base hits. They combined for 42 steals in 53 tries). During a road game against the Shreveport (Louisiana) Sports, a heckler shouted at the Sports manager, "When you gonna get yourself some niggers so we can win some ballgames?"

"That tickled me," Harmon explained. "He's gonna call you a nigger, but he appreciated how good you were."

Their teammates marveled at the black players' ability to perform despite the constant pressure and aggravation. Once, a white Tulsa teammate told Harmon: "You don't know where you're gonna stay the next night; you don't know how you're gonna get to the ballpark; and you don't know where you're gonna eat. This game is hard enough. All I got to worry about is that damn curveball. You guys got to worry about all this other stuff, and still hit over .300."

---

3.   They lost Lawrence to the Cardinals in the 1953 minor league draft, then reacquired him in January 1956. He won his first 13 starts as a Red, and was elected to the Reds Hall of Fame in 1976.

Other teammates were more naive, not even realizing that the team hotel was for whites only—they had vaguely noticed that Harmon was never around, but just assumed that he had remarkable success chasing the local women.

In fact, Harmon had married Daurel "Pearl" Harmon in 1947. Pearl Harmon was of mixed heritage, and her light skinned, blonde beauty confused the authorities in Jim Crow–era Tulsa, especially when she came to games with the couple's daughter, whose skin was the same tone as her father's. The Oilers staff didn't know where to sit them in the segregated ballpark—with the other players' families or in the "colored" section? They called Gabe Paul for advice, but were told to "work it out," and warned not to distract Harmon's development. Unable to hit, throw, or run—to fight back in the way Chuck could—Pearl Harmon didn't attend many games, but would sit in her car and listen to the action on the radio.

The discrimination and the hate hurt Harmon. How could it not? He told himself that one day, things would be different, better. One day he'd make it to the major leagues, and out of segregated towns like Tulsa.

He was close. Back in Cincinnati, Hornsby abandoned the Reds with eight games left in the 1953 season, after Paul had refused to renew his contract.[4] It was probably not a coincidence that Harmon's contract was purchased by the Reds just days later. However, with only three games left in the season, he didn't actually join the club.

By 1954, the Reds had 10 black players in their system, with Harmon, Escalera, and 35-year-old Negro League–veteran Willie Powell vying to make the club in spring training.[5] While there was some discussion about Harmon breaking the Reds' color barrier, the emphasis was more on his skills than his skin. Harmon had appeared on several lists of 1954 rookie prospects, and *Enquirer* sports editor Lou Smith noted the "strong possibility" that Harmon would make the team. Smith's scouting report: "The lanky Negro speedster can do a workmanlike job at first and third, along with a fair job in the outfield. There's no question about his hitting. He's been a consistent .300 hitter all spring. Yes, the outlook is encouraging."

---

4. Hornsby later blamed his exit on an anti-Semitic slur he'd uttered in Paul's presence. Hornsby hadn't noticed that his boss was Jewish.
5. Powell actually appeared in the Reds' official Opening Day team picture, but was sent to the minors late in camp.

Harmon did make the club, as did Escalera. New Reds manager Birdie Tebbetts offered advice that wasn't much different from what Jackie Robinson had received seven years earlier. "Walk away [from a fight], fold your arms. If not, you'll get beat up and blamed for starting it."

Neither rookie appeared in the Reds' first two games, but on Saturday, April 17, 1954, at Milwaukee's County Stadium, Tebbetts called on Escalera to pinch-hit to lead off the seventh inning. He singled to center field off the Braves' Lew Burdette. Harmon then pinch-hit for the pitcher, but popped out to first.

With that, the Reds were officially integrated. The event, while historic, went largely unnoticed, at least by the mainstream press. (Baseball fans nationally had been cheering black players for nearly a decade; the Reds and the Cincinnati media may not have wanted to call too much attention to the fact that the Reds were just now integrating.)

Neither man made a significant impact on the field in 1954, as the Reds struggled to a fifth-place finish. Harmon hit only .238/.277/.304 and Escalera fared even worse (.159/.234/.203). In the field, Harmon saw most of his action at third base, while Escalera served almost entirely as a pinch-hitter or pinch-runner. He started only 9 of the 73 games he appeared in, and logged just 77 plate appearances and 98 innings in the field.

The struggles might've made for a rough year, but Harmon didn't remember hearing any negative remarks in Crosley's cozy confines. In fact, the Reds held a "Chuck Harmon Day" in August, welcoming Harmon's family and friends on the field before the game. Chuck celebrated with three hits.

By 1955, Escalera was back in AAA, where he'd play five more seasons, most with the Havana Sugar Kings. But Harmon had been accepted as part of the big league team, a fact illustrated in scary circumstances. One July day in New York, Harmon's ninth-inning pinch-single broke up Giants pitcher Jim Hearn's no-hit bid. The next day, Harmon received a death threat via letter. The Reds informed the FBI, but nothing more could be done. Before the next game, Harmon would need to take the long walk from the Polo Grounds clubhouse (located beyond the center-field fence) to the dugout—a path that allowed players and fans to intermingle.

Teammates Wally Post and Gus Bell first engaged in the requisite teasing, comically distancing themselves from Harmon. But they quickly returned and walked side-by-side with Harmon. The trip to the dugout was uneventful, but the gesture meant a lot to Harmon.

By 1956, eight black players suited up for the Reds—the most in baseball. Twenty-year-old Frank Robinson was the star, of course, hitting 38 home runs in one of baseball's all-time best rookie seasons. Surrounding him were veterans of a very specific type—black players acquired by the Reds not only for their play, but for their leadership abilities. The Reds wanted to build a foundation to ease the path for Robinson and the next generation of black players, and they gathered a group of truly remarkable men to do it.

(The Reds' "mentoring" approach even extended into the minor leagues. In 1955, they went all the way to the AAA Pacific Coast League to get 35-year-old Negro League–veteran Marvin "Tex" Williams—then sent him to Class A Columbia (South Carolina) to serve as Robinson's mentor. It was a great investment. Williams, who had been one of integrated baseball's first black managers (helming an independent league team in 1952), gave Robinson batting tips, talked him out of quitting the game entirely, and once stopped a bat-wielding Robinson from heading into the grandstand to confront a racist heckler.)

In addition to Harmon, they had pitchers Brooks Lawrence (back from St. Louis) and Joe Black, first baseman George Crowe, and outfielder Bob Thurman. All had played in the Negro Leagues, all were in their thirties, and all except Thurman were college men. Taking cues from these leaders, the Reds black players supported each other, but not by isolating themselves—they insisted that the black players' lockers be interspersed with the whites'. They felt an obligation, both to protect their own and to educate the baseball world. "We always felt that we were the first coming along and that we had to set an example so that the whites could see what the blacks were really like," Thurman said later. Lawrence echoed the sentiment, saying, "It was a totally new experience for [the white players] too."

Thurman was almost 38 when he finally made it to the majors in April 1955,[6] but he was still an exceptional power hitter. He was also

---

6.   The Reds, along with everyone else in baseball, thought Thurman was four years younger—a deception that certainly made his big league career possible.

extremely popular, both with teammates and Cincinnati fans. Thurman, who had learned how to play the game—and how to be a professional—on a Homestead Grays team that included three Hall of Famers (Josh Gibson, Buck Leonard, and Cool Papa Bell), was able to pass those lessons on to young black players like Frank Robinson, Vada Pinson, and Curt Flood.[7] That mentorship extended beyond the field; Thurman helped the Reds' black players arrange lodgings and meals when they weren't able to stay with the team. Robinson called their post-game conversations "an oral encyclopedia of baseball."

The Reds had been one of the last teams to integrate, but when they did, they did so aggressively and successfully. Building on the foundation laid by Harmon, Escalera, and the others, Robinson and Pinson led the 1961 team to the pennant, and by 1964, half the team's regulars were black.

---

7. Flood played a handful of games for the Reds as a teenager in 1956–57. He was traded to St. Louis after the 1957 season.

29

HOMER BAILEY

BAILEY

DOES IT AGAIN

After a spring training game in 2013, Joey Votto and Homer Bailey were idly chatting in the Reds' clubhouse, and the topic turned to repeating past performance. "You think you can throw another no-hitter?" Votto asked. The previous September, Bailey had authored a gorgeous no-hit game against the Pirates, in the heat of a pennant race.

Homer raised an eyebrow: "Do you think you can win another MVP?"

"Yes," Votto answered, and Bailey nodded, as if his answer were the same.

Bailey would later say that he was just joking, that he never thought he could actually do it again. But fast-forward three months (just 17 starts after that first no-hitter) and there he stood on the Great American Ballpark mound, three outs away from his second no-hitter.

Just getting to this point had been quite an odyssey for David DeWitt Bailey, the tall, lanky Texan with the nickname more suited to a slugger. Homer had been a schoolboy phenom. Scouts drooled over his blazing fastball and dynamite curve, and he was selected by the Reds with the seventh overall pick of the 2004 amateur draft.[1] Though he experienced some ups and downs in the minors, by 2006, Bailey was one of the top two pitching prospects in all of baseball.

So in 2007, Bailey (still barely 21 years old) was called up to the majors. The Reds were in the midst of a span of nine consecutive losing seasons, and fans were desperate for something, anything, that might provide a little hope for their favorite club. Homer represented that hope, and if he didn't quite understand at first how eager the Queen City was for his arrival, he soon did. As he drove north from Louisville (home of the Reds' AAA club), Bailey saw his picture on a roadside billboard just outside Cincinnati. On the billboard, he was holding a flaming baseball.

Bailey's debut went well, and it appeared as if he were on the short road to stardom. Little did anyone know that years of frustrations,

---

1. Bailey was the national high school player of the year after his senior season. During his high school career, Bailey was 41-4 with a 0.98 ERA, striking out 536 hitters in 298 innings.

INSIDE THE MOMENT

While being interviewed on live television, on the field after the game, Homer was asked about walking Blanco to lead off the seventh, and whether Bailey's sixth-inning plate appearance had led to the walk. "No man, I mean, I just [expletive] walked a guy. This game's pretty tough, regardless of those guys up there that make it sound pretty easy," he said, with a nod to the radio booth that had been so critical of him earlier in his career. Bailey didn't realize his faux pas until after the game, when his father told him that he'd cursed on live TV. "I had no idea until I left the park, like zero idea," Homer said. "[My dad] was kind of laughing about it, like, what can you do?"

seasons full of trials and tribulations, lay ahead. Bailey didn't make the Reds' Opening Day roster in 2008, and when he was finally called up, he was a shadow of the phenom he had been, going 0–6 with a 7.93 ERA in eight starts.

The next three seasons were equally frustrating. Bailey was jerked back and forth between AAA and the big leagues, suffered through some injuries, and—like most young pitchers—was inconsistent as he learned how to pitch at the game's highest level. Through his first five seasons in the big leagues, Bailey never won more than nine games in a season, and never posted an ERA lower than 4.43.

Fans who had considered him the savior just a few years before began to get impatient, taking their cues from broadcasters and writers who were hyper-critical of Bailey's struggles. In 2012, however, Bailey began to put it all together, leading the league in starts and posting a 3.68 ERA. By the time 2013 rolled around, Bailey—now 27—was consistently throwing with more velocity than he ever had, and his split-fingered fastball had become lethal. Homer was finally pitching like the ace everyone had been expecting.

All the work, all the struggle, culminated on July 2, 2013, when Bailey faced the defending world champion San Francisco Giants. The previous October, the Giants had come back to defeat the Reds in a heart-breaking NL Division Series. Bailey started Game 3 of that series, with the Reds up two games to none, on the verge of a sweep. Homer was magnificent, allowing just one run on one hit and striking out 10

Homer Bailey celebrates after pitching a no-hitter against the San Francisco Giants.
(AP Photo/Al Behrman)

Giant batters over seven innings, but was left with a no-decision in a game that the Reds ultimately lost in extra innings.

Bailey hadn't faced the Giants since that October evening, but he picked up right where he left off, retiring the first 18 San Francisco hitters before issuing a walk to Gregor Blanco leading off the seventh inning. Catcher Ryan Hanigan visited the mound after ball four, reminding Bailey of a mechanical cue to keep his fastball from moving out of the strike zone.

The little chat must have worked, because Blanco would be the only Giant to reach base all day. He was, however, involved in a key play moments later that almost buried Bailey's no-hit chances.

Blanco had advanced to second on a groundout and Buster Posey reached the plate. On an 0-2 pitch, Posey hit a soft line drive toward first base. Votto ranged far to his right and fielded the ball on a hop, but Homer—thinking Votto would catch the ball in the air—was late getting over to cover first. Meanwhile, Blanco had drifted off second and decided to break for third when he saw Votto step toward the first base bag. Sensing that neither he nor Bailey would beat Posey to first base, Votto turned and threw the ball across the diamond to third baseman Todd Frazier, who slapped the tag on Blanco. The no-hitter was still alive.

"Joey had a great heads-up play," Bailey said. "I was almost a little late getting to the bag."

"That would have been a sad way to lose a no-hitter," Reds manager Dusty Baker said. By that time, the Reds were up 3–0, far more than Bailey would need.

After retiring the Giants easily in the eighth inning, Bailey retreated into the tunnel leading to the Reds clubhouse. As his teammates batted in the bottom of the eighth, Bailey paced back and forth, talking to himself. "I kind of said to myself, 'I've already done this. I know what to expect.... It's one pitch at a time.' At the end, I just looked at the [catcher's] glove and threw it as hard as I could."

Reds broadcaster Thom Brennaman described a buzz around the ballpark as early as the sixth inning, as fans noticed that the "H" column in the Giants line score still read "0." By the time the top of the ninth rolled around, the crowd of 27,509 was on their feet, cheering Homer's every move.

Outwardly, Bailey appeared calm. He paused behind the mound and cleaned his spikes before stepping up and wiping off the rubber with his right foot. Bailey peered in, got Hanigan's sign, and delivered a 96-mph fastball to Brandon Crawford for strike one. After another strike, Crawford chopped one back up the middle. Homer timed his leap perfectly, stabbed the ball, and threw quickly to first for out number one.

Next, Bailey struck out Tony Abreu on a high fastball, clocked at 97 mph. Bailey stalked all the way around the mound, chest puffed out, body pumping with adrenaline. The crowd was delirious.

The final hitter was Blanco. On a 1-2 pitch, Blanco grounded meekly to third. Frazier fired over to first, and the no-hitter was secured. Homer stood tall next to the mound, both arms raised to the sky. His teammates mobbed him, 20 men jumping up and down in unison. Then, one by one, each teammate and coach shook Bailey's hand and gave him a hug. Just before leaving the field, Bailey removed his cap, and tipped it to the fans.[2]

Homer had authored the 16th no-hitter in Reds history, and the first in Cincinnati since Tom Browning's 1988 perfect game. It was also the first no-hitter in the history of Great American Ballpark. Bailey became the third Cincinnati pitcher to throw more than one no-hitter in his career; the others were Johnny Vander Meer and Jim Maloney.

"He was dealing. He had a dynamite fastball," Baker said. "I'm so glad for Homer. He's worked so hard to get to this point."

It was as dominating a performance as you're likely to see. Of Bailey's 109 pitches in the game, 84 were fastballs and 74 were strikes. Five of Homer's last six pitches were 97 mph; the other—Bailey's next-to-last pitch of the night—was clocked at 98.2 mph. The average speed on his fastball throughout the game was 95.32 mph, which is fast, but makes it apparent how much he dialed it up in the ninth inning. "It was all adrenaline," Homer said.

It took six long, trying years, but the flaming baseball from that billboard had finally arrived in the Queen City.

---

2. After Bailey's first no-hitter, he presented a gift to his catcher: a "real nice" watch, according to Hanigan. In speaking about the second no-hitter after the game, Hanigan said, simply, "I'm going to look at watches on the internet tonight, for sure."

30

POWERHOUSE REDS PLAY FIRST TELEVISED GAME

On August 26, 1939, the Reds split a doubleheader against the Brooklyn Dodgers, winning the first game 5–2. Bucky Walters, who would go on to win the 1939 NL MVP, threw a two-hitter for his 21st win, but otherwise, nothing about the box score even hints that this game would be talked about 85 years later.

But like many reality television "stars," this game is famous for no reason other than *being on TV*. It was the first professional baseball game ever broadcast on the then-experimental technology.

In the 21st century, television is the single most important force in baseball. It's the essential economic engine that drives the sport, from the major leagues to Little League. Every year, MLB takes in over $1.76 billion in national TV revenue, with local team deals adding another $2.3 billion.

That TV money impacts nearly every aspect of the game. Because of TV, the average value of a franchise in 2023 was $2.32 billion. Because of TV, teams at the back of the pack in attendance can still sign marquee free agents. Because of TV, playoff games end—and sometimes even start—well after most young fans have gone to bed.

It's hard to imagine now, but there was a time when baseball owners were steadfastly opposed to broadcasting games, convinced that it would hurt attendance. One man who saw the future was Larry MacPhail. In 1939, MacPhail was president of the Dodgers, but from 1934 to '37, he'd been the Reds' general manager.

MacPhail was perhaps baseball's greatest innovator. He was most famous for introducing nighttime baseball to the world, in a 1935 game under the new lights at Crosley Field. But MacPhail also introduced or popularized season tickets, air travel and pension plans for ballplayers, "knothole gangs" for kids, and batting helmets.[1] He installed lights in

---

1. And, as a young Army officer at the close of WWI, MacPhail was involved in a harebrained plot to kidnap German Kaiser Wilhelm II.

Ebbets Field and vastly increased the Dodgers' radio presence, breaking a "no radio" gentleman's agreement among New York's three teams.[2]

It was this increased radio presence that led to the televised game. Very few people owned TVs in 1939—there were only about 400 in the entire New York area. While the technology had been in development for a number of years, it had only been introduced to a mass audience earlier that spring, at the 1939 New York World's Fair, when experimental station W2XBS aired President Franklin Roosevelt's speech opening the fair.

On May 17, 1939, the same station (which eventually became WNBC-TV) telecast a college baseball game from the Columbia University campus in upper Manhattan, a site selected in part because there were few tall buildings around to interfere with the signal.

By late summer, RCA (which co-owned the station with NBC) was interested in televising a major league game. They asked Dodgers radio announcer Red Barber, who had broadcast football for NBC radio, to broker the deal with the Dodgers. The publicity-loving MacPhail was thrilled to notch another "first," and invited the station to cover a sold-out Saturday doubleheader with the league-leading Reds.

Barber was quite familiar with the Reds, having been the team's radio voice from 1934 to '38. That Saturday afternoon, he took a seat alongside one of the two cameras being used to capture the action—high in the third-base grandstand. (The other camera was at ground level, behind home plate.)

Though *The Sporting News* described the setup as "elaborate equipment," Barber had no video monitor, and no communication connection to the broadcast's director. Barber simply guessed what the audience was seeing by peeking to see which camera's red light was on, and where it was pointed. Barber had doubts about the picture quality, so he just provided the same play-by-play as he would've on radio.

That turned out to be wise, because the primitive TV technology had trouble with moving objects. While the players could be seen, both bat and baseball alike were blurry at best, invisible at worst.

---

2. In 1934, the three New York teams had made a five-year pact not to broadcast their games. When MacPhail announced the Dodgers' intention to end the self-imposed embargo in 1939, the other clubs half-heartedly followed suit. But because the Yankees and Giants shared a flagship radio station, the Dodgers were the only team to broadcast all their games live on radio.

Only a handful of New Yorkers were able to watch at home, but hundreds more saw the broadcast at the World's Fair Television Building, a Broadway theater, and the Ebbets Field press room.

Mostly to fill the time, Barber spun the camera around between innings and offered ads for the Dodgers' three radio sponsors: Ivory soap, Mobil gas stations, and Wheaties cereal.

The action on the field didn't fill much airtime. Mostly thanks to Walters' two-hit, one-strikeout performance, the game lasted only 76 minutes. (Modern World Series games will typically have almost that much time in commercial breaks.) After the Reds quickly closed out the ninth for the win, Barber hustled down to the field and interviewed Walters, Reds manager Bill McKechnie, and several Dodgers. Essentially, Barber created the template for a baseball telecast that is still used today—a framework that *Radio News* magazine described as "very pleasing, indeed," predicting that telecasts of live events like sports would be "greatly instrumental in selling sets."

They were right. Baseball grew television, and television grew baseball. Later in life, Barber was very aware—and concerned—with the impact that television had on sports, and the world in general. "Nobody had any idea, any comprehension as to the enormous impact, the unbelievable amount of money that was coming," as a result of TV. Barber may not have recognized today's game, but television—and its money—is what lets today's fan watch almost every game in baseball, every night of the season, on his TV, computer, or phone.

31

SPARKY AND GEORGE

George "Sparky" Anderson was the most accomplished, decorated manager in Cincinnati Reds history. He was a kindly grandfather figure to millions of Reds fans, accessible to media, fans, and players alike.

He was also, at least in his early years managing the Reds, a rigid taskmaster, whose first spring training camp was called "Stalag 17" by Johnny Bench. And, of course, he was a fiery competitor who earned the "Sparky" nickname as a minor leaguer.

He was a huge national celebrity, who met presidents and the Pope, but who was happier chatting with his neighbors at the local Albertsons grocery in Thousand Oaks, California.

In short, he was two people. "There's Sparky Anderson, he's the one who manages a baseball team," he told one writer. "He talks to the nation and appears all over the country. Baseball is show business. That's the way it should be. And that's where Sparky belongs. Then there's George Anderson. He's the guy from Bridgewater, South Dakota. He's the guy who knows he's no smarter or no better than the guy next door. George Anderson is me."

Stated another way: "I know I'm the real Sparky," he wrote. "But Sparky ain't the real me."

Reds fans didn't know Sparky *or* George in October 1969, when Anderson was introduced as the replacement for recently fired manager Dave Bristol. The newspaper headline may have read "Sparky Who?" but the man was no stranger to the Reds braintrust. Anderson had first worked for general manager Bob Howsam and player personnel director Sheldon "Chief" Bender in the St. Louis Cardinals' system in 1965–66, then followed them to the Cincinnati organization when Howsam was hired as the Reds GM for the 1968 season. Sparky won titles in all three seasons, and earned a good reputation for working with young talent.

But like every minor leaguer, Sparky wanted to wear a big league uniform, so he left the Reds organization for a coaching job with the 1969 expansion San Diego Padres. When the Reds managerial job opened a year later, Sparky's name came up in deliberations. Surprisingly, he was suggested not by Howsam, Bender, or one of the team's scouts, but by Reds publicity director Tom Seeberg, Sparky's old friend from Dorsey High in Los Angeles. Seeberg's pitch: Sparky knew Howsam's system and expectations as well as anyone, and was just as obsessed with detail as Howsam was. Howsam liked the idea and offered Sparky the job.

This was just another stunning example in a life full of moments where character met opportunity. Anderson's baseball career started with another. Walking home from his first day of third grade in Los Angeles, little Georgie Anderson retrieved a home run ball from the bushes outside the University of Southern California baseball field. But rather than keeping the ball (as USC's student manager suggested), Georgie insisted on returning it to the coach. Impressed, 28-year-old head coach Rod Dedeaux—who would go on to win 10 national championships at USC—invited Georgie to serve as the Trojans batboy, beginning a mentorship that would last until Dedeaux's death in 2006.

With guidance from Dedeaux and local scout Lefty Phillips, Georgie Anderson became a pretty good high school shortstop, signing with the Brooklyn Dodgers in 1953. Coming up through the Dodgers system made a major impact on Anderson. He didn't talk about it much later, but Sparky had internalized the "Dodger Way," Branch Rickey's comprehensive approach to the game that emphasized attention to detail, direct personal communication, and above all, a commitment to winning. The lessons stayed with Sparky long after his playing career was over.

Sparky never took the credit for his players' success, but his style had quickly taken the pressure off a talented, but until-then underachieving team. "He wanted to win as badly as Bristol did," Johnny Bench said, "but he went about it a lot differently." Sparky had presence, charisma...that ineffable *something* that made men want to follow him.

He worked to get to know every player—not just their playing strengths and weaknesses, but what made them tick as men. "If I understood them," he said, "I could basically deal with almost any kind of problem."

"Sparky didn't kick a guy that needed patting [on the back]," Pete Rose said, "and he didn't pat those that needed kicking. And he didn't do either one to guys who just needed to be left alone."

Although deeply empathetic, Sparky never put a ballplayer's feelings above the team's needs. "Sparky refuses to cater to the individual, [but] he cares very much about the individual as a person," Joe Morgan explained. "Because he was close to you and cared about you as a person, you were always willing to do more for him than you were for somebody else. I never thought of him as my manager. I thought of him as part of my family."

Despite the folksy demeanor, Sparky (like Howsam) was a progressive thinker in some ways. When the Reds were planning the Joe Morgan trade, Howsam and Sparky's primary focus was on-base percentage. Morgan and Denis Menke both took a lot of walks, and more base runners meant more runs. Sparky also embraced technology and new thinking—he wanted to "take every possible advantage," even if it meant rejecting tradition.

In other ways, he was a dyed-in-the-wool conservative. The Reds' famous rule requiring short hair and a clean shave was Howsam's, but Sparky supported it 110 percent. While Howsam thought in terms of team image and marketing, Sparky saw the rule as fostering team cohesion. It also matched Sparky's ideas about individual discipline.

"We don't have many rules on this club," he'd tell a new arrival, "and we've been successful, so wouldn't it be silly to rock the boat over something so trivial?" Almost everyone went along. Of course, it was easy to sacrifice for the chance to play on the Big Red Machine, and who was going to buck a system supported by Rose, Morgan, Bench, and Tony Pérez?

Some of the team's lesser lights came to resent Anderson for having two sets of rules: one for the superstars and one for the backups. Anderson's view was that the Hall of Famers had earned some leeway— and he'd be thrilled if the others would earn the same privileges.

In his autobiography, Morgan quoted Sparky's more direct response to a player who complained that the stars operated under a different set of rules: "You're damn right they do and don't expect me to treat you the same. When you contribute to the team what they do, then you'll get the same kind of consideration."

Another quirk that drove some Reds pitchers crazy was Anderson's then-innovative propensity to rely on his bullpen as much as his starting staff. It started right away—the 1970 Reds had more saves than complete games[1]—but Anderson didn't get his "Captain Hook" nickname until 1975, during a then-record 45-game stretch without a complete game.

This wasn't just a quirk, it was a way to leverage the assets he had and minimize the Reds' weaknesses.[2] "Top to bottom, our staff would beat any other," reliever Pat Darcy told the *Enquirer* years later. Even though other teams may have been blessed with more elite starters, Anderson coaxed value out of everyone. "Most staffs had two or three guys they hardly ever used," Darcy explained. "Not Sparky. He used everybody."

That included "Sparky" himself—the chatterbox persona he could use to needle, boost, or shield his players, depending on the situation. As Detroit sportswriter Joe Lapointe wrote about one conversation with Sparky, "Reporters exited his crowded office feeling somewhat chastised, perhaps enlightened, and a little confused." That was by design. Sparky acknowledged that reporters needed to wear "high boots" to wade through the rhetorical bull droppings he spread around to distract attention from struggling players.

He'd even use the Sparky persona to protect his team. If a player had made a mistake that cost a ballgame, Sparky would extend his postgame media remarks a bit longer than usual, a filibuster that gave the player a few extra minutes to cool off and prepare for his own questioning from the press.

But Sparky would also remind his players that reporters were people too, just doing their jobs like anyone else. Treating reporters (and everyone else) with respect was important to George Anderson, as was simply being nice—values that Midwesterners could understand. "It doesn't cost a nickel to be nice to people," he'd say. "It's something you can give away for free and it means more than a million dollars."

Sparky led the Reds to heights that are almost unimaginable to present-day fans. Over nine seasons, his Reds won almost 60 percent of their games, capturing four National League pennants and two World

---

1. The National League as a whole wouldn't have that ratio until 1977.
2. For example, blessed with a healthy, deep rotation in 1970, Anderson's Reds had 24 complete games in the first half. But as injuries mounted after the All-Star Break, Anderson relied on the bullpen much more—only eight complete games.

Series titles. He had become an institution in the Queen City, and with his distinctive white hair and approachable charm, he was as famous as the on-field cogs of the Machine.

But after a listless and disappointing 1978 season (92 wins and second place passing for disappointing), the Reds' new general manager Dick Wagner wanted to make some changes. One of those changes was firing Sparky Anderson. Wagner flew out to L.A. to deliver the news in person—and with tears in his own eyes.

After taking a year off, Anderson took the job managing the Detroit Tigers, and in 1984, became the first manager to win the World Series in both leagues. He ended his career with 2,194 wins, which at the time ranked third in history, and was elected to the Hall of Fame in 2000.

In retirement, George took precedence over Sparky once again. Anderson, who *Sports Illustrated*'s Ron Fimrite once called a "determinedly ordinary man," reveled in retirement, leading a life of golf matches with old friends, daily walks with neighbors, and lots of time helping the baseball team at nearby California Lutheran University.

The places where George and Sparky overlapped—maybe those are the truest expression of the man's character. He was usually optimistic, choosing to see the best in people and situations. He relished both teaching and learning. And whether Hall of Fame player or corner grocery clerk, Anderson treated everyone he met with kindness and genuine respect.

Ultimately, George Anderson was that rarest of individuals—the man who reached life's pinnacle and kept his soul. "I'm a nice man," he said in 1984. "I like myself." Almost everyone he met seems to have agreed.

32

THE WHIP'S FINEST MOMENT

It was 1947, and for the first time in his life, Ewell Blackwell was struggling.

A long, lean right-handed pitcher, Blackwell had worked hard for years to master his control. As a schoolboy back in San Dimas, California, he constructed a wooden frame approximately the size of the strike zone in his back yard, and spent day after day, hour after hour, firing baseballs through the frame from different arm angles—including the sidearm twister that made him famous.[1]

He took everything he'd learned in the back yard onto the sandlots and schoolyards of Southern California, where he played against the likes of Ted Williams. In 1941, after spending one season pitching for LaVerne College, Blackwell was playing for Vultee Aircraft in the semi-pro California Industrial League, when he began to attract the notice of big league scouts.[2] One scout for the Dodgers, Andy High, thought Blackwell was a sure thing and approached the lanky 18-year-old. Blackwell, demonstrating supreme confidence in his abilities, said he had only one condition to signing: an invitation to spring training with a big league club. "After the trip is over, you send me wherever you think I ought to pitch," Blackwell told the scout.

High immediately wired his report back to Dodgers GM Branch Rickey in Brooklyn, recommending that the Dodgers give Blackwell anything he wanted. Rickey ran the request up the ladder to club president Larry MacPhail, who rejected the young pitcher's modest demand outright. "I don't want anybody in camp who isn't a candidate for the Brooklyn club," MacPhail reportedly said.

Shortly thereafter, Reds scout Pat Patterson came sniffing around. The Reds had no qualms about offering the youngster a train ticket to spring camp in Tampa. Blackwell eagerly accepted and wasted no time in proving that he was right to bet on his own ability. After he pitched three scoreless innings in early March, Reds manager Bill McKechnie began

---

1. Later, Blackwell described his pitching education thusly: "I'm just a country boy from a town which doesn't even have a movie theater, who is trying to learn all he can about this pitching business."
2. He worked as a riveter in the Vultee plant, and played on the company team.

singing Blackwell's praises. The Cincinnati papers quickly got in on the act: "Blackwell, the 6-foot, 5-inch...pitching giant looks a fine prospect. He's a bit awkward, but he can fire the ball, which is what counts."

As the Reds came north, McKechnie made the decision to keep the 19-year-old on the club and, one week into the 1942 season, Blackwell made his major league debut to rave reviews. From the *Cincinnati Enquirer* the following day: "Ewell Blackwell, [19]-year-old stringbean right-hander, replaced the hit-shocked (Bucky) Walters in the seventh, and limited the hard-hitting Cards to one scratch single during the one and two-third rounds he worked. For a youngster, playing his first year in pro-baseball, Blackwell looks like a future great. He doesn't swear, and gets plenty on the ball."

After a couple of outings, Blackwell was sent to Syracuse in the International League for some seasoning, where he pitched exceptionally: 15–10, 2.02 ERA, 20 complete games, four shutouts. Reds' management was enthusiastic about Blackwell's potential, and expected him to join the Cincinnati staff for good the following year. Big things appeared to be in store.

Then came the war.

In January of 1943, Blackwell was drafted into the Army, and he was deployed to Europe almost exactly two years later.[3] By the time he returned to the Reds in 1946, he had grown another inch—to 6'6"—but he was three weeks late for spring training. No matter: McKechnie was thrilled to have him back, predicting that Blackwell would be "one of the truly great pitchers, one of the all-time greats."

But one year later, in the spring of 1947, Blackwell was facing a crisis of confidence. He had pitched reasonably well in 1946—well enough to be named to his first All-Star Game—but he wasn't happy with his 9–13 record, especially with the way big league hitters were hammering his usually reliable changeup.

One day late in spring training, Blackwell was scheduled to pitch a Grapefruit League contest against the Boston Red Sox. His old friend Ted Williams had a field day at the plate, and after the game, Williams sought out a dejected Blackwell. "When you throw your change of pace,"

---

3. Blackwell's pitching prowess was even touted throughout Germany during his stint in the Army. A reporter for the Associated Press, Whitney Martin, later noted that "Everywhere we went in that war-crushed country, we heard his name."

Williams said, "I can see the palm of your hand. It's a dead giveaway. You better change your grip, or all the hitters will get the tip."

Blackwell began working on concealing his changeup better, but the results weren't immediate. After five starts in the regular season, Blackwell was just 2–2 with a 5.09 ERA. Then something clicked. Beginning with his outing on May 10—a complete-game victory over the Cubs—Blackwell started cruising. When he stepped out onto the mound on June 18, his record was 9–2 with a 2.48 ERA, and he had won seven in a row. Blackwell was once again striking fear into the hearts of opposing batters, but his finest performance was yet to come.

There was rain and a low-hanging fog at Crosley Field as Blackwell slowly made his way to the mound. It was the first night game he had started in his entire career, and he would be facing the hottest team in the league, the first-place Boston Braves. In their four previous games, the Braves had scored a total of 42 runs, including an 11–1 drubbing of the Reds one day before.

When right fielder Tommy Holmes led off the game with a base on balls, the Braves looked to be off and running again. Johnny Hopp sacrificed him to second, then Bama Rowell hit a scorching line drive over Reds shortstop Eddie Miller's head that looked to be heading into the gap for the first hit and the first run of the game. The 5'9" Miller, however, leaped high into the air and snagged the liner for out number two, then calmly flipped the ball to second for the double play. Inning over: no runs, no hits, no errors.

Cincinnati took the lead in the bottom half of the first inning on first baseman Babe Young's three-run home run, his first homer of the season. Staked to a 3–0 lead, Blackwell went to work. He had been nicknamed "The Whip" for his sidearm delivery, a release that came after a high leg kick, with arms and legs flailing, that intimidated opposing hitters,[4] but Blackwell had another advantage working for him: the foggy night. "I took advantage of the night in sticking to fast balls," he said. He threw only three or four curves during the entire game.

The fastball was enough. He retired the next 16 Braves hitters in order before surrendering another base on balls in the seventh inning.[5]

---

4. "I realized my sidearm delivery was intimidating," Blackwell once said. "I took advantage of it any way I could. I was a mean pitcher."
5. Catcher Ray Lamanno took the blame for that walk. "I called for a curve after Johnny was fouling fast balls, and Blackie condescended, losing Johnny on the pitch."

A FLY ROD WITH EARS

Describing Ewell Blackwell's physical appearance seems to have been one of late-40s baseball's great delights. Besides "The Whip," he was known as "Young Bones" and "Skeleton." The Associated Press said he was "built like a vaulting pole." *The Sporting News* called him "Cincinnati's Thin Man." The *Cincinnati Enquirer* was known to call Blackwell a "human windmill."

Coach Hank Gowdy said he was "a great long strip of whalebone with the pitching motion of a tarantula and a sidearm sinker that could break your bat. [He] coiled up his right arm like a rattlesnake." Red Smith, a columnist for the *New York Herald Tribune*, called Blackwell "a fly rod with ears." Another New York writer, Joe Williams of the *World-Telegram*, described Blackwell's appearance as that of "a Picasso impression of an octopus in labor."

Players and the media were just as colorful in describing Blackwell's performance. Stan Musial once said that he'd rather try to talk extra contract money out of St. Louis' miserly owner than face Blackwell with men on base. Another Hall of Famer, Ralph Kiner, said many times that Blackwell was the toughest pitcher he'd ever hit against.

Waite Hoyt was the Reds play-by-play broadcaster during Blackwell's career (he had also been a Hall of Fame pitcher). Years later, he was emphatic that the Whip was among the best pitchers baseball had ever seen. "There was a time," Hoyt said, "when Blackie was as close to unbeatable as a pitcher can get. Yes, he could knock the bats out of their hands—and he did. I've seen him do it.... The right-handed hitters of today can thank their lucky stars that they don't have to hit against that string bean."

In early June 1947, a couple of weeks before Blackwell's no-hitter, Phillies pitcher Schoolboy Rowe was bragging about his hitting in the dugout. His manager, Ben Chapman, overheard Rowe. "Yes, you're a great hitter," Chapman said. "We need your punch in the lineup, Schoolboy. The next time we hit Cincinnati, you can chuck against Blackwell."

Rowe sat up straight and shook his head. "Not that guy," he objected. "I've asked waivers on him as an opponent. He's too tough for even a great hitter like me."

That walk came one batter after Cincinnati's third baseman, Grady Hatton, robbed Holmes of a hit on a sharp grounder that he scooped up and tossed to first for the initial out of the inning. Then, with Hopp on first and one away, Rowell hit another screaming line drive, but right fielder Frank Baumholtz was able to snag it just before it hit the bleacher screen. For the second time in the game, Rowell had been robbed of a hit and an RBI, and Blackwell's no-hitter remained intact.

By this time, the crowd of 18,137 had been worked into a frenzy, despite the rainy conditions. Beginning in the sixth inning, fans cheered every single Blackwell pitch, and every subsequent Boston out was met with a roar of approval. When Babe Young repeated his heroics in the eighth inning—another three-run homer over the right-field fence—the crowd clamored for Blackwell to come out and finish the job.

Blackwell admitted that he was "a trifle nervous" during the last two innings. He actually issued two walks in the eighth before retiring the final two hitters in that frame.[6] Holmes led off the ninth, working the count to 2-1 before Hatton once again robbed him of a hit, making an incredible play on Holmes' hard smash down the third-base line. With one away, Hopp—Boston's speedy center fielder—laid down a bunt that Ray Lamanno pounced on, firing to first to retire Hopp by three steps. Two outs.

Bama Rowell stepped into the batter's box, feeling like he was due after hitting the ball hard two times earlier in the game. With the count 0-2, Blackwell had Rowell right where he wanted him. He looked in and got Lamanno's sign—fastball, of course—and gave a quick nod. Blackwell kicked and threw, and Rowell took a vicious cut...but the ball settled into Lamanno's glove for strike three.

The no-hitter was complete! Blackwell's teammates mobbed him on the mound, lifted him onto their shoulders, and carried him into the Cincinnati clubhouse. Later, photographers were baffled when Blackwell's teammates refused to give the pitcher a hug for the cameras. Eventually, Grady Hatton clued them in: Blackwell had not washed his sweatshirt since his winning streak began some five weeks before. "Frankly, it stinks," said Hatton.

In his next start, Blackwell nearly matched Johnny Vander Meer's incredible feat, holding the Brooklyn Dodgers without a hit until Eddie

---

6.   The Braves' third out in the eighth was made by pinch-hitter and former Red great Frank McCormick.

Stanky bounced a single through Blackwell's legs with one out in the ninth inning. Blackwell's streak of consecutive no-hit innings ended at 19, but he continued to win game after game after game. When he triumphed over Philadelphia on July 25, it was his 16th consecutive victory, which still ranks as the third-longest such streak in the big leagues since 1900. During that historic run, which encompassed 17 starts, Blackwell pitched 16 complete games and 151 innings, giving up only 110 hits and a 1.61 ERA. Even more impressive, the Reds were 17–0 in Blackwell's games during that streak, but were 17–37 when another pitcher started. After the season, Blackwell narrowly lost the MVP vote, finishing a close second to Braves third baseman Bob Elliott. (Elliott was 0-for-3 with a strikeout in Blackwell's no-hitter.)

The Whip was the most feared pitcher in baseball, a fact that was confirmed when he started for the NL in the 1947 All-Star Game, his second of six consecutive All-Star appearances. Blackwell pitched three scoreless innings in the midsummer classic, striking out four American League hitters. With two outs in the first, he faced Ted Williams, whose tip back in the spring launched Blackwell into the stratosphere. Williams struck out looking.

History didn't record whether or not the pitch was a changeup.

33

UNSUNG HEROES: STOWE AND SCHWAB FAMILIES

Baseball has long been a family game, passed down from fathers to sons. It's true on the field, where Ken Griffey Jr. and Buddy Bell echoed their father's legacy; and off, with fathers introducing their sons (and daughters) to the surreal green of the Riverfront AstroTurf and GABP's manicured grass.

In Cincinnati, the generational ties also extend behind the scenes, where two families, largely unsung, have done the hard day-to-day work that literally made the games possible, and in the process created the glue that binds over a century of Cincinnati Reds history. The Schwab family tended the field and grounds of the ballpark ultimately known as Crosley Field for nearly a century, and three generations of Stowes have manned the Reds clubhouse (in three ballparks) for more than 70 seasons. Between them, the Schwab and Stowe families span over 130 years of Reds history, with no end in sight.

The Schwabs

John Schwab was the head groundskeeper at Cincinnati's League Park, starting when it opened at the corner of Findlay Street and Western Avenue in 1884. In fact, he was the *only* groundskeeper at League Park. At least, he was the only paid groundskeeper. John was assisted by neighborhood boys, including his son Mathias—the Schwabs lived just across the street from the ballpark. The boys picked up trash, mowed the field with an old-fashioned hand mower, and tied up horses behind the fence. Sometimes, they'd even take an old wagon tongue over to the barber pole factory, to be turned into a baseball bat. In exchange, the boys got free passes to the Red Stockings games.

As a 15-year-old, Mathias (known as "Matty") built the first scoreboard for League Park—as he later admitted, it was "just some boards against the wall."

Matty grew up throwing batting practice to the Reds, and even pitched professionally for Natchez in the Cotton States League. But by

1903, he'd returned to take up his true calling, replacing his father as groundskeeper at the new Palace of the Fans.[1]

In 1912, the Reds moved into the new Redland Field (which would later be renamed Crosley Field). Once again, Matty designed a scoreboard for the new ballpark, but this one included the type of information we've come to expect, including out-of-town scores. The design was so popular that Schwab was hired to design scoreboards for seven major league parks, including all three New York ballparks.

Schwab's innovation didn't stop there. He invented bases anchored by straps and pegs, built the first template for lining a batter's box, and designed baseball's first semi-automatic watering system. He was, as Lonnie Wheeler and John Baskin wrote in *The Cincinnati Game*, "the Edison of baseball technology." Schwab didn't invent underground drainage, but with Crosley's flood-prone location, he was constantly tinkering with his own system.

As baseball became a more professional affair (and as civic reforms discouraged child labor), Matty was able to hire a staff, led by his three brothers and his son, also named Matty (Mathias Jr. was known as "Buddy" in Cincinnati.). Matty was park superintendent; his much younger brother Leonard was the head groundskeeper; Buddy was an assistant.

Leonard was hired away to work the Schwab magic on the Ebbets Field turf in 1928. He eventually returned to Cincinnati, but a decade later, former Reds general manager Larry MacPhail hired Buddy Schwab to do the same job for the Dodgers, thus kicking off another legendary career on the turf.

The Schwabs were the gold standard of big league ballpark groundskeepers. Matty became as famous as a groundskeeper possibly could be—the *Enquirer* said he was as good at his position as Joe DiMaggio was in center field. There was a near revolt among Reds fans when the 1939 club voted Schwab only a $500 World Series share, compared to the $750 given to batboy Joe Hurst. The following year, the Series winners upped Schwab's share to $750, same as the batboy.

Schwab's greatest impact on the Reds came in 1945, when, due to wartime restrictions, the Reds held spring training on the Indiana

---

1. League Park partially burned down in 1900, and the extravagantly designed (but cheaply rebuilt) replacement at the same Findlay & Western location was known as the Palace of the Fans.

University campus. The Schwab brothers joined the club in Bloomington, to get the Hoosiers' waterlogged fields into some semblance of big league condition, with the help of student laborers, some of them athletes themselves.

After the Reds workouts, the Hoosiers baseball team—including members of the Schwabs' makeshift grounds crew—would practice, and then the crew would drag and rake the field for the next day's action. Waiting and watching, Matty Schwab noticed that one member of his crew—a sophomore with still-growing biceps—was launching home runs to places the Reds' feeble hitters could only dream of.[2] Schwab quickly shared his find with Reds manager Bill McKechnie, and the Reds eventually signed the big center fielder with the difficult name—Ted Kluszewski. Old Matty Schwab had flushed out the Reds' best hitter of the 1950s.

In 1947, the Reds clubhouse was dedicated to Matty Schwab. After all, he'd designed and supervised its construction. The Reds threw Matty a retirement party in 1953, but he actually stuck around for another decade, until he was 83 years old.

Schwab eased the transition to his grandson Mike Dolan, who'd already served a lengthy apprenticeship under his grandfather by the time he took over officially at age 23. Dolan managed the Crosley Field turf through the 1968 season, leaving for Ohio State University once it became clear that the new Riverfront Stadium would have AstroTurf, and thus had no need for a groundskeeper. Dolan's departure ended the Schwab family's nine-decade run as caretakers of Cincinnati's most precious diamond. Matty Schwab Sr. died in April 1970, just as the final touches were being put on Riverfront, where green-dyed plastic turf made groundskeepers obsolete.[3]

The Stowes

Bernie Stowe grew up about four blocks from Crosley Field, going to ballgames occasionally with his older brother George. Bernie's neighborhood pal Ralph Tate had every boy's dream job—he was the visiting team's batboy at Crosley Field. One day, an under-the-weather

---

2. For the entire 1945 season, the Reds hit only 56 home runs.
3. Technically speaking, Riverfront had a grounds crew. They used brooms to push the infield dirt back into the base "pits," leaf blowers to clear the field of debris, and a modified Zamboni machine to vacuum rainwater from the turf.

Tate asked 12-year-old Bernie to fill in for him. That was 1947, and Stowe never left the clubhouse.

The boys became friendly with new Dodger Jackie Robinson on Brooklyn's first trip to Cincinnati. Batboys were paid $3.00 a game—$3.50 for a doubleheader—but the tips...oh, the tips. The high-rolling Dodgers stood out: Robinson and Roy Campanella each tipped $5 per game, and Carl Furillo gave $20 for a three-game series.

The money was good and the perks were incomparable, but the hours were long. The batboys worked into the night, shining shoes and organizing for the next day's game. This posed a problem. The Cincinnati Board of Education didn't like middle schoolers standing on street corners waiting for the 1:00 AM bus. The Reds had an answer for that. Reds general manager Gabe Paul personally marched Bernie down to the Board offices and obtained the necessary work permits.

Stowe spent three years in the visitor's clubhouse, then moved over to the Reds' side in 1953. Cincinnati's manager at that time was Rogers Hornsby. The Hall of Fame player was in his late fifties and had been retired as a player for 15 years, but he still took batting practice every day—and insisted that Stowe pitch it. "Hell, I couldn't throw worth a damn," he told John Erardi and Greg Rhodes 50 years later, "but I tried." Hornsby wasn't one to praise effort alone. "You throw like a girl," he'd yell.

Though not apparently blessed with athletic ability (Stowe once shot 203 over 18 holes in a 1970s-era Reds golf outing),[4] Bernie Stowe worked as hard as any player, putting in 15-hour days, eventually advancing from batboy to clubhouse attendant, to equipment manager, and finally to senior clubhouse and equipment manager.

In the process, he carved out a unique, valued place in the culture of the clubhouse, and the larger Reds family. First as little brother, then as a supportive peer (and class clown), and finally as a surrogate father—or, as Mario Soto once put it, "He's like everybody's mom."

"He was one of us," Pete Rose said years later. "He wasn't a player, but he was like a player."

"A man that raised us, in a sense," Johnny Bench said. "The constant in the turmoil."

---

4. "That was the first time I've ever played golf," he explained to nodding heads, "and the last."

INSIDE THE MOMENT

Old John Schwab was a real character. He was dedicated to his job, to a fault. He once chased down and confronted Reds shortstop Germany Smith, who had pocketed an old practice baseball...and got knocked out for his trouble. Bernie Stowe echoed this moment eight decades later. Faced with a three-day rain delay between World Series games, the 1975 Reds worked out at the Tufts University gym in Boston. College kids filtered in to watch the Big Red Machine, and maybe snag a souvenir. The Reds later remembered how entertaining it was to watch Bernie Stowe chase college kids around for pilfered baseballs.

Marty Brennaman remembered that "nobody had greater respect inside that clubhouse than he did. I don't care if you were Pete Rose or Johnny Bench or Joey Votto, whoever it was, nobody had a greater level of respect than Bernie Stowe did."[5]

Stowe wasn't above lording that authority over people, at least for fun. The first day Sparky Anderson walked into the Reds clubhouse in 1970, Stowe introduced himself with a joking warning: "Let's get one thing straight. I was here before you got here and I'll be here after you're gone, so don't give me any crap."

Stowe kept the clubhouse in order, but also kept it light. His running banter with close friend Joe Nuxhall—another Reds lifer—entertained generations of Reds. Nuxhall would harass Stowe about the quality of the day's clubhouse buffet, while Stowe would respond with teasing about Nuxhall's famous malaprops.

"I looked forward every day to the Bernie Stowe–Joe Nuxhall show," Sean Casey said after Stowe's 2016 death. "It was like Abbott and Costello."

Like it was for the Schwabs, baseball is the Stowe family business. Bernie's son Mark started working for his dad—and the Reds—in 1975. He's now the Reds clubhouse assistant. Brother Rick was going to take a different path, but took a part-time job as a batboy while a college student in the early 1980s, and was hooked. College classes couldn't compare to spending evenings with Rose, Bench, and Tom Seaver.

---

5. Unlike Matty Schwab, Bernie Stowe was typically awarded a full share of Reds playoff money, receiving $19,060.45 (the same as Rose, Bench, and Morgan) after the World Series win in 1975. Bernie's son Mark, in his first season working as a clubhouse boy, received a ⅙ share of $3,176.74.

He's now the senior director of clubhouse operations. Rick's son Luke even joined the family business, working as a batboy and clubhouse attendant.

As Brennaman said, perhaps with a hint of self-interest, "I think that's the greatest compliment that a son or daughter can pay a parent—I want to do what you did. That in itself says a lot about the man."

Mark and Rick do the job their father did, which is much, much more than washing uniforms and polishing spikes. They solve problems, smooth the path, and create a vital home away from home for the long, long baseball season.

"Bernie had a way of making you feel welcome. He relaxed you," said Rose. Bernie retired in 2013 and died in 2016, but his sons have maintained their father's same high standards, and created that same environment. "I don't think they've missed a beat," Brennaman said. "I don't think you can put a value, in words, on what the Stowe family has meant to this organization."

Reds owner Robert Castellini called Bernie "generational glue," but that definition fits all three generations of Stowe men, just as it did three generations of the Schwab family.

34

OVER AND DUNN

As a high schooler in Texas, Adam Dunn was one of the most highly sought after athletes in the country—as a football player. According to some analysts, Dunn was the number three quarterback recruit in the entire country in 1998. After a protracted recruiting battle, Dunn ultimately committed to play QB for the University of Texas, choosing the Longhorns over other premier football schools like Notre Dame, Tennessee, and Texas A&M.

You probably already suspect that Dunn was a pretty good baseball prospect, as well. If it weren't for football, however, Dunn may never have become a Cincinnati Red.

Every big league team passed on Dunn in the first round of the 1998 draft, allowing the Reds to snap him up in the second.[1] The consensus was that Dunn was a surefire first-rounder, but he made it clear to every club that he was Texas-bound. "That's what I let everyone know," Dunn said, "that I was going to play football, but I'd like to play baseball, too. I guess that scared a lot of teams off."

Dunn signed with the Reds, with the stipulation that he'd be allowed to continue playing football. After a redshirt season, Dunn was the backup quarterback for the Longhorns and seemed to be on track for a career in football. Then Texas signed the nation's top quarterback recruit and the coaches asked Dunn to move to tight end. The writing was on the wall, and Dunn made the decision to focus strictly on baseball.

Football's loss was Cincinnati's gain. By the time he left the club in 2008, Adam Dunn had cemented his place as one of the greatest sluggers in Reds franchise history.

Over his eight-year career with the Reds, Dunn hit .247/.380/.520, with an OPS+ of 130 (or 30 percent above average).[2] His 270 homers as a Red ranks fifth on the all-time franchise list, behind only Johnny Bench (389 HR), Joey Votto (356), Frank Robinson (324), and Tony Pérez (287).

---

1.   The Reds took Lexington, Kentucky high schooler Austin Kearns in the first round in 1998.
2.   That's the eighth-best OPS+ in Reds history, among all hitters who played at least 800 games with the club.

And each of those Reds legends played in at least 400 more games in a Reds uniform than Dunn.

During his time in the Queen City, however, Dunn was also one of the most underappreciated players ever to wear the Cincinnati Red and White. Yes, Dunn had his limitations (defense mainly; his glove left something to be desired, as Dunn readily admitted). Among certain talk-radio listeners, Dunn was also criticized for "not being a clutch player," whatever that means. Many were given their cue, it must be said, by Marty Brennaman. Brennaman, in the authors' humble opinion, is perhaps the greatest baseball broadcaster ever (at least in the non–Vin Scully division), but his criticism of Dunn always seemed off the mark, minimizing Dunn's strengths and all the ways Dunn helped the Reds win (occasionally, anyway), and focusing on the strikeouts and other odd "shortcomings" (like the time Dunn went a full season without hitting a sacrifice fly...though he did have 46 home runs and 102 RBI).

During the last week of June 2006, Dunn put that talk to rest (temporarily, at least). On June 29, he came to the plate with two outs in the bottom of the eighth, with the Reds and Royals tied 5–5. With runners on first and second and the count 0-2, Dunn delivered a hard line drive to right field, resulting in a double and the go-ahead run. The Reds won 6–5.

But the real fireworks happened the following night.

Reds fans were upbeat that Friday evening. Nearly 35,000 people crowded into Great American Ballpark as the cross-state rival Cleveland Indians came to town for a weekend series. At first pitch, the temperature was a comfortable 81 degrees and the Reds, who hadn't finished above .500 since a second-place finish in 2000, were riding high at 43–36, only one game behind the Cardinals in the NL Central division. It was a good night.

It didn't take long to become an awful night. In the top of the first inning, Reds starter Elizardo Ramirez surrendered six consecutive hits, and the Reds were down 5–0 before they could record the game's second out.

Ramirez stayed in the game and actually settled down somewhat; he only allowed one more run in his five-inning stint. But after the Indians tacked on another run against the Reds bullpen, Cincinnati trailed 7–0 and the game appeared to be all over but the crying. Most fans chose to stick around, if only for the postgame firework show.

Through seven innings, the Reds were 1-for-13 with runners in scoring position. Reds center fielder Austin Kearns finally got the home team on the board with a solo home run. Second baseman Brandon Phillips and catcher Javier Valentin followed with singles and the Reds, still trailing by six runs, were beginning to make a little noise.

Reds manager Jerry Narron sent light-hitting infielder Juan Castro—a .229 hitter over the course of his 17-year career as a utility guy—to the plate to bat in the pitcher's spot. With the count at 1-1, Cleveland reliever Rafael Betancourt left a pitch out over the plate and Castro made him pay with a line-drive three-run homer. It was only the second pinch-hit homer of Castro's career, and it cut Cleveland's lead to 7-4.

The Indians stretched the lead back to 8-4 in the top of the ninth, and Cleveland manager Eric Wedge brought in his closer, Bob Wickman, to finish the game. With one out, Kearns worked the count to 3-1, then drilled a liner into right-center field for a single. The Reds, given up for dead after seven innings, were still alive.

Kearns stole second and moved to third on Phillips' single. Wickman then uncorked a wild pitch that sent Phillips to second, and Valentin followed with a groundout to first base that scored Kearns. The score was 8-5, but Wickman had two outs and only one runner on base. Over the course of a 15-year All-Star career, Wickman had worked out of any number of similar jams.

But that's when the wheels fell off, as Narron suspected they might. "It was set up by early at-bats in the inning," Narron said. "Our guys worked the count on Wickman. When you get him up to about 30-some pitches, you'll have a chance to get something to hit."

Wickman walked pinch-hitter Ryan Freel on five pitches, then issued a four-pitch walk to Felipe Lopez. He had thrown 33 pitches in the inning when Adam Dunn walked slowly from the on-deck circle towards the plate. With bases loaded and the Reds trailing by three runs, Dunn was feeling confident.

"When Felipe walked, I knew it was one swing away," Dunn said.

Dunn took the first pitch for a ball, the sixth straight ball Wickman had thrown. It would be his last. Wickman next delivered a fastball and Dunn pulled it hard down the right-field line. "I knew I hit it good enough," he said later. "I didn't know if I hit it high enough. Fortunately, it got out."

It did get out, a line-drive homer that barely cleared the wall in right field for a grand slam. The Reds had rallied for a 9–8 victory that was almost unfathomable just a few minutes earlier. Even better, the Cardinals had lost earlier that evening, so the grand slam also lifted the Reds into a tie for first place in the National League's Central division.[3]

Reds fans went berserk, and Dunn's teammates were just as excited. As Dunn rounded third, he saw that his fellow Reds were waiting for him at home plate. They mobbed him, smacking his helmet and nearly pulling the 6'6", 285 lb. Dunn to the ground in celebration. Eventually, Dunn made his way back to the dugout and began collecting his equipment to take back to the clubhouse. Great American Ballpark remained a madhouse, however, and the crowd continued the standing ovation until Dunn emerged from the dugout, carrying three bats, for a curtain call.

This game marked only the third time in Reds history that the club had overcome a seven-run deficit in the eighth inning or later. The first time was against the Boston Braves on June 4, 1951; the other was against the Mets on May 6, 1995.[4]

It was Dunn's sixth career grand slam and his fifth career walk-off home run. For one night, at least, he was the most popular guy in Cincinnati, but he treated the situation with his customary humility and humor.

"I hit [a homer] in Little League that was pretty cool," Dunn said. "This one is probably second."

---

3.   The Reds stayed in the pennant race for much of the 2006 season, before fading to a record of 80–82. The club wouldn't post a winning record until the magical division championship year of 2010.
4.   When these dates were recited to Dunn the next day, he deadpanned: "That's stuff that, if you know, you're a nerd."

35

RETURN OF THE (HIT) KING

In the waning days of the 1983 season, Pete Rose sat in a Philadelphia coffee shop with his longtime friend and advisor Reuven Katz. Pete was desperately unhappy. He was suffering through the worst season of his career, and it was clear that the Phillies had no intention of re-signing the aging star.

Katz took a sip of coffee and looked at his friend. "I don't want you to think about this," Katz said. "Just give me a quick answer. If you had your choice, where do you want to go next year?"

Pete didn't hesitate. "I want to go home."

You can't go home again. That's what they say, right? For a long time, that's precisely how things looked to Pete Rose.

You see, Pete never wanted to leave Cincinnati. He was heartbroken in 1978 when the Reds refused to sign him to a new contract after 16 dazzling seasons. So Rose trudged off to Philadelphia, where he appeared in four All-Star Games and won another World Series. But after five seasons, Pete was once again a free agent.

Katz, a lawyer who had informally represented Rose and Johnny Bench in negotiations with the Reds in past years, reached out to Bob Howsam. Howsam, the legendary architect of the Big Red Machine, had recently returned to an active role with the team as team president. Katz told him that Pete was open to discussion about coming back.

Howsam wasn't interested. The Reds had just lost 189 games in the previous two seasons and, in Howsam's mind, the last thing they needed was a 43-year-old first baseman with a .286 slugging percentage.

No, he didn't see how Rose the player could help a rebuilding team. But the conversation with Katz did get Howsam thinking.

Howsam had been around Cincinnati for a long time, and he understood very well what Rose meant to the town, and what Cincinnati meant to Rose. Across the city, people still told tales of little Pete playing baseball at Boldface Park on River Road, and of his exploits in Knothole baseball. The stories of Rose as a player for

Pete Rose is welcomed at the podium by Bob Howsam at the start of a press conference at Riverfront Stadium on August 16, 1984, where Rose was named player-manager of the Reds. (AP Photo/Al Behrman)

Western Hills High School and local American Legion teams had long grown into legends.[1] Pete was the hometown boy who grew up to be a star for the Reds. As far as Reds fans were concerned, Rose was one of their own.

Pete felt similarly. Even during the press conference in January 1984 after signing with the Montreal Expos, Rose spoke openly about his disappointment.

---

1. Rose's high school coach, Paul Nohr, was one of the few who refused to engage in any hyperbole when speaking about his former player. "He was just average. A good high school player. But the kid hustled."

"It sure seems that they just don't like me—the people who run the Reds," Rose said. "I can't think of any reason why. I'll always be a Reds fan. I sort of hate to sit back and see how that thing has deteriorated. I know how many great fans they've got, and how much hell they've been going through."

Over the 1984 All-Star break, Howsam bumped into Katz at a wedding reception for Reds pitcher Jeff Russell. Very casually, Howsam broached the topic of bringing Rose back to Cincinnati. At the time, Rose was struggling at the plate with Montreal, despite collecting his 4,000th career hit earlier in the season.

Katz's ears perked up, and he confirmed that Pete remained interested in returning.

That's when Howsam dropped the bomb: he wanted Pete to retire as a player, and come back to Cincinnati to manage the Reds.

Katz shook his head. He knew Pete wasn't ready to stop playing, and as he walked away from Howsam that day, he assumed the subject was closed.

Except that it wasn't.

Later that month, the Reds traded first baseman Dan Driessen to Montreal. That transaction ultimately relegated Rose, who was hitting just .286, to a bench role for the Expos.

A couple of days later, Expos president John McHale called Howsam about the possibility of a trade involving Rose. The wheels began turning, and a few days later, Katz himself called Howsam. But the same sticking point existed: Howsam wanted Rose only to manage the Reds.

Rose was adamant that he could still play. Initially, Howsam wouldn't budge. Finally, Rose got a chance to speak with Howsam personally, and he put the Reds' team president on the spot.

"Do you think I can hit?" asked Rose.

Howsam responded, "I think you can hit."

"Well," Rose said, "if you think I can hit, and I think I can hit, and a lot of my personal friends think I can hit, then why should I retire as a player?"

Eventually, Howsam relented, and negotiations moved quickly to bring Pete back as a player-manager. Howsam made it very clear, however: it was a nonnegotiable condition that Rose would play only sparingly, and would focus primarily on his managerial duties. Rose eagerly accepted that condition, saying: "I can still do the things I could do 10 years ago. I just can't do them every day."

On August 15, 1984, the trade was announced. Pete Rose was returning to the Queen City after five and a half years in exile.

Rose-mania immediately consumed Cincinnati. The front-page headline in the next day's *Cincinnati Enquirer*, in letters an inch and a quarter high, read simply: "Pete Comes Home."[2] That same morning, by 7:30 AM, fans had begun lining up at the ticket windows, eager to secure tickets for the homecoming game. By 6:00 PM, about 8,000 tickets had been sold, not including telephone orders (421-REDS) that kept the club's 10-person sales staff swamped all day long.

Rose was introduced at a press conference on the Riverfront Stadium turf that afternoon. Howsam was quick to remind everyone—and especially Pete—that Rose was a manager first, even using the term "manager-player" on numerous occasions. "Pete is coming mainly to be a manager, and also pinch-hit and fill in a few times," Howsam said. "What I expect from him is what I always expect from a manager—to work hard and lead a winning team."

Pete, wearing a Reds jacket and cap, standing behind a podium adorned with a Reds pennant, couldn't have appeared any happier to get the opportunity to help turn the Reds around. "Somewhere along the line, the winning attitude escaped this ballclub. I don't know why.... Things can change if you got the right personnel and the right attitude."[3]

On the playing time issue, Pete initially agreed with Howsam. "I'm not going to play every day," he said, but he was also quick to leave the door open as to how much he'd pencil himself into the lineup.

"I didn't say I was going to be strictly a pinch-hitter," Rose said. "I'll use my own discretion as far as playing's concerned."

Rose continued: "If I couldn't hit, I wouldn't waste Bob's time as a player-manager. I wouldn't waste anybody's time. [But] if I retired as a player and had a feeling inside that I still could hit, then I really didn't give it a good effort to get everything out of the game I could. It would be a tough life for me."

---

2. Jim Ferguson, Reds' vice president for publicity, cracked, "'Nixon Resigns' was slightly bigger, but not much."

3. Legendary Cubs broadcaster Harry Caray attended the press conference and his reaction was typically understated. "Truly dramatic," Caray said. "This is the Pete Rose Story. Bringing back Rose is the greatest objective thing the Cincinnati Reds have ever done."

Rose noted that he was looking forward to meeting with each of the players individually in the coming days. "I want them to realize I am just like them," he said. "I have two arms, two legs, and 4,000 hits."

Pete knew that he still had something left in the tank. The next night, he proved it.

Relief pitcher Tom Hume was one of the first to arrive at the ballpark prior to the Friday night game against the Cubs.[4] "I just wanted to get down here and see what it was like," he said.

"When I walked in here, you could feel it. It was like there was a buzz in the air. Amazing. Just amazing. You know what, it's like Opening Day again. It's like all those games we played (the Reds were 51–70, and 21 games out of first place at the time) are gone, they don't even matter."

During batting practice, Rose saw his old friend and teammate Johnny Bench on the field. Bench had retired the previous year, and the Reds had already retired his uniform No. 5, but Pete couldn't resist. "John, I've got a uniform for you in there," he said, pointing toward the clubhouse.

Fellow Big Red Machine veteran Tony Pérez had returned to Cincinnati at the beginning of the 1984 season, and he was excited. "I never thought I would play with Pete again, and I *never* thought he would be my manager. He will help the attitude here."

Before the game, Rose called a team meeting. It only lasted 15 minutes—"I just told 'em to play hard, have fun, and do a good job," Rose said—but it ended in applause. The players were fired up. As game time approached, Dave Concepción, a nine-time All-Star and one of the few remaining links to the Big Red Machine, was seen running down the tunnel toward the field.

"I've got to hustle now," Concepción said. "If I don't, the manager will fine me."

Riverfront Stadium began filling up from the moment gates opened, but outside, people were still trying to buy tickets. First pitch was pushed back 10 minutes to get all those fans into the park, and by the time Rose walked to home plate with the lineup card, a crowd of 35,038—each of whom had received a certificate proclaiming "I Was There"— was ready to rock.

---

4.   It was appropriate that the Cubs were the opponent on this historic night. Chicago's manager, Jim Frey, and their third-base coach, Don Zimmer, had been high school teammates at Western Hills High School, Pete's alma mater, in the late 1940s.

THIS IS A GREAT GAME

Around 10:00 PM on the night of Rose's return, a phone rang in the *Cincinnati Enquirer*'s newsroom.

"Hello, is this Cincinnati?" the caller asked. "I'm calling from Portland, Oregon, and I'm watching the Cubs game on the Chicago cable station and I want to know if this is a rerun."

"No, it's live," responded a baffled staff reporter.

"Then what the hell is Pete Rose doing playing first base for the Reds?"

The staffer explained that Rose was back, and was the player-manager of the Reds. The caller let out a yell, and reported the news to the people who were watching the game with him.

"That's great," he said. "I love it. This is a great game."

On that lineup card, Rose had written his name second. He wouldn't be pinch-hitting this evening. "A lot of people are going to be here tonight," Rose said before the game. "They didn't come to see me take the pitcher out of the game."

The Cubs took the lead early as Cincinnati's starter, Mario Soto, gave up a run on a couple of Chicago hits in the top of the first inning. The Reds' leadoff hitter Gary Redus led off the bottom half with a clean single.

Pete Rose strode to the plate in Riverfront Stadium as a Cincinnati Red for the first time since October 1, 1978. (Rose's last at-bat in a Reds uniform, though not official, had actually occurred on November 21, 1978, in an exhibition tour of Japan.)

The crowd rose in unison. A fan near the Reds dugout tossed four long-stemmed red roses onto the field. Rose took a couple of practice swings, tipped his helmet to acknowledge the ovation, then stepped into the batter's box.

On the first pitch from Cubs starter Dick Ruthven, Rose faked a bunt as Redus stole second base. The next pitch was a called strike.

Rose stepped out of the box and took a deep breath before resuming his familiar crouch from the left side of the plate. And at 7:54 PM, he showed everyone that Pete Rose was back.

Rose laced a line drive over the head of Chicago shortstop Tom Veryzer. Rose rounded first, saw that the ball had skipped past center fielder Bob Dernier, and kept going.

"I haven't been playing much lately," Rose said later. "When I got to second base, third looked like it was at Fifth and Vine." But he wasn't about to stop.

"Rose is racing around second," Ken Wilson said on the television broadcast. "Rose digging for third. There's that head-first slide, and this crowd goes *bananas*!"[5]

In the Reds dugout, the players high-fived each other in genuine excitement. Third baseman Wayne Krenchicki looked over at Concepción. "I've got to get a hold of myself," he said. "I've got tears in my eyes."

"Well, look at this," Concepción replied, holding out his arms. They were covered with goose bumps.

Meanwhile, Rose stood on third base, soaking up his fourth standing ovation of the night. A huge smile crossed his face and dirt covered the front of his brand-new Reds uniform. Cincinnati had its hometown hero back.

But Rose didn't stop there. With the Reds leading 5–4 in the seventh inning, Rose came to the plate for the fourth time (he had grounded out in his previous two trips to the plate). With the crowd chanting, "Let's Go Pete," he slapped a double down the left-field line that plated the Reds' final run in a 6–4 victory. True to form, Rose slid head-first into second on the double.

The night was an unmitigated success. When he finally returned to his office, Rose had to clear dozens of roses off his desk in order to take a phone call. The call was from his old manager, Sparky Anderson.

"Pete, never change," Sparky told him. "Just be Pete Rose."

Rose went on to get three hits in each of the next two games against the Cubs, and even Howsam couldn't complain about Rose being in the starting lineup for the entire series. "When you have a person holding the hot hand," he said, "you play that hand."

Rose continued to hold the hot hand for the rest of the season. He collected 24 hits in his first 58 at-bats, and by season's end, Rose had hit

---

5. Outside the stadium, local resident Larry Price was collecting beer and soda cans. "I heard the roar and I knew Pete had come through," Price said. "This is his town. He owns it. And everybody's going to benefit. I've already collected about 900 cans and I haven't even gone down in the garage yet. I ain't seen cans like this since '76."

.365/.430/.458 in a Reds uniform. As if trying to prove to Bob Howsam that he wasn't just a pinch-hitter at this point in his career, Rose reached base in all 23 games he started.

The fun didn't stop in 1984. The following season, 52,971 fans packed into Riverfront for Opening Day, despite snow flurries that twice interrupted the game. Pete doubled, singled, scored a run and drove in three more in a 4-1 Reds win. The chase for Cobb was on.

Even better, after three consecutive losing seasons, Pete's return also marked the return of a competitive ballclub. In his first full season at the helm, Rose's Reds went 89-72 and finished in second place, an improvement of 19 wins over the previous season.

Cincinnati baseball was back, and it was fun again. The (Hit) King had returned.

36

BIG APPLE DRAMA: 1973 NLCS

The loss to Oakland in the 1972 World Series was especially frustrating to the Reds, because they felt they had the better team. While they struggled in the first half of the 1973 season, three consecutive walk-off wins against the Dodgers in early July kicked off a 62–29 finish, giving the Reds their third National League West division title in four seasons.

The Reds entered the National League Championship Series brimming with confidence. The New York Mets' record was only 82–79; they would've finished tied for fourth in the West, 17 games behind the Reds. While talented, the Mets had been beset with injuries all summer. As late as August 31, the Mets were in last place in the NL East, 10 games under .500. Only a sizzling 21–8 finish put them in the playoffs.

Cincinnati had offense (only the Braves in their "Launching Pad" stadium scored more runs), but New York had pitching (1973 Cy Young winner Tom Seaver, Jerry Koosman, and Jon Matlack anchored the rotation). The Reds tried to lower expectations—"It ain't no mismatch," said manager Sparky Anderson—but the Reds were heavy favorites.

In a thrilling series opener, Reds veteran starter Jack Billingham matched pace with Seaver. The Mets snatched an early 1–0 lead, but Billingham recovered to retire 19 of the final 20 hitters he faced. Seaver, though battling a stiff shoulder, shut the Reds out through the first seven innings before Pete Rose homered to right in the eighth, waking up the home crowd. An inning later, Johnny Bench lined a Seaver fastball over the left field wall for a 2–1 walk-off win.

In the second game, Jon Matlack dominated the Reds, shutting them out on two singles. The Series was tied, but more disturbingly for Anderson, the Reds were playing the Mets' game—low-scoring pitcher's duels. And the confident, even-keeled Reds hitters were getting a little frustrated.

The outcome of Game 3 at Shea Stadium was a foregone conclusion even before the Reds batted a third time. Starter Ross Grimsley had pitched well in the 1972 postseason, and put up a 3.23 ERA in the Reds

1973 rotation, but on this particular Monday afternoon in Queens, he had nothing. Grimsley faced 11 hitters: six of them reached base. It was his worst start of the year, and Anderson once again earned his "Captain Hook" nickname, pulling his starter with one out in the second inning.

When Grimsley left the mound, the Reds were in a 3-0 hole. By the time he reached the showers, the deficit was 6-0; reliever Tom Hall gave up a three-run homer to the very first batter he faced.

With one out in the fifth inning, Rose singled. Joe Morgan then grounded hard to John Milner at first for a tailor-made double-play ball. Milner threw to Harrelson, whose quick return throw easily beat Morgan at first to end the inning. The Mets began to run off the field, before noticing a commotion in the middle of the diamond.

Rose had slid hard into Harrelson, trying to break up the double-play. By objective accounts, the play was tough but not dirty (by 1973 standards, anyway). As Rose popped up, his elbow clipped Harrelson's head. The shortstop understandably took exception, and called Rose a few unprintable names. The 200-pound Rose responded by shoving the 146-pound Harrelson, and the two men locked up and tumbled to the ground.

Within seconds, both teams had rushed in to protect their guys. Mets third baseman Wayne Garrett was closest to the scrum, so he took a few shots at Rose. Quickly realizing he was outnumbered, Rose rolled onto his back, holding onto Harrelson as a sort of shield. While some of the largest peacemakers wore red—Johnny Bench and Ted Kluszewski were quick to protect Rose—the infield was, in the words of the *New York Times'* Arthur Daley, "a free-for-all of sprawling immensity," with "private fights as well as impersonal wild-swinging melees."

The most notable of those private fights began when Reds reliever Pedro Borbon arrived from the bullpen and took a hearty swing at New York reliever Buzz Capra.[1] The two exchanged a few wild haymakers, but were eventually separated. As he walked away, the still-steaming Borbon retrieved his baseball cap from the ground and returned it to his head. But as his teammates quickly pointed out, Borbon had mistakenly picked up Cleon Jones' Mets cap. Enraged once again, Borbon pulled off the hat and chomped out a giant bite, spitting the blue wool onto the

---

1. According to the *Enquirer*, Borbon was late to the brawl because he couldn't open the bullpen gate. "He tugged at it twice," said teammate Clay Carroll. "Then he just tore the thing off the hinges."

green of the infield. (This incident, combined with a 1974 brawl where he actually bit the neck of a Pittsburgh reliever, earned Borbon the nickname "the Dominican Dracula.")

Having blown off their steam, the teams calmed down. Incredibly, no one was ejected. The only permanent damage was to Harrelson's eyebrow (cut when his sunglasses broke in the scrum) and Jones' ball cap.

Mets fans, however, were just getting started. When the Reds took the field for the bottom of the fifth, debris joined the boos and jeers launched at the Reds—and at Rose, in particular. Beer cans, programs, batteries, and bottles rained down on the outfield throughout the inning. A short delay didn't help—a whiskey bottle buzzed Rose's head, and pitcher Gary Nolan took a beer can (Schlitz) to the head, while sitting in the bullpen.[2]

Sparky had seen enough. He pulled his team from the field, announcing: "That's enough for us today. Let's go." In phrasing that could come only from Sparky, he told the umpires, "Pete Rose has contributed too much to baseball to be allowed to die in left field at Shea Stadium." Telling the umpires to call him when they got things straightened out, Sparky led the Reds into the clubhouse, where they stayed for 20 minutes.

NL president Chub Feeney eventually prevailed on the Mets to dispatch a set of all-star ambassadors to quiet the crowd. Out walked manager Yogi Berra, Seaver, Willie Mays, Jones (as left fielder, closest neighbor to the most unruly fans), and first baseman Rusty Staub (carrying a bat in case the situation really deteriorated).

Although the 42-year-old Mays was struggling through his final season, and hadn't played at Shea since Labor Day, his appearance broke the tension, giving Berra the chance to explain to the crowd that the Mets were facing the possible forfeit of a playoff game they were leading 9-2. Yogi's persuasion, plus the timely appearance of several of New York's Finest in the left-field stands, calmed things down just enough to finish the game.

Afterward, Rose was unapologetic: "I'll be honest. I was trying to knock him into left field," he said, promising, "I'll play the same way

---

2. The *Enquirer* reported that the can was "half full," but Nolan probably had a "glass half empty" mindset about the experience.

Pete Rose fights Mets shortstop Bud Harrelson after Rose failed to break up Harrelson's double play in Game 3 of the NLCS at Shea Stadium on October 8, 1973. Both benches and bullpens emptied in the ensuing brawl. (Marty Lederhandler/AP Images))

tomorrow." The *Cincinnati Enquirer's* Bob Hertzel described it as "Pete Rose...being Pete Rose," but a closer look shows that there was more going on.

For starters, Harrelson had made comments after Game 2 that gave the struggling, frustrated Reds hitters a focal point for their anger. When told of Harrelson's observation that "the Reds are just swinging from the heels," Rose shouted across the Reds clubhouse to make Joe Morgan aware of the slight.

Morgan (0 for 8 in the Series, to that point) first responded philosophically: "I'm not hitting anyway. Not off the heels, toes, or anything else." But he quickly got around to torching Harrelson. "What the hell's he, a hitting instructor?" Morgan asked. "What did he hit? I'll tell you, .253. Only in New York would anyone like that be a superstar."

Before Game 3, Morgan had confronted Harrelson during batting practice. According to Harrelson, Morgan told him, "If you ever say that about me again, I'm going to punch you." Staub broke up the confrontation, but not before Morgan reportedly promised Harrelson that neither he nor Rose would forget the snub.[3]

Harrelson was already extra-sensitive to contact around the base at that point, having missed most of June with a broken hand after a takeout slide by Reds catcher Bill Plummer, then another 16 games in August after colliding with Pittsburgh's Rennie Stennett during a rundown.

Rose himself was on edge in the fifth inning, having been brushed back by a Koosman pitch minutes before. (Koosman had great control that afternoon, not walking a batter all day.)

Aftermath

With the city still on edge the following day, Mets officials rerouted the Reds team bus and added a perimeter of guards. The combination of universal hatred and high security led Rose to quip, "Now I know how Nixon feels."[4]

Shea Stadium was full of anti-Rose banners, with sentiments like "Rose is a Weed," and "Roses Die, Buds bloom." The Mets organization, hoping to calm matters with a goodwill gesture, asked Rose and Harrelson to shake hands at home plate prior to Game 4. Rose declined, explaining that he had no hard feelings, but wanted the focus on baseball. The Reds did hold Rose out of outfield drills and the lineup card exchange (as the Reds captain, Rose would've delivered the card).

After Game 3, Rose had denied that he'd acted out of frustration, and promised to take out his frustrations on Game 4 starter George Stone. Morgan and Bench were a little worried, though. Morgan spent the evening with Rose, having dinner and watching *Monday Night Football*—while sprinkling in reminders for Rose to "not try to do too

---

3. Staub and Morgan were teammates and close friends for six seasons with the Houston Colt .45's/Astros. Both debuted as 19 year-olds in 1963.
4. Coincidentally, Nixon's Vice-President, Spiro Agnew, resigned at 2:05 PM on October 10, almost exactly the time Seaver threw the first pitch of Game 5.

much." Bench kept an eye on Rose during Game 4, reminding him to be patient and wait on a hittable pitch.

As it would for the better part of the decade, the unique relationships between the Machine's superstars let each man play better than he might've on another club. On this day, it was Rose who was supported by his teammates, and Rose who took his revenge on the Mets, going 3 for 5 with a walk, and hitting the game-winning home run in the 12th inning—punctuated by a jump onto home plate.[5]

Game 5 rematched Seaver and Billingham, but there was no repeat pitcher's duel. Seaver was great, as usual, but the Mets touched Billingham for five runs in four innings and coasted to a 7–2 victory. Shea Stadium was rocking with a strange mix of exhilaration and anger, combined with the sense of chaos and lawlessness that had settled over early-70s New York.

Late in the game, fans began to leave their seats, filling the aisles and massing near the field, in anticipation of the postgame field mobbing that was so common in the 1970s. Reds officials and families, many wearing team colors, became targets for jeers, thrown objects, and worse.

As the Reds mounted a rally in the ninth, loading the bases against Seaver, things broke loose, literally. A retaining wall actually collapsed, spilling fans onto the field. Members of the Reds traveling party took some of the worst of it. A few wives had their hair pulled, and Lois Ballou, wife of the team doctor, was pushed to the ground and trampled. The game was delayed as security tried to herd the fans back into the grandstand. When a string of firecrackers in the upper deck created a diversion, the Reds party evacuated their box seats and hustled across the field, through the dugout, and into the clubhouse.

When Mets closer Tug McGraw stifled the rally to lock up the pennant, thousands of fans streamed onto the field. And this was no ordinary mob. They pulled up the infield turf, flattened the pitcher's mound, stole all three bases *and* home plate, and destroyed sections of the outfield fence and grandstands. Meanwhile, the Reds base coaches and baserunners (including Rose) sprinted through the crowd for the

---

5.   The iconic image of Rose's home run trot—rounding second with his right fist raised—was used for the Reds 1974 "Poster Day" promotion, and graced many a Midwestern bedroom for the next decade. In an incredibly fortunate quirk of photographic composition, Rose's fist is aligned just below the chin of Harrelson, who is standing in the photo's background at his shortstop position.

dugout steps—where Anderson, Bench, and a dozen others stood guard, a phalanx armed with baseball bats.

The Mets had completed a remarkable six-week journey from the cellar to the pennant, while the Reds were once again disappointed. Four years into the '70s, and the Big Red Machine had three Western Division titles and two NL pennants, but still no ring.

37

COME FLY WITH ME

They call it "All-Star Week," but when Cincinnati hosted the festivities surrounding the 2015 Major League Baseball All-Star Game, it might well have been called "Hometown Heroes Week." The city had been abuzz for days, reveling in its role as host to baseball's elite. Just before the All-Star Game began, Cincinnati baseball took center stage.

First, Johnny Bench was honored as one of baseball's four greatest living players.[1] Moments later, Bench was joined on the field by the rest of what MLB called the "Franchise Four"—the four greatest Cincinnati Reds of all time, as chosen by a fan vote. Bench, Joe Morgan, Barry Larkin, and Pete Rose took turns waving to the standing-room-only crowd. Rose, the Cincinnati boy, permitted to participate in an official baseball activity for one of the very few times since his banishment from the game 26 years before, received the loudest cheers of the evening so far.

But the cheers for Rose were soon dwarfed by the enthusiastic reception given to Todd Frazier.

No, really: *Todd Frazier*.

To understand why, you'd have to go back about 22 hours, when an even louder roar had enveloped Great American Ballpark as Frazier etched his name in Reds history with a thrilling performance in the Home Run Derby.

It was Frazier's second try at the Home Run Derby; he had lost in the finals of the 2014 contest in Minnesota.[2] Though Frazier was the highest-ranking returning contestant, he wasn't the favorite in a contest that included Albert Pujols, Josh Donaldson, rookie-phenom Kris Bryant, and two-time champion Prince Fielder. Frazier was, however, the most excited man at the event.

"I'd be in [the Derby] every year if I could," Frazier said. "It should be a lot of fun. I'm looking forward to it in front of the Cincinnati fans."

---

1. The other three: Willie Mays, Hank Aaron, and Sandy Koufax.
2. It was also his second All-Star selection, and the first time he had been elected to start.

INSIDE THE MOMENT

Later, Frazier noted that, in addition to finishing second in the 2014 MLB Derby, he had also finished second in a home run derby back in high school. "I lost to a kid from Keansburg High," he said.

The night began on a good note, when former Reds star Ken Griffey Jr. threw out the first pitch for the Derby. Junior's catcher was another former Reds star: his dad, Ken Griffey Sr.

In the first round of the competition, Frazier faced Fielder, still one of the game's most fearsome sluggers. With his very first swing of the night, Fielder ripped a line drive into the outfield seats, 434 feet from home plate. His second swing resulted in a 474-foot blast that very nearly cleared the right-field bleachers, and caused the partisan Cincinnati crowd to begin to murmur. By the time he was finished, Fielder had hit 13 balls over the fence, and the cameras flashed to Frazier, who had a nervous smile on his face.

Nervous or not, the smile didn't leave Frazier's face as he grabbed his bat and approached the plate. With his customary walkup music—fellow Jersey boy Frank Sinatra's "Fly Me To The Moon"—blaring over the loudspeaker and his brother Charlie doing the pitching, Frazier proceeded to hit just one home run in his first seven swings.

With 90 seconds to go in the timed event, Frazier was still five home runs behind Fielder. With a minute remaining, he was down by four. Then Frazier got hot. Boom: a line drive into the left-field stands. Bam: a moon shot into the upper deck. Crack: a long fly ball that just cleared the fence in left-center.

Then, with one final swing as the last second of regulation time ticked off the clock, Frazier drilled a 420-foot line drive that tied Fielder with 13 home runs.[3]

Chants of "Let's Go Frazier" echoed through every corner of the park. Frazier stepped out of the box, looked up at the seats and applauded the fans. The party had officially started.

---

3.   Each hitter was given four minutes to hit as many home runs as he could. The timer stopped after every homer during the final minute. If a batter hit two home runs that exceeded 420 feet, he was given 30 seconds of bonus time. A home run of more than 470 feet added 30 more seconds.

Under rules that had just been put in place that year, Frazier had earned 30 seconds of bonus time. The Cincinnati third-sacker crushed a homer—his 14th—on his first swing in the bonus period to pass Fielder and advance to the second round. "Honestly, I was thinking '14.' That's Pete Rose['s jersey number]. I can't let him down,'" Frazier said.

In the next round, Frazier would face Toronto's Josh Donaldson, his third-base counterpart on the American League side. In the first round, Donaldson had dispatched Anthony Rizzo, but his most notable blast didn't count in that total. Donaldson's longest hit was 468 feet, but the ball went just foul...where it was caught by former Reds All-Star Sean Casey, sitting in the crowd.

In the second round, Donaldson—who would go on to win the 2015 AL MVP Award—again finished with nine.[4] No sweat for Frazier, right? Well, Frazier put himself behind the eight ball once again: after his first 12 swings, he had just two homers. When Frazier finally started hitting them, the park got even louder, if that's possible,[5] and he pulled to within one homer with a minute remaining.

Then, with a nation's fans urging him on, he failed to hit a single homer with his next eight swings. Only 13 seconds were left on the clock. But right on cue, Frazier hit a liner to dead center field, followed by a 444-foot blast that landed in the Reds bullpen just as time expired.

Fireworks exploded above the park, and Frazier—that patented broad grin painted across his face—tried to wave to every single person in the stadium.

"There are baseball gods out there," said Bryant. "And they were on his side today—as they should be."

But for all the drama, Frazier had only earned a return ticket to the finals. Dodgers rookie Joc Pederson had cruised into the championship round with more homers than any other participant, and didn't slow down in the finals. Pederson set the bar at 14 home runs, equaling Frazier's first round as best of the night.

Frazier's work was cut out for him. In two Derby appearances, Frazier had never hit 15 homers in a single round. Once again, he

---

4. "Honest to God, I didn't even know who I was going up against in the second round," said Donaldson, "but after 30–40 seconds into it, I could start to hear people boo me. Then mid-swing, I was like, 'Oh, I'm going up against Frazier.' Good for them. He put on an awesome performance tonight."

5. One reporter tweeted: "That sound you hear when the ocean ebbs in and out of the seashore, crashing against the rocks? That's the ballpark right now, for Frazier."

Todd Frazier celebrates winning the 2015 Home Run Derby at Great American Ballpark.
(Frank Victores-USA TODAY Sports)

INSIDE THE MOMENT

Frazier, of course, had been in the American baseball consciousness since he was 12, when he was the best player on a Toms River, New Jersey, team that won the Little League World Series and captured the heart of a nation. He had also been a big league All-Star and an integral part of a Central Division championship squad. But the Home Run Derby title was special to him. "This is up there," he said. "I wanted to bring this hardware home. It's an unbelievable feeling."

started slowly in the final. With 90 seconds remaining, he was still down 14–7, and he was visibly exhausted. That's when Reds fans—who had been on their feet for every Frazier swing all evening—kicked it into yet another gear, pushing Frazier to finish strong.

"It had a big-time impact," Frazier said. "Just hearing the crowd roar, calling my name, the adrenaline kicked in. It really picked me up. I was able to drive the ball out of the park a lot more. It was really fun. I appreciate that a lot."

Frazier hit four homers in his next five swings. With 30 seconds to go, he had 13 and, once again, Frazier beat the buzzer with a long fly to left-center. Frazier waved it across the fence, and when it settled into the crowd, the Derby was tied at 14 apiece.

Again, Frazier had earned 30 seconds of bonus time; all he would need was just one home run to capture the title. He toweled off, took a deep breath, and settled back into the familiar batter's box. For once, Frazier didn't wait for a buzzer-beater. With the first swing of his bonus time, Frazier drilled a line drive over the left-field fence and raised his hands in triumph. Teammate Aroldis Chapman came out to hug Frazier, who blew a couple of kisses to a crowd that had been whipped into a frenzy by the night's excitement.

Frazier had become just the second player ever to win the Home Run Derby in his home park, and he had accomplished it with a home run on his last swing in each and every round.

The Jersey boy lifted the championship belt over his head like a heavyweight champion. Above the wild cheering by the Ohio River, you could hear the strains of Sinatra's "My Way" playing.

CINCINNATI REDS

Frazier had certainly done it his way, and for one week at least, he was Cincinnati's pride and joy. And every fan who had been lucky enough to attend would never forget the night that they formed an integral part of one of the most exciting moments in the history of the Cincinnati Reds.

38

THE GREATEST BATTING PERFORMANCE IN REDS HISTORY

The 2017 version of the Cincinnati Reds wasn't expected to contend. General manager Dick Williams had developed—and was sticking to—a plan to rebuild the organization into a pennant contender, but the plan was not expected to bear fruit until 2018 or later. The 2017 season was one for evaluating and developing young players.

So it was a slight surprise when, just days before Opening Day, the Reds claimed 26-year-old utility man Scooter Gennett off waivers from the Milwaukee Brewers, to provide infield depth and a left-handed bat off the bench. Gennett was a solid hitter (career .279/.318/.420), but hardly the type of guy you build a team around.

Plus, he wasn't cheap, at least to the Reds. Gennett immediately became the sixth-highest-paid player on the Opening Day active roster. By signing Gennett, the Reds were adding about $2 million to their $92 million payroll. But with the Reds planning to carry only four bench players, Williams saw the appeal. "My team in the front office thought it was a fit strategically for us: a left-handed bat with power, a guy who could play some positions we needed," Williams told WCPO's John Fay.

Ryan Joseph "Scooter" Gennett took his nickname from a character on the Muppets, in one of the more interesting nickname stories you'll hear. As a preschooler, Gennett was defiant and refused to wear his seat belt. His frustrated mother finally drove him to the nearest police station to scare him straight.

Young Ryan was quick thinking (if not exactly honest), and gave the officer an alias: "Scooter Gennett."

"I didn't answer to Ryan, my given name, for a year-and-a-half because I thought I'd get in trouble or get arrested," he told the *Enquirer*. "You know some kids have imaginary friends and stuff. I had an alias."

In many ways, it was inevitable that Scooter would play for the Reds someday. Born in Cincinnati during the championship season of 1990,[1]

---

1. Gennett was born on May 1, the day the Reds lost an afternoon game to the Phillies. Todd Benzinger had three hits in the loss.

Gennett moved to Florida at age nine, though he remained a lifelong fan of the Redlegs. One summer in high school, he returned to play for a Cincinnati-area travel team, before being drafted by the Brewers in the 16th round of the 2009 draft.

Gennett paid dividends immediately upon his return to the Queen City, homering on Opening Day, and he was hitting .315/.344/.522 on May 28. But Gennett faced a rough patch late in the spring. In the midst

WHAT ARE THE ODDS?

General manager Dick Williams had been approached just before the game by a longtime fan who had brought his three granddaughters to their first ever Reds game. As the girls pored over their newly-purchased media guide, they recognized Williams and asked their grandfather to see if the GM would sign their "First Game" certificates.

"I was flattered and agreed to sign," said Williams. "But I felt terrible that they would only have a GM certificate." Williams had to do an on-field presentation pregame, so he asked if he could keep the certificates and take them to the field to get more autographs for the girls. The gentleman was skeptical, but relented.

When he went out through the dugout, however, no players were around. They were either out on the field stretching or back up in the clubhouse getting ready for the game. Finally, just before Williams left the field, one player came walking down the tunnel. Yep: Scooter Gennett.

Williams asked Gennett to sign the certificates and returned them to the girls. Sheepishly, he apologized to the gentleman. "I told him I was so embarrassed that I could only get one player autograph in the limited time that I had," said Williams. The certificates had been signed only by Scooter and the GM that had claimed him for the Reds.

Two weeks later, Williams received a sweet thank you note from the grandfather. He thanked Williams for getting the autograph, and said they were all ecstatic over how rare and valuable the certificates were. After all, those were the only "First Game" certificates signed that night by Scooter, and the only items he signed at all before his historic game.

Later in the season, Williams remembered the episode: "It's crazy how a small good deed that I thought was a disappointment actually turned into something amazing."

There's no better word to describe everything about that evening. Amazing.

of his first extended slump as a Red (0-for-19 with nine strikeouts), Gennett was unintentionally embroiled in a mini-controversy, when former Red Brandon Phillips made his first return to Great American Ball Park after an off-season trade to Atlanta, and declared that Gennett's wearing of Phillips' former uniform No. 4 was "a slap in my face."

Gennett was deferential—"I think he's got a right to feel that way"—and explained that he had tried to change numbers, but doing so would've required him to purchase each and every "Gennett 4" jersey in the Reds team shop's inventory.

Gennett went 0-for-10 against Phillips' Braves, but broke out of his slump with a game-winning two-run double in a June 5 game against St. Louis. The following night, Gennett started in left field and batted fifth, as slugger Adam Duvall got the night off against the Cardinals' longtime ace Adam Wainwright.

In the first inning, Gennett came to the plate with two outs. He flared a single to left, scoring Billy Hamilton from second base for the game's first run. One at-bat, one RBI. But Scooter was just getting started.

When Gennett next came to the plate, in the third inning, the bases were loaded with Reds. With a full count, Wainwright threw a devastating curveball in the dirt—Gennett barely fouled it off. Wainwright returned with a cut fastball down the middle of the plate, and the left-handed hitting Gennett crushed it deep into the right-field seats for a grand slam. After three innings, his RBI total already stood at five for the night.

One inning later, a bases-loaded triple from Eugenio Suárez chased Wainwright from the game. Gennett greeted reliever John Gant with a two-run homer, making the score 10–1. In the sixth inning, Gennett turned a good night into Reds immortality, tying the club record with his third home run of the game—this one a line drive into the left-field stands. The crowd of 18,620 insisted on a curtain call from the recently returned hometown hero.

By the bottom of the eighth inning, the game was a laugher. The Reds were ahead 11–1 and the only question was whether Gennett would get a chance to seize the club record with a fourth home run—he was set to bat fourth in the inning. With one out, pinch-hitter Scott Schebler coaxed a walk from Cardinals rookie John Brebbia. Scooter would bat one more time.

With the crowd on its feet, Gennett took a fastball on the inside corner for strike one. Brebbia came back with another fastball, this one low. Gennett took a massive swing, but came up empty. With an 0-2 count, Brebbia's next fastball came in at 93.3 miles per hour—and was sent back out at 104.2. The only question was whether it was high enough to clear the right-field wall. It was, landing in the third row 377 feet from home plate, and making Scooter Gennett the 17th—and perhaps most unlikely—man to hit four home runs in a major league game.[2]

"Usually when I hit a home run I consider myself lucky," Gennett said afterward, "but it's hard to get lucky four times in a row. So I think I might be on to something here."

In a span of less than 24 hours, Gennett chalked up six hits, four home runs, 19 total bases, and 12 RBI. In addition to the single-game HR record, Gennett claimed the Reds record for total bases (17) and tied the club mark for RBI (10). In one night, he improved his season hitting line from .270/.308/.450 to .302/.336/.578.

The 2017 Reds were young and exciting, just as advertised. And the season's most memorable moment came from the most unlikely source.

---

2. Gennett joined Mark Whiten as the only players in baseball history to have a four-homer game where one of the homers was a grand slam. Whiten, of course, perpetrated the feat for the Cardinals against the Reds on September 7, 1993.

39

ARCHITECT OF THE BIG RED MACHINE

When Bob Howsam was introduced as Cincinnati's new general manager on January 21, 1967, the Reds were coming off a seventh-place finish and the franchise was in a state of flux. A group of local business leaders had purchased the club just over a year earlier, and when they went looking for an experienced baseball man to run the show, they found Howsam, who had spent the last two years as the general manager of the St. Louis Cardinals. Hired and given total authority over baseball matters, Howsam set about drawing up the plans for the Big Red Machine.

Raised on his family's honeybee farm in rural Colorado, Howsam had served as a Navy flier during WWII, but spent his service stateside. One of his earliest strokes of good fortune came when he married the daughter of Edwin "Big Ed" Johnson, who represented Colorado for three terms in the U.S. Senate and in two separate stints as the state's governor. After the war, Bob went to work as his father-in-law's administrative assistant in Washington.

A few months later, the Western League re-formed to bring minor league baseball back to the Great Plains. Senator Johnson was the league's nominal president, but would Bob be interested in getting the league up and running as executive secretary? He was, and did.

One year later, Howsam—along with his parents (who sold the honey business) and brother—scraped together the money to buy the league's Denver Bears. Bob soon realized that the Bears' stadium situation was untenable, a problem he solved with stunning efficiency. First, he bought the old Denver city dump for $32,000. Then he built a 19,000-seat stadium for $400,000, and he accomplished all this in just 110 days... including the time needed for the grass to grow.[1]

The effort was a huge success. In the first full season in their new park, Howsam's Bears led all minor league teams in attendance, despite spending most of the season in last place.

---

1.   This Bears Stadium eventually took on a different name. As Mile High Stadium (and with additions and renovations), it served as home to Denver's professional baseball and football teams for the next 53 years.

Howsam kept learning, seeking out mentors from the Bears' major league affiliates, including Pittsburgh, where he learned talent evaluation from scout Billy Myers,[2] and everything else from legendary exec Branch Rickey. In 1955, Howsam purchased the Kansas City club and moved it to Denver, stepping up to the AAA level and hooking up with the Yankees organization and its own organizational genius, George Weiss (like Rickey, a member of the Baseball Hall of Fame).

Wildly successful but unfulfilled in the minors, Howsam joined Rickey and several millionaires in a plan to create a third major league, to be called the Continental League. That plan fell apart when the major leagues agreed to expand by four clubs, satisfying at least some of the investors.

Howsam's ambition led him to the one major setback in his life. He'd expanded Bears Stadium in anticipation of the Continental League crowds, and needed a product to fill those seats. Denied an NFL team, he became the original owner of the Denver Broncos, when the American Football League began play in 1960. It was a disastrous move for the capital-light Howsam. An unfamiliar product, a lousy team, and bad fall weather combined to give Howsam's ownership group an enormous loss for the first season.[3]

Unable to sustain such hefty losses, Howsam sold the Broncos, and also had to part with the stadium and the Bears team. After 14 years, it appeared that Howsam's professional sports career was over. He went into business selling mutual funds.

Three years later, however, his old mentor Branch Rickey reached out, offering the St. Louis general manager's job. Howsam was not only back in baseball, this time he was in the major leagues.

But Howsam chafed under the Cardinals' corporate structure (the Cards were but one subsidiary in the larger Busch family business), and was open to a change. Meanwhile, the Reds' ownership group was searching for a new general manager in late 1966, with four "must have" criteria. They needed a candidate who:

1. Had experience as a major league general manager;
2. Was "promotion-minded," and dedicated to making the ballpark experience an exciting, family-friendly entertainment option;

---

2. The same Billy "Jaguar" Myers who played shortstop on the Reds 1939–40 teams, and is a member of the Reds Hall of Fame.
3. Estimates ranged from $270,000 to $1,000,000 in 1960 dollars, just for that one season.

3. Was willing to focus on building the farm system; and
4. Had experience planning and moving into a new stadium.

Those were basically the top bullet points on Howsam's resume; he was offered the job in January 1967.

Finally given the freedom to run a major league team *his way*, Howsam quickly got to work. His stated goal: "Build the number one organization in baseball." As in Denver, that meant putting as much focus on the "back of the house" as on the major league roster. His first hire was Dick Wagner, an efficient, bloodless expert in the business of sports who, like Howsam, had once been honored as a *Sporting News* minor league executive of the year.

In Denver, Howsam had made the ballpark an attractive family entertainment option, independent of the product on the field. He quickly went to work doing the same thing in Cincinnati. Even though Crosley Field was slated for destruction, he invested money in renovations and improvements. Fans marveled over the spotless ballpark.

Understanding that the Reds were a regional team, Howsam and Wagner developed baseball's first professional marketing shop, branding the *Big Red Machine* and tapping into the fertile region they called "Reds Country." They built a network of regional ticket offices and rapidly expanded the Reds radio network fourfold. The Reds were the first to do significant market research, and to use computers to crunch the data. They launched a speaker's bureau and a preseason radio caravan, giving far-flung fans (and local radio advertising buyers) the chance to rub elbows with the team's stars.

The team gave free tickets to straight "A" students, a program that introduced the Reds into every schoolhouse in the region, while filling unused seats with hot dog buyers, and selling seats to their parents (and less-studious siblings).

Always conscious of their regional appeal, Howsam's Reds opened an official souvenir store in downtown Cincinnati (fans might not be able to find a Reds hat in their Louisville Sears), and developed a Zamboni-style machine to vacuum the rainwater off the Riverfront turf. (Nothing spoiled a weekend trip like a rainout.)

When Howsam arrived, the Reds had all of 900 season ticket holders. By the early '70s, that number was more than 15,000. In 1966, they ranked ninth out of 10 NL teams in attendance, with only 742,958 fans visiting Crosley Field. By 1970, when Riverfront opened midway through the year, the Reds had jumped to second, with 1,803,568 fans. By 1973, their annual attendance topped 2,000,000, a level they would exceed for eight consecutive years.

For the farm system, Howsam turned to Sheldon "Chief" Bender, who had run player development for the Cardinals.[4] Before long, Howsam had doubled the size of the Reds front office, hiring an advertising director, a sales department, and promotions staff. He boosted the scouting department from 16 to 24 full-time scouts, led by the Bowen brothers. Expert evaluator Rex served as Howsam's head scout; little brother Joe, an organizational genius in his own right, was director of scouting.

Howsam quickly worked to develop a deep, Rickey-style farm system. In 1966, the Reds had selected 27 players in the amateur draft. In Howsam's first year, that total jumped to 72.[5] Most of these players would never see the major leagues, but like Rickey, Howsam believed in "developing quality from quantity."

The Reds organization already had a strong talent base at the major league level: Pete Rose and Tony Pérez were established in the lineup, along with Vada Pinson, Tommy Helms, and Deron Johnson. Prospects Johnny Bench, Lee May, and Gary Nolan were close behind.

But after observing for a season, Howsam began to reshape the organization to match his vision. Gone were Pinson and pitcher Milt Pappas, who were too independent/rebellious for Howsam's conservative sensibilities.[6] But Howsam wasn't dealing out of spite. Pinson returned 23-year-old speedster Bobby Tolan; the Pappas deal brought starting pitcher Tony Cloninger, reliever Clay Carroll, and shortstop Woody Woodward.

Overall, Howsam made 10 trades in his first three years at the helm, adding 18 new players to the Reds organization. Many were key pieces in the Reds' 1970 and 1972 pennant-winners; some even stuck around to contribute to the 1975–76 champs. But Howsam's biggest move—the one that truly made the Big Red Machine—was the 1971 trade for Joe Morgan.

---

4.   Bender would run the Reds minor league system for 22 years, then spend another 17 years with the club in various capacities. His system produced Griffey, Concepción, Gullett, Soto, Larkin, Davis, and O'Neill.
5.   In those days, there was no limit on the number of players a team could draft.
6.   "Many years ago, I came to the conclusion that complainers and malcontents have a debilitating effect on your team," Howsam once said.

The Reds' biggest priority, at least after moving into Riverfront Stadium, was speed. Howsam bought into Rickey's maxim that speed is the only common denominator between offense and defense, and given Riverfront's spacious gaps and artificial playing surface, it was vital. A slow player just couldn't stick with the Reds. Hal McRae had gap power and great on-base skills, but he wasn't fast enough, so he was traded off to Kansas City.[7] Similarly, the Reds passed on talented, but slow-footed local infielders Mike Schmidt and Buddy Bell.

Regardless of a few isolated misses, Howsam's organizational philosophy was an enormous success. From Morgan's arrival in 1972 through 1976, the Reds led the majors in stolen bases—and more importantly, won three pennants and four division titles in five years. In 34 postseason games over this period, the Reds out-stole their opponents 48–2. Speed kills.[8]

The Reds were also famous for Howsam's dress code—short hair, no beards or mustaches, and uniforms that were actually...*uniform*—everyone's pants the same length, their shoes the same color (black, with logos blacked out with shoe polish). Set against the counter-culture of the early '70s, this approach was a perfect fit for conservative Cincinnati, but it was also a perfect match for Sparky Anderson and his players, who saw the dress code as a way that *they* could reinforce discipline and conformity in service of the team.

To Howsam, it was also about serving and entertaining the fans. Yes, Cincinnati fans may have rejected a team with mustaches like the Oakland A's, but Howsam took issue with their footwear. "The movement of the white shoe detracts from the flight of the ball, and in watching the game, the ball should be the center of attention."

He hated distractions and looking second-rate. Every day, the batting helmets were cleaned and shined. And the Cincinnati Reds simply didn't wear stained or torn uniforms. "He's a stickler for presenting the best possible image," said equipment manager Bernie Stowe. "We probably order more uniforms than any big league team."

Howsam was, in the words of author Daryl Smith, "the quintessential American businessman of the postwar era." But his management style

---

7. McRae had nearly 2,000 hits for the Royals over a 15-year career, though he still may never have cracked the Big Red Machine lineup.

8. As did Johnny Bench. From 1970–76, the Reds' postseason opponents were caught stealing in 13-of-15 attempts—just a 13 percent success rate.

wasn't as autocratic as his button-down look may have implied. Like many exceptional leaders, Howsam actually listened to the people who worked for him. The buck stopped with Bob Howsam, but he *wanted* differing opinions from his staff, as long as they were expressed behind closed doors. (Once a decision was reached, he insisted on public unanimity.)

While the Machine was winning back-to-back titles, a new era dawned in baseball, in the form of free agency. No longer were players eternally tied to the team that drafted them. Howsam was deeply disturbed by the change, and sincerely thought it would ruin the game. At least from his vantage point, this was true. A team like the Big Red Machine could never exist in the free agent era. It would be impossible to preserve even the core of four veteran, Hall of Fame–level superstars, let alone the rest of the dominant roster.

Rather than adjust, Howsam first chose to ignore the sea change.[9] The Reds tried to re-sign their free agents, but when it came to the formal free agent draft, Howsam sanctimoniously passed in every round, both in 1976 and 1977. (From 1976 to 1980, the free agent process wasn't entirely free bargaining. There was a formal draft, where teams bid—in inverse order of the standings—on the free agents they wished to sign. Teams were limited in how many players they could bid on, and ultimately sign, and there was a similar cap on the number of teams that could make an offer to a single player.)

"In fairness to the players who have won the world championship for us two years in a row, and considering the way our organization is structured, we do not think it would be right for the Cincinnati club to get into bidding contests that must come out of this draft," Howsam read aloud, when the Reds' turn to draft came.

While Howsam pontificated, the talent exodus began. Don Gullett was the first to leave, just weeks after the '76 Series. The Yankees gave him $2 million over six years. Others soon followed.

The most important loss was only indirectly caused by free agency. Facing Gullett's departure and the expected loss of Gary Nolan after the 1977 season (Nolan had made his plans clear), Howsam felt the need to add pitching. Perhaps more important, he wanted to get Dan Driessen

---

9. Author Joseph Preston called Howsam's Reds a dinosaur—perfectly evolved to dominate a long era, but also highly susceptible to a dramatic, fundamental change in its environment.

into the everyday lineup. Still just 25, Driessen had hit .281/.356/.401 in four seasons, plus a sizzling .357/.438/.714 in the 1976 World Series.

Remembering Rickey's adage that it was better to trade a player a year too early than a year too late, Howsam looked at Tony Pérez. Closing in on 35, Pérez had driven in 90 or more runs for 10 consecutive seasons and showed no signs of slipping. But moving him was the most logical way to clear a spot for Driessen, who had proven that he couldn't play anywhere but first base. (Howsam approached Pérez with the idea of platooning, but Pérez understandably declined. He wanted to remain a Red, but he'd rather start for a contender than sit the bench in Cincinnati. Howsam later said that out of respect for Pérez and his family, he honored that wish.)

So in December 1976, Howsam traded Pérez (and reliever Will McEnaney) to the Montreal Expos for pitchers Woodie Fryman and Dale Murray. It was definitely "a year too early"—Pérez had four more years as a regular first baseman left in him. But more than losing his most consistent RBI man, Howsam had traded away the heart and soul of the Big Red Machine. "I don't think Howsam understood Tony's value," Rose later said. "I know he did as a player, but not as a leader."

Driessen replaced Pérez, but the Reds didn't bid on a single free agent until after Howsam handed the reins over to Dick Wagner, which happened in February 1978. At 60, suffering from a bad back and existential dread over the free agent revolution, Howsam stepped down from the day-to-day running of the team.

That fall, Wagner tried but failed to sign pitcher Tommy John and outfielder Lee Lacy. The Reds wouldn't actually sign a free agent until 1981.

While Howsam had given up operational control in February 1978, and lived in semi-retirement in Colorado, he retained the title of vice chairman of the Reds board of directors. He still represented the team at league meetings, and was a close advisor to ownership. His contract also required him to help select Wagner's replacement, if and when the time came.

It came sooner than either man expected. The Dick Wagner era had been an abject disaster, at least in the opinion of Reds fans and the local media. Even when the Reds won, it felt like failure—the 1979 playoffs ended with a whimper, and a self-awarded "Baseballs [sic] Best Record" banner was cold comfort for being shut out of the 1981 playoffs. Wagner presided over a series of public relations disasters, from the inexplicable firing of Sparky Anderson after the 1978 season, to the departures of Rose, Morgan, Griffey, Foster, and Seaver, and concluding with embarrassing seasons in 1982–83.[10] Attendance dropped, front office morale suffered, and the fans were in open revolt.

Wagner was fired in July 1983, and ownership called Howsam. Either find us a new general manager or come back and do it yourself, they said. Batteries recharged and ready for the challenge, Howsam came back. And he was finally ready to swim in the free agent pool, which had only gotten deeper in Howsam's five-plus years away. "Baseball has changed and maybe I have a bit, too," he said.

Howsam brought stability to the front office, hired key behind-the-scenes talent, and reversed some of Wagner's penny-pinching decisions. In an effort to atone for his single biggest mistake, Howsam brought Tony Pérez back to the Reds in 1984. But his biggest move was later that summer, when he brought Pete Rose back to the Reds as player-manager. Stability reestablished, Howsam began planning his second exit. In October 1984, he secretly informed ownership of his plans to leave, and hired Bill Bergesch as general manager (Howsam retained the title of team president). While the 67-year-old Howsam publicly denied any intention of retiring ("If anything, I'm going to be able to do more"), Bergesch quickly stepped into a prominent role.

Two months later, minority owner Marge Schott purchased the controlling shares of the Reds. While hailed as saving the team for Cincinnati, Schott quickly proved tough to work for.[11] Howsam was too old to put up with nonsense, and his back troubles weren't getting any better. He announced his retirement a month later.

"I feel like I've accomplished what I set out to do," he said. A man perfectly suited to his times and his job, Bob Howsam re-retired to Colorado, where he finally helped bring major league baseball to Denver as a consultant for the expansion Rockies. He was elected to the Reds Hall of Fame in 2004, and died in 2008, just shy of his 90th birthday.

---

10.   Behind the scenes, things were a little better. Chief Bender and the Bowen brothers stuck around, and the Wagner-era Reds drafted the foundation of the 1990 World Series champs: Eric Davis, Paul O'Neill, Barry Larkin, Tom Browning, Chris Sabo, and Joe Oliver.

11.   She referred to Bergesch as "Whatchamadoodle" in her first press conference.

40

ERIC THE RED

"Eric Davis flat-out frightens me more than any player I've ever seen."
                                        —Tommy Lasorda, Dodgers manager

Shirley Davis saw her son approach from a distance. Slender and wiry even as a child, Eric had always been a precocious athlete, able to keep up with the older kids on the 68th Street Elementary School playground and down at the Baldwin Hills Recreation Center in South Central Los Angeles. Eric's lean frame hinted at his incredible agility, and since the age of 12, he had dominated the local basketball courts against the likes of future Laker Byron Scott and Eric's most ferocious opponent: his father, Jimmy.

As Eric walked toward his mother, however, the boy was clearly unhappy. "Here," Eric said, thrusting a red ribbon into his mother's hands. "This is yours."

Shirley looked at the ribbon, which bore the words "Second Place." "Oh, good!" she said with a broad grin. "But don't you want to keep it?"

Eric shook his head. "No, that's not what I wanted. It's yours. I wanted first place."

"I don't want the world. I just want a piece of it. I want people to remember Eric Davis."
                                                —Eric Davis, 1987

Basketball was Davis' first love, and his stardom on the court was never in question. Davis had always played baseball too, but when he first went out for the high school team, the coach sent him home, saying Eric was just a basketball player. Fremont High had an impressive baseball tradition; alumni included Hall of Famer Bobby Doerr, renowned manager Gene Mauch, and big league All-Stars Chet Lemon, Bob Watson, and George Hendrick.[1] Fremont took its baseball seriously.

---

1. Another Fremont alum, Bobby Tolan, had been a member of the early Big Red Machine.

Undeterred, Davis showed up at baseball practice again the next day. When he came home on the third day, he was carrying his new uniform.

"I thought they weren't going to let you play," remarked his father.

"After they saw me play," Eric said, "they changed their minds."

By the time his senior year rolled around, Davis was a two-sport star. As a point guard, he averaged 28 points and nearly eight assists per game, and received basketball scholarship offers from Arizona and Arizona State, among others.

Playing shortstop for the Fremont Pathfinders, Davis hit .635 in the 19-game season, with 50 stolen bases in 50 attempts (he slid "only because I didn't want to embarrass the catcher"). Despite those gaudy numbers, big league scouts largely ignored him. "There were not a whole lot of scouts that wanted to come down to my neighborhood," Davis said later.

Davis' neighborhood—he lived at 66th & Denver in inner-city Los Angeles—was not a destination that most scouts were eager to place on their schedule. Reds bird-dog Larry Barton Jr., a Fremont alum who lived in nearby Torrance, was the only scout to watch Davis in high school.

"I knew the coach pretty good," said Barton later, "and I'd sit next to him on the bench, so it wasn't too bad. There was a lot of gang activity in that area when Eric was in high school."

The Reds selected Davis in the eighth round of the 1980 amateur draft, and he signed for $18,000, almost on a whim. "I didn't really get a chance to think about it," said Davis. "I was playing baseball, and then I signed."

"There's got to be a stick of dynamite in that body.... He's got more talent in that body than any one player I've ever seen."
—Reds pitcher Ron Robinson

Davis hit only .219 in his first taste of pro ball, but he took off like a shooting star after being shifted to center field in his second minor league season. Before long, Cincinnati newspapers—almost comically, in retrospect—declared Davis "Cincinnati's hottest prospect since Paul Householder."

CINCINNATI REDS

Davis made his Cincinnati debut in 1984, and after bouncing between the majors and minors for a couple of seasons, he finally began to make his mark in the big leagues in 1986. Davis was inserted into the Reds' lineup for good in mid-June…and was National League Player of the Month for July. Through the end of the season, he hit .297/.398/.568 with 23 home runs and was, by all accounts, the best player in baseball. He was a 24-year-old revelation, finishing with 27 home runs and 80 stolen bases for a Reds team that finished in second place.

As the 1987 season approached, Davis was not just the talk of the town, he was the talk of baseball. *Sports Illustrated*, *Sport* magazine, and *The Sporting News* all predicted that Davis would be the National League's Most Valuable Player.

"Nobody in this league has any more talent than Eric Davis," said Giants manager Roger Craig. "He can hit the ball five hundred feet and run like a deer. He's just like Hank Aaron when he came up."

More prevalent were comparisons to Willie Mays. "Eric has more talent than any player I have ever seen in my life, including Willie Mays," said Davis' manager, Pete Rose. "I think everything said about him is justified."

The previous August, the Reds were playing a series against the Giants in San Francisco's old Candlestick Park. Mays just happened to be at the game, and Rose approached him. "I got a kid who can do all the things you could, Willie," said Rose.

Mays squinted at Pete. "Where is he?"

When Davis, 6'3" and rail-thin, walked over to be introduced, Mays was not particularly impressed. "I saw no similarities," he said later. "Let the kid play. In the end, they'll compare numbers on paper."

For his part, Davis responded to the plaudits with his customary modesty. "Not even close," says Davis. "I've got a long way to go. I'm being compared to the impossible…. Why not compare me to my peers?"

Very soon, it would begin to seem that Eric Davis had no peers.

"A player like Eric might come around every 70 years. Sometimes I feel guilty because I don't have to pay to watch him. Speaking in terms of the overall package, there isn't a guy in either league who can touch him."
—Reds outfielder Dave Parker

Eric Davis (44) celebrates with Billy Hatcher (22) after hitting a two-run homer in Game 1 of the 1990 World Series. (AP Photo/Mark Duncan)

CINCINNATI REDS

Opening Day, 1987: Eric Davis tore out of the gate as if he were hell-bent on proving all the predictions correct. In an 11–5 Reds win over Montreal, Davis reached base five times, going 3-for-3 with two walks, two stolen bases, three runs scored, and a towering second-inning home run.

After the game, he was asked if there was anything else he could have done. "Sure," Davis responded. "I would like to go 12-for-12 if I could."

Davis didn't slow down the entire month of April.[2] He won another NL Player of the Month award, hitting .364/.437/.727 with seven homers and 16 RBI. It was the following month, however, that the Legend of Eric Davis reached impossible heights.

Cincinnati was just a half-game out of first place when the Reds traveled to Philadelphia for a three-game weekend series beginning on May 1. In Friday's game, Davis went 3-for-4 and hit two home runs, one of which was a grand slam, driving in five runs as the Reds downed the Phillies 8–5.

The next day, Davis "only" went 2-for-4 with a double. In Sunday's finale, however, "E"—as his teammates called him—hit three homers, including another grand slam. In the series, Davis had nine hits in 13 at-bats, five home runs (two grand slams), seven runs scored, and 11 RBI. The Phillies had been completely dismantled by the newest star in the game.

"What we should have done," said Phils pitcher Don Carman, who took the loss in the first game of the series, "was slip some kryptonite into his locker before the game. Maybe that would have weakened him."

When America woke up the next morning, the papers had the specifics: Davis was leading the league in every major hitting category. Batting average: .411. On-base percentage: .475. Slugging percentage: an almost-inconceivable .900. Davis had 12 home runs, 27 RBI, and 27 runs scored.

But just when it appeared things couldn't get any better, Davis showed that he was more than a typical power hitter. In Cincinnati's next game, against the Mets in New York, Davis stole three bases and scored another run, but the big highlight came in the sixth inning. With the Reds

---

2.   Well, that's not quite true. In late April, Davis struck out nine times over the course of back-to-back games against Houston, setting a major league record (which has since been tied); just a blip on the radar of Davis' brilliant 1987 season.

clinging to a slim 1-0 lead, Davis' childhood friend Darryl Strawberry launched a blast to deep left-center field. Davis sprinted back to the fence, near the 410-foot mark, leaped high into the air and reached over the wall. When he landed, the ball was in his glove for the third out of the inning.

"I didn't think Superman could get to that ball," said Rose. "I guess I forgot who was going after it."

The following day, Willie Mays had reconsidered his position. "It's an honor to be compared to Eric Davis," Mays said. "I hope Eric is honored."

"Name me another cleanup hitter who can steal 100 bases. Name one. It's like having an atomic bomb sitting next to you in the dugout."
—Pete Rose

On the final day of May, Davis hit his third grand slam of the month, a National League record. The blast was his 19th homer of the season, which also set a league record for most home runs through the end of May. The previous record had been held by Reds legend Tony Pérez, Cy Williams, and—you guessed it—Willie Mays.

"Congratulations, Eric," said Pérez, who had joined the Reds as a coach after retiring. "You [bleep]. My record stood for 17 years!"

Davis was a national sensation, appearing on the cover of *Sports Illustrated*, and being named NL Player of the Month once again in May. *The Sporting News*, in a cover story on Davis—headline: "ERIC THE GREAT(EST)—declared: "We have observed the blossoming of perhaps the greatest baseball player ever."

Again, Davis balanced his feats at the plate with equal heroics in the field. In early June, he made game-saving catches in consecutive games against St. Louis, both times robbing Cardinals slugger Jack Clark of home runs. "He's the Ozzie Smith of the outfield," said a frustrated Clark. "He can probably do flips, too."

In mid-season, Davis was elected to start his first All-Star Game. Less than a month later, with a walk-off 11th-inning home run in a 5–4 Reds win over San Francisco, Davis joined the exclusive 30/30 club: 30 homers, 30 stolen bases. (Before Davis joined the club, only six players had ever produced 30 home runs and 30 steals in the same season. Two of those players were named Hank Aaron and Willie Mays.) The home run was a mammoth shot off the facing of the red seats at Riverfront Stadium, estimated at somewhere just shy of 500 feet.[3]

"Eric Davis has unlimited ability—awesome ability. I don't think he'll be Willie Mays. That would take some doing. But, on the other hand, I don't think he has a weakness, either."

—Hank Aaron

On September 4, the Reds were in a bit of a slump, but still battling with the Giants and Astros for the top spot in the NL West. Cincinnati scored four runs in the top of the ninth to take a 4–3 lead over the Cubs, in a game they needed to win in order to keep pace in the title race.

Reds closer John Franco struck out the leadoff hitter in the final frame before permitting an infield single. After retiring Cubs standout Ryne Sandberg on a fly ball, Franco gave up another infield single (to another future Hall of Famer, Andre Dawson).

With the winning run on first base, the Cubs' Brian Dayett smoked a long, deep fly ball to right-center field. Davis tracked it and made a game-saving catch, crashing hard into the ivy-covered Wrigley Field wall. The grab secured the victory, but Davis jammed his left shoulder.[4]

The injury provided a microcosm of what would become an all-too-familiar story during Davis' career: a brilliant season interrupted by a max-effort injury. But what a brilliant season it was. In only 129 games, Davis hit .293/.399/.593 with 37 home runs, 100 RBI, and 50 stolen bases. After the season, he was awarded a well-deserved Gold Glove, as well as a Silver Slugger award.

From 1986 to 1990, Davis averaged 30 homers and 41 steals a season, with rate stats of .277/.371/.527. Unfortunately, he was only able to average 131 games per year, as various injuries continued to pile up.

In 1990, Davis hit one of the most memorable home runs in Reds franchise history, a first-inning blast off Oakland's Dave Stewart in Game 1 of the World Series that catapulted the Reds to their first championship since the Big Red Machine. Again pairing brilliance with injury, Davis also lacerated a kidney while making a diving catch in the Series' decisive Game 4.

---

3. "It's already halfway down to One Lytle Tower," Rose said after the game. "I mean, that was a rocket. I don't know how a man can hit a ball that far. It ought to be against the law to hit a ball that hard."
4. As you would expect, Cubs fans poured beer on Davis as he lay injured on the warning track.

In 1991, Davis was traded to his hometown Dodgers, and he also spent a year and a half with Detroit before retiring after the 1994 season. After taking a year off, Davis returned to the Reds in 1996, winning the Comeback Player of the Year Award for hitting .287/.394/.523 with 26 home runs.

Halfway through the following season, Davis—now playing with Baltimore—announced that he had been diagnosed with colon cancer. He underwent immediate surgery, and drew praise from all corners for his dignity and fighting spirit in the battle against cancer. Davis made a dramatic return in September, even hitting a game-winning homer in Game 5 of the ALCS. In 1998, Davis put together one of the best seasons of his career at age 36, hitting .327/.388/.582 with 28 home runs and 89 RBI for the Cardinals.

Ultimately, Davis retired after 17 seasons in the big leagues. In 2005, he was inducted into the Reds Hall of Fame. Many Reds fans will always consider his career one of the great "What might have been?" stories in franchise history. For that one season, however, in 1987, Eric Davis was the brightest star in the baseball universe.

41

THE
YOUNG RUNNIN'
REDLEGS

The first weeks of 2023 were certainly among the lowest points for Reds fans in the history of this storied franchise. After slogging through ten years without a division title, the 2022 Reds had lost 100 games for just the second time in club history. The owner's son riled fans on the field in the moments before the home opener—"Where ya gonna go?"—and management slashed payroll in a cynical effort to "align our payroll to our resources," in the words of general manager Nick Krall.

In mid-January 2023, that same owner's son, club President Phil Castellini, stuck his foot squarely in his mouth again. In a presentation to the Rosie Reds, Castellini claimed that the Reds operated like a "nonprofit" and presented a slide show in which he argued—to a Reds fan club—that the team simply could not compete with other teams in Major League Baseball.

Fast forward to April. Krall had been unable or unwilling to improve the pitching staff in the off-season, resulting in an Opening Day roster with only three legitimate big league starters. On the offensive side of the ledger, someone named Jason Vosler was batting fifth on Opening Day. Surprising no one, the Reds started the season 7-15, culminating in a four-game sweep at the hands of the Pirates that saw Cincinnati score just six runs. Fans responded to yet another poor start to a season by avoiding Great American Ball Park in droves. During one game in this span, only 7,375 showed up for a win over Tampa Bay. Another depressing 100-loss season looked inevitable.

Inside the clubhouse, however, the mood was different. Reds players had been convinced for weeks that they had something special going.

As spring training unfolded, Jonathan India, Tyler Stephenson, and Hunter Greene stepped forward to take leadership roles, despite their tender ages (at 26, with 190 big league games under his belt, Stephenson was the graybeard of that group).

"I said at the beginning that I thought this season would be special," India later recalled. "I knew we were going to be a winning organization this year just because of the way that everyone bonded in spring training. You could tell we all were there to win. We had a motive every day. We worked really hard in practice. We didn't take a day off."

Few recognized it at the time, but India had set that tone in the first moments of the Cactus League schedule. In the first inning of the long, long baseball season, India had been hit by a pitch, advanced to second on a wild pitch, then stole third, sliding in headfirst both times..

Things began to change on April 24, when outfielder TJ Friedl's line drive single scored India for a walkoff win against the Rangers. The Reds reeled off a five-game winning streak, sweeping the Rangers (a club that would go on to win the World Series). That was the canary in the coal mine.

"We realized how we have to play," Friedl said later. "We have to play free, play loose and play with excitement. I always look back at that, even now, as one of the defining moments of our season. We started playing good baseball after that. It was a really big turning point for this group."

Cincinnati was beginning to show some encouraging signs, but by mid-May, they were still mired in fourth place, four games under .500, when the Reds made the first of a series of transactions that would almost instantly redefine the franchise. Before a game in Colorado, 2021 first round pick Matt McLain was called up to join the Reds. A slick infielder from UCLA, the 23-year-old McLain had been dominating at Triple-A Louisville, hitting .340/.467/.688 with 12 doubles, 12 homers, 10 steals, and 40 RBIs in only 40 games.

McLain's first big league hit was a harbinger of things to come. He looped a little flare over the Rockies shortstop, a single for almost any player in the league. But playing aggressively in his very first game, the speedy McLain never slowed down, sprinting around first base and sliding headfirst into second. In retrospect, this was the precise moment when everything began to change about the Cincinnati Reds.

McLain quickly established himself in the heart of the Reds lineup. Over his first 40 MLB games, McLain hit .316/.371/.538 with 12 doubles, four triples, six home runs, and 25 runs batted in. A series of hot-shot kids would follow him to the majors in short order, supercharging the Reds roster and changing the face of the franchise.

Lefthanded pitcher Andrew Abbott was called up for his first big league appearance on June 5. Drafted one round behind McLain in

2021, Abbott had similarly shot up everyone's prospect rankings after a brilliant start to the 2023 minor league season. He actually began the campaign in Double-A, where he posted a 1.15 ERA in three starts, striking out 36 hitters while walking just three. The Reds wasted no time in promoting him to Triple-A Louisville, where he was 3-0 with a 3.05 ERA and a 54:14 strikeout-to-walk ratio in seven starts.

Just two years after dominating in the College World Series for the University of Virginia, Abbott was dazzling in his big league debut. After throwing 53 pitches in the first two innings, Abbott settled in and looked like a confident veteran. He didn't allow a hit until the fifth inning, and by the time he left the field to a standing ovation, he'd tossed six shutout innings, allowing just the one hit.

Much like McLain, Abbot didn't slow down, looking much more like a veteran than a kid in the big leagues for the first time. The Reds won each of his first six starts; Abbott surrendered only five runs in those starts, posting a 1.21 ERA that was the second-lowest for any Reds pitcher over their first six starts.[1] A couple of weeks later, Abbott became the first pitcher of all time with an ERA under 2.00 and at least 60 strikeouts over his first ten starts.

One day after Abbott's debut, Elly De La Cruz arrived. Born in Sabana Grande de Boya in the Dominican Republic, De La Cruz was only 6 years old when he moved away from home to pursue a baseball career. The Reds first encountered him as a 16-year-old who was as skinny as he was tall. He was also raw, which means the Reds were able to sign him for just $65,000 in the summer of 2018.

By 2023, De La Cruz was the top prospect in all of baseball, combining light-tower power, an otherworldly throwing arm, and athleticism that made him the fastest player in the game. When his promotion to the big leagues was announced, Reds fans overwhelmed the team's ticket website, causing a brief outage. Once the game started, the crowd gave De La Cruz a standing ovation before he ever saw a pitch in the majors and fell deathly quiet during pitches—whether to avoid distracting the kid or simply out of rapt attention, the silence was shocking, but completely understandable. All eyes were on Elly, because he could literally do anything at any time.

---

1.   Another lefty, Tom Browning, had a 0.95 ERA after his first six starts in the big leagues.

Elly De La Cruz, Matt McLain, and Andrew Abbott pose after McLain's first-inning home run in a July 2023 game against the Giants in Cincinnati. (AP Photo/Jeff Dean)

He walked in that first at-bat, but later in the game Elly doubled to the gap in right-center. It was his first big league hit, and it was also the hardest hit ball of the season for any Reds player. The next day, he collected his first big league homer, a moon shot to the last row of the seats in right field. It went 458 feet, the longest Reds home run of the season. By the time the dust had settled on his first MLB series, the 21-year-old De La Cruz had become just the second player in league history to hit a single, a double, a triple, and a homer plus steal a base in his first three games. We're talking the stuff of legends here.

It took less than a week to see just how dramatically Elly had altered the DNA of the team. In one win over St. Louis, he had two hits and two walks (one of the hits was an infield single on a grounder to first base!), but it was his game-winning run that left everyone astonished.

After walking to lead off the eighth inning, De La Cruz advanced to third on a groundout and a passed ball. With one out in a tie game, the Cardinals pulled their infield in so as to potentially cut down the runner advancing home. They got their wish, as Stephenson grounded the ball sharply to the shortstop. Running on contact, Elly still somehow beat the throw home. Stephenson couldn't believe it. "I was just as shocked when I turned around and saw safe," he said. "He's an incredible talent."

The Reds were already fun, but now they were electric. And the buzz was just as loud in the dugout as it was in the grandstand and around the league. "This whole team has some type of vibe, and a really positive vibe, too," De La Cruz said. "It's kind of like vibes of going to the World Series."

In a matter of a month, a listless fourth place club featuring retreads like Will Myers and Kevin Newman had transformed into one of MLB's most exciting and entertaining teams. The Reds reeled off 12 consecutive victories and climbed back to .500 by mid-June, and they sat atop the NL Central. Other than the first few days of a season, it was their first time leading the division since 2012.

While the rookies were making waves—in all, 16 players would make their big league debuts for the Reds in 2023—a veteran returned to cheers, as well. Reds legend Joey Votto had been rehabbing from a shoulder operation he underwent in August 2022, and finally made it back to the lineup in mid-June. When he stepped to the plate for the first time, fans rose in unison, causing the 39-year-old Votto to step out of the box and tip his helmet to the crowd. He then proceeded to play like vintage Votto, with a fifth-inning home run and the go-ahead two-run single in the sixth inning.

The twelfth and final win of the streak was perhaps the most entertaining game any team played all season long. After the first half-inning, the Reds were down 5-0 to an Atlanta team that would go on to win 104 games. But inspired by a sellout crowd of 43,086, these Reds kept battling.[2] Votto had two home runs but it was Elly who stole the show once again.

Wearing the uniform number 44 made famous in Cincinnati by Eric Davis decades before, De La Cruz led off the second inning with

---

2.   That "never-say-die" attitude was a hallmark of the 2023 Reds. During the season, they collected 48 come-from-behind wins, and grabbed victories in their final plate appearance 24 times. Ten of those were walk-off wins.

a double, had a two-run homer in the third, and drove in a run with a single to center in the fifth. Then, in the sixth inning, he tripled, becoming the youngest player to hit for the cycle since 1972, and only the third player since 1901 to hit for the cycle within his first 15 career games.

"That's special stuff right there," India said that night. "It's a special time in Cincinnati and we're enjoying every part of it."

The last Reds player to hit for the cycle, of course, had been Eric Davis in 1989.

The 12-game winning streak was Cincinnati's longest since 1957. By the first week of July, the Runnin' Redlegs were 10 games over .500 and two games ahead of their nearest competitor in the NL Central. And Cincinnati was excited. "We came back home during that huge winning streak, and this ballpark was packed," rookie Spencer Steer said. "We started to get the trust and the belief from the fans. We had the trust and belief that we were going to be good. We had to prove that to the city. That was the first time they really responded and said, 'We believe you can be good again.'"

One day over the summer, Steer was at a local coffee shop when a man approached him. The man had been spending evenings with his father in the hospital, watching the Reds together every night. The winning streak and the excitement surrounding the team had given a boost to both father and son.

Though the other rookies often dominated the headlines, Steer was arguably the team's most valuable player. He selflessly played five positions over his team-leading 156 games, moving around the field wherever he was needed. No matter where he played, he was productive, finishing with a .271/.356/.464 slash line, and leading the team with 23 home runs and 86 RBIs.

There were more highlights to come. In early July, De La Cruz stole second, third, and home in the same inning. In fact, he accomplished the feat in only two pitches, the first player in 50 years to steal three bases in a single plate appearance. When he caught Milwaukee pitcher Elvis Peguero sleeping and swiped home, Elly skipped to the dugout where he was met by his astonished teammates. De La Cruz highlights were a nightly staple on both SportsCenter and social media.

Slugger Christian Encarnacion-Strand made his debut in July, and he struggled initially. But over his last 18 games, CES hit .318/.375/.682

with 8 homers and 18 runs batted in. Noelvi Marte didn't arrive until mid-August, but he quickly became one of Cincinnati's most dependable hitters, slashing .316/.366/.456 over 35 games the rest of the way.

With youth came exuberance, aggression, and an athleticism the club hadn't seen in decades. The fastest team in baseball, the Reds led the majors with 190 stolen bases—24 more than the next-best team and a staggering 132 more than the 2022 Reds. Part of this was the result of rule changes that encouraged stolen bases, but it was more than that. The Reds were among the league leaders in stretching singles into doubles, and doubles into triples, and ranked second in baseball in adding extra runs on the basepaths, after finishing tied for last the season before.

The Reds ultimately missed a wild card spot by two games, eliminated from the race on the next-to-last day of the season. Cincinnati finished 82-80, a resounding success given the depths to which the organization had descended just months before.[3] The future seemed brighter than it had ever been. Fans had turned from anger and resignation to excitement and hope (with perhaps a bit of leftover anger).

"So much has happened this year," manager David Bell said. "Our players deserve all the credit. They've been amazing from day one. It's the best team I have ever been a part of. There's a lot to be built on when you have a team like that. That's our players. They worked hard to create that. They created a great experience that will really change everyone that's been a part of it and sees how you go about it. I will be forever grateful to every single guy on this team. Hopefully we stay together for a long, long time."

---

3. Preseason gambling lines predicted that the Reds would win 65 games.

42

TOM TERRIFIC'S NO-HITTER

Tom Seaver and Jerry Koosman made their major league debuts for the Mets on successive days in April 1967. For the next 10½ seasons, they were teammates, All-Stars, and mainstays of the New York rotation.

They were also good friends who enjoyed poking fun at each other. Every so often, Koosman would approach Seaver in the clubhouse and drop into a seat next to him. "Hey, Tommy," Koosman would say, "when are you going to pitch a no-hitter?"

Seaver wouldn't even look up at him. "Anytime I feel like it," he'd say. "I just never have felt like it."

By the time Seaver, already a 10-time All-Star, was traded to Cincinnati in a blockbuster deal in June 1977, he had pitched five one-hitters. Three times, he had taken a no-hitter as far as the ninth inning, but ultimately surrendered a hit each time.

As the Reds and Cardinals squared off on Friday, June 16, 1978—one year and one day after the trade—Seaver was on a roll. He had posted a 1.63 ERA in winning six straight starts, and he would be facing the woeful Cardinals, who were destined to finish the year with the second-worst record in the NL.

Seaver wasn't particularly sharp at the outset. He did retire the first four Cardinals on infield groundouts, but then walked Keith Hernandez in the second. Seaver immediately began paying close attention to the St. Louis first baseman.[1] The first pitch to Jerry Morales was a pitch-out, but Hernandez wasn't going. Seaver then threw over to first twice, trying to keep the runner close. Before delivering the next pitch, Seaver took a longer pause than normal.

When he finally pitched, Hernandez took off for second. The throw from Reds catcher Don Werner—starting in place of the injured Johnny Bench—bounced in front of the bag and skidded into center field. Hernandez scampered to third base, and the Cards were in business in inning number two.

---

1. Hernandez was relatively fast for a first baseman, but entered the night with only three steals.

Seaver was able to strike out Morales, but St. Louis third baseman Ken Reitz worked another base on balls. Cincinnati's ace didn't have his best stuff, but he forced Mike Phillips to break his bat on a grounder to second to end the nascent Cardinals rally.

After that inning, Seaver began to settle into a groove, and when Tom Terrific got into a groove, he was as good as any pitcher in baseball history. "I didn't have a super fastball," he said after the game. "[After the first two innings] I had very good control. That was the big thing."

Reds manager Sparky Anderson agreed. "Seaver's right. He had great control. He didn't go to his heater too much."

He didn't have to; his slider and curveball were doing most of the work. On the rare occasion that Seaver made a pitch that wasn't exactly where he wanted, he could be seen pacing behind the mound, talking to himself before stepping back onto the rubber.

Whatever he was saying, it worked. The Cardinals were retired quickly in the third, fourth, and fifth innings. Only once in that span did they even threaten to collect a base hit. It was Hernandez again, this time in the top of the fourth. He ripped a ground ball into the hole between first and second base. Reds second baseman Joe Morgan moved quickly to his left, stabbed the one-hopper and threw to Dan Driessen at first base for the third out of the inning.

Unfortunately, the Reds weren't mustering much offense against Cardinal starter John Denny. Cincinnati hitters didn't get a ball out of the infield until the fourth inning, and didn't collect their first hit until César Gerónimo lined a single to center leading off the fifth. Werner followed that up with a hard single to left, making amends for his earlier throwing error.

With two runners on, Denny struck out Seaver, then abruptly left the field and ran into the clubhouse. There was a long delay, with players and coaches standing around, staring at each other, utterly baffled at the sudden interruption of a game that had been proceeding quickly to that point. Eventually, Denny returned, and the mystery was later revealed: Denny's jockstrap had snapped on a pitch to Seaver, and Denny understandably needed to replace it immediately.

Whether the replacement athletic supporter was too tight is a question that is lost to history but, whatever the reason, when Denny finally returned, the Reds started scoring runs. Pete Rose roped a double

INSIDE THE MOMENT

Seaver appeared on WKRC Channel 12 for a live interview shortly after 11:00 PM to discuss the no-hitter. Unfortunately, just as the station went live, the transmitter went on the blink and the station went off the air unexpectedly. The interview was not seen outside the studio.

The WKRC anchor who conducted the interview was Nick Clooney. Clooney, of course, is the father of actor/director George Clooney and the brother of singer/actress Rosemary Clooney.

to left-center field, scoring Gerónimo and Werner to give the Reds a 2–0 lead. One batter later, Morgan pulled a rocket down the right-field line for a double of his own, scoring Rose.

In the sixth inning, Driessen crushed a home run on a 3-1 fastball from Denny. Those four runs were more than enough for Seaver, who was cruising.

Beginning with the seventh inning, the crowd of 38,216 rose to their feet every time Seaver walked to the Riverfront Stadium mound. Seaver noticed. "I got stronger at the end of the game," he said afterward. "From the seventh inning on, I began to feel the excitement of the fans."

Seaver threw only six pitches in that seventh inning, to the delight of the assembled masses. He retired the first two hitters on two pitches. With two outs, Hernandez—who else?—came close once again to getting the first hit of the night; he drilled a ball hard up the middle, but Seaver was able to just barely get his glove on it. That deflection was enough to permit shortstop Davey Concepción to smother the ball and nab Hernandez at first.

Seaver benefited from another good defensive play in the eighth. Ray Knight had just entered the game as a defensive replacement for Rose at third base, and Morales hit a high chopper in his direction to lead off the inning. Knight charged hard, fielded the ball cleanly on the bounce and made a strong throw to first to get Morales by a half-step. After another groundout and a fly out, Seaver walked slowly off the mound to yet another standing ovation.

As he sat in the Cincinnati dugout, watching the Reds bat in the bottom of the eighth, Seaver's mind wandered back to one of the three games earlier in his career in which he had entered the ninth with a no-hitter. He thought of a late-September game against the Cubs back in 1975. He could still see it. He had opened up the ninth with back-to-back strikeouts, and quickly got to a two-strike count on Chicago right fielder Joe Wallis,[2] one pitch away from a no-hitter. Seaver then delivered a "darn good curve ball," that Wallis lined into right field.

As he walked to the mound for the bottom of the ninth, Seaver replayed that game and made a decision. "No curve balls," he said to himself. "They'll have to hit fastballs."

Just before Seaver returned to the field, Sparky pulled him aside for the first time all day. "I never talked to him until he went out there in the top of the ninth," Anderson said later. The advice was purely tactical. "I told him that if anyone tried to bunt, not to worry about the left side of the infield. Ray [Knight] would cover that. I told him to take the right side and be sure to cover first if one got past him."

Pinch-hitter Jerry Mumphrey led off the ninth. Pressure didn't often get to Seaver, but all of a sudden, his control started to falter. He threw three straight balls to Mumphrey, and eventually walked him on five pitches. That was the first Cardinal baserunner since the second inning; Tom Seaver had retired 19 consecutive hitters.

Sparky ordered Doug Bair to begin warming up in the Reds bullpen. A no-hitter is fun, but Anderson knew by 1978 that a pennant is even better. No reason to take any chances.

If Seaver noticed the reliever warming up, he didn't show it. Lou Brock settled into the box for a battle of future Hall of Famers with history on the line. Brock—who would collect his 3,000th hit one year later—fouled off four consecutive two-strike pitches before flying out to George Foster in left field.

That brought up Garry Templeton, who grounded meekly to shortstop, forcing Mumphrey out at second. Templeton hustled down the line, though, and prevented a double play that would have ended the game.

With two away, George Hendrick came to the plate. With everyone in the stadium on their feet, Hendrick took a called strike, then fouled one off. The next pitch was a ball, high.

---

2.   It was fresh in Seaver's mind that 1978 evening because he'd just told the story to teammate Bill Bonham a few hours earlier. As the two drove to the stadium together before the game, they discussed the fact that Wallis had been traded that day, and Seaver told Bonham about Wallis' role in spoiling his earlier no-hit bid.

INSIDE THE MOMENT

Pete Rose had two hits in this game, giving him a modest two-game hitting streak. Take a look at Chapter 25 to see what happened next.

Seaver took the return throw from Werner, and toed the slab once again. A little smile crossed his face as he looked in for the sign; it was almost like Seaver was confirming that he had things under control and he knew what was coming next. The windup and the pitch: fouled straight back.

Quickly, Seaver got the ball and delivered the last of his ninth-inning heaters. Hendrick swung and grounded to first. Driessen gloved it, stepped on first base, and immediately reached for Seaver's hand to shake it. The smile that crossed Seaver's face at that moment was as large as the pitcher's place in baseball history.

In the stands, Seaver's wife, Nancy, was overcome with emotion. "Tears of joy," she said. "I burst out crying when Danny stepped on first base for the final out."

Seaver's Cincinnati teammates mobbed him at first base. His hat askew, Seaver tried valiantly to shake everyone's hand as they made their way to the dugout. Before disappearing from sight, he ripped the red cap off his head and thrust it high in the air, a salute to the home fans at the first no-hitter ever at Riverfront Stadium.

The following morning, Seaver arrived at the stadium and spent the hours before the Saturday game reading all the telegrams from well-wishers. He also received more than a few phone calls, one from his old pitching coach with the Mets, Rube Walker. "Tell those coaches there not to get too big for their britches," said Walker. "Remember, we got you started, 12 years ago."

Those comments were relayed to Sparky Anderson. He shouted, so Walker could hear him on the other end of the line. "Thirteen years you guys had him and nothing" said Sparky. "My guy [Reds pitching coach Larry Shepard] has him one year and he breezes to a no-hitter!"

Everyone was having fun, but the highlight of the entire experience, for Seaver at least, didn't occur until that night. The great Frank Sinatra was on tour at that time, and he just happened to be performing at

Riverfront Coliseum (now Heritage Bank Center) on that Saturday night. During the concert, Sinatra spotted Seaver sitting in the audience and congratulated him on the heroics of the previous evening.

The Sinatra crowd stood in unison, a final standing ovation in honor of one of the greatest performances from one of the greatest pitchers in the history of baseball.[3]

---

3. Seaver wasn't playing hooky. The Reds had played an afternoon game.

43

BILLY WHO?

After the Reds' dominant victory in the opening game of the 1990 World Series, Game 2 was a tight affair. Twice the Oakland Athletics had taken a lead, and twice the Reds had battled back to tie things up. As the game stretched into extra innings, manager Lou Piniella faced a critical decision.

The pitcher's spot in the order would come up second in the bottom of the 10th, and Piniella needed a pinch-hitter. He had a few options left, but settled on the most unlikely one: rookie Billy Bates.

Bates had been a college baseball star, a two-time All-American at one of the country's true powerhouse programs, the University of Texas Longhorns. As a freshman, the Longhorns won a College World Series title and Bates was named to the All-Tournament Team.

Bates had great speed,[1] but had found it difficult to stick in the big leagues. Back in June, Bates was traded to Cincinnati—along with Glenn Braggs—from Milwaukee, where he had hit just .140/.208/.163 in 21 games over two seasons.

Cincinnati assigned Bates to AAA Nashville, but in September, he was called up to the big club. Upon walking into the clubhouse for the first time, some of the Reds players mistakenly thought that the 5'7" Bates was a new clubhouse attendant. (Though that was better than his first spring training with the Brewers, when his teammates replaced his rental car with a tricycle, and would refer to a baseball hat lying flat on the ground as "Billy.") Serving mostly as a pinch-runner, the speedy Bates appeared in eight games for the Reds down the stretch, and didn't collect a single base hit. Bates' only notable moment that September was when he raced a cheetah in an on-field promotion for the Cincinnati Zoo.[2]

When second baseman Bill Doran suffered an injury, Bates was named to the Reds' postseason roster. In the NLCS against Pittsburgh,

---

1. Bates still holds the Longhorns record for career triples, and is tied for fourth (with former Red Drew Stubbs) on their all-time stolen base list.
2. Bates won that race, partly because the cheetah became distracted—and slowed down momentarily—when Bates' cap flew off.

Bates appeared twice as a pinch-runner, scoring one run, but had no plate appearances.

He had little hope of getting a chance to bat in the World Series either, but in the bottom of the 10th of Game 2, with Eric Davis approaching the plate, Piniella yelled for Bates to start getting loose. It was a surprising move, given that Piniella still had Luis Quinones—Cincinnati's top pinch-hit threat in 1990—available on the bench.[3]

"I was kind of shocked they had me pinch-hit when they had other guys on the bench," Bates said. "I didn't think I'd get to bat in this series." Shocked or no, Bates grabbed his bat and his helmet and walked to the on-deck circle.

In the stands, a group of Rosie Reds weren't impressed.[4] "Who is this swinging the bat?" said one little old lady who was memorably captured on video. "Bates? What's he put him in there for? Where's Quinones? I don't know about that move, Piniella!"

Meanwhile, there was drama taking place off the field. In the bottom of the seventh inning, Rick Stowe, the son of Reds' equipment manager Bernie Stowe, brought an urgent message to pitcher Tom Browning: Tom's wife, Debbie, was going into labor and was leaving the stadium to go to the hospital. Browning didn't hesitate; he left the clubhouse in full uniform, accompanying his wife to the hospital. After all, Browning was scheduled to start Game 3 of the Series, so there was no way he'd get into Game 2.

Except that the score was tied late, extra innings were a possibility, and Piniella began to worry. The number of pitchers he had at his disposal was dwindling, since Lou had been forced to dip into his bullpen early after starter Danny Jackson had been unable to escape the third inning. He turned to his pitching coach, Stan Williams, and told him to make sure Browning didn't go anywhere, just in case. Williams assured the manager that Browning would be there. Neither of them knew that he was already gone.

When Williams discovered that Browning wasn't in the dugout or clubhouse, he and Piniella decided to send a message up to Marty Brennaman in the Reds' radio booth.

---

3. A diminutive reserve infielder, Quinones had hit a remarkable .361/.390/.500 as a pinch-hitter during the 1990 season. Just another reason the Reds were the biggest surprise that season.

4.   The Rosie Reds are an all-female club, formed in '64, when it was thought the Reds might move out of Cincinnati. "Rosie" is an acronym for "Rooters Organized to Stimulate Interest and Enthusiasm in the Cincinnati Reds."

Glenn Braggs (left), Billy Bates (helmet), Eric Davis, Jose Rijo, and Billy Hatcher (right) celebrate after the Reds beat the Oakland A's 5–4 to go up two games to none in the 1990 World Series. (AP Photo/Mark Duncan)

"We have a rather unusual message," Brennaman told thousands of radio listeners. "We understand Tom Browning's wife, Debbie, has gone into labor and he has left the ballpark. And a call apparently has come up from the Reds' clubhouse to make an appeal over our airwaves to have Tom Browning come back to the ballpark in the event they will have to use him to pitch tonight."

A strange night was about to get even stranger. Back on the field, Billy Bates would be facing one of the most fearsome closers in baseball history, Oakland's Dennis Eckersley. A future Hall of Famer, Eckersley was nearly unhittable in 1990, posting an ERA of 0.61 while racking up 48 saves. In his last 11 postseason appearances, Eckersley had allowed just a single run, while holding opposing hitters to a .167 batting average.

"How in the world are the Reds going to score against him?" asked CBS play-by-play man Jack Buck. "We might be here forever tonight."

Seven minutes later, the game was over.

With one out, the left-handed Bates stepped into the box and settled into a deep crouch. Bates took two quick strikes without removing the bat from his shoulder. Finally, on the third pitch, he made contact, fouling a ball off. Then, with the count still 0-2, Bates chopped one off the plate. It bounced high and Athletics third baseman Carney Lansford was unable to make a play. Bates had delivered with a pinch-hit infield single.

Next up was Chris Sabo, and he singled sharply to left field, advancing Bates to second. Joe Oliver was due up next.

Oliver was a light-hitting catcher with an excellent defensive reputation who was in his first full season as a Reds regular. In the fourth inning, he had doubled and scored on Ron Oester's pinch-hit single. Now it was his turn to try to drive in a run.

Eckersley appeared unperturbed by the tense situation. He got his sign and delivered a first-pitch slider for strike one. Pitch number two was a fastball, and Oliver got the bat around quickly. The ball skipped over the third base bag, just out of Lansford's reach, and rattled around in the A's bullpen. Oliver raised first one hand, then the second in triumph, as Bates sped around third and scored easily. The Reds had a 5-4 win and an unexpected 2-0 lead in the World Series.

Bates' Reds teammates met him at home plate, where Braggs lifted him into his arms. For one night, Billy Bates was the talk of the town.

The pinch-hit single would be the only hit Bates would ever collect as a Red. In fact, after his World Series heroics, Bates never played in another major league game.

Afterward, like most of the baseball world, Eckersley was shell-shocked. "Oh my God, Billy Bates," he said. "Who would have ever thought it?"

Forty minutes after Oliver's game-winner, Tucker Thomas Browning was born. The proud papa, Tom, held him for the first time, still wearing his full Reds uniform. (Tom had ignored the call to return to the park.)

The Reds had done the improbable and taken a 2–0 lead against the mighty A's. Bates was a hero, Browning was a father, and center fielder Billy Hatcher had even set some all-time World Series records. Hatcher had reached base the first eight times he batted in the Series, including seven consecutive base hits—both World Series records.

Joe Oliver echoed the sentiments of the elated Reds fans. "You always dream about something like this," Oliver said, "but there's a lot more excitement and fulfillment when you experience it. We're not in dreamland anymore."

The Reds, confident and poised, may not have been in dreamland anymore. On the other hand, after the exhilarating high of that Game 2 victory, Reds fans everywhere began having *sweep* dreams.

44

THE FIRST STEP FOR THE OL' LEFT-HANDER

As the ninth inning approached, Reds manager Bill McKechnie scanned the players available to him in the home dugout and made a decision. He was going to put the kid into the game.

The game had been nothing short of an abject disaster. The powerhouse Cardinals—who would go on to win the World Series that fall—had slugged their way to a 13-0 lead through eight innings. No more than 3,500 loyal Reds rooters remained in the Crosley Field stands on that muggy June 1944 day, and there was little hope that the Reds could mount any type of a comeback on a Cards team led by Hall-of-Famer Stan Musial.

In fact, the Reds didn't come back. The final score was a brutal 18-0, the worst shutout loss in the National League in nearly four decades.

But that's not why the game remains memorable after all these years.

Near the end of the eighth inning, McKechnie pointed in the general direction of a 6'3", 195-pound teenager sitting in the Reds dugout. "Warm up, Joe," he said, then repeated himself when young Joseph Henry Nuxhall didn't move. "Go warm up," the manager insisted.

"I thought Mr. McKechnie was kidding," Nuxhall said on the 30th anniversary of his first major league appearance. "But he wasn't."

Indeed, he wasn't, so Joe Nuxhall hurried his 15-year-old body to the bullpen and warmed up. When McKechnie inserted the kid into the game to pitch a short time later, Nuxhall made history by becoming the youngest player to appear in a major league game in the 20th century.

Nuxhall had graduated from Wilson Junior High School in nearby Hamilton, Ohio, only 48 hours earlier. The Reds had actually signed the youngster back in February, but Nuxhall had spent the early part of the season simply sitting on the bench during weekend day games and night games after school (although, given special permission by his junior high principal, he had been allowed to skip school and attend the Reds' Opening Day contest).

Just a ninth-grader at the time, Nuxhall had been discovered while playing in the same Cincinnati amateur league as his father. "The scouts had come to watch my dad," Nuxhall said. "And it just so happened that our game started before his on another diamond. I was pitching and the scouts wanted to know who the kid was. That's how it all started."

With a World War raging, and professional baseball players away serving their country, Major League Baseball was facing a serious manpower shortage, and it has always been assumed that Nuxhall's signing was a byproduct of the war. At the time, however, Reds general manager Warren Giles insisted that wasn't the case. "Nuxhall is a great prospect," Giles said. "We are not signing him because of the war situation. Two other clubs wanted him, and he would have been signed, war or no war."

Early on, the hard-throwing left-hander was a curiosity, but no one really expected him to get into any games. McKechnie considered the youngster a nice prospect, and wanted to give him a taste of pro ball by allowing Nuxhall to spend time with the club. "I plan to keep him all summer, if he continues to show promise, whether he gets into any games or not," McKechnie said, prior to the 1944 season. "He'll get every opportunity to be a big leaguer."

Still, even Nuxhall was surprised when the manager ordered him to prepare to enter an actual big league game. "I was nervous," he said after the game. "Sure, I had watched 'em as they came to bat, thinking I ought to know their weakness. But I sure never expected Mr. McKechnie [to pick] me. Gee!"

After throwing a few warm-up tosses, Nuxhall was summoned to the pitcher's mound. "I felt fine warming up on the sidelines," Nuxhall recalled. "It didn't get to me until I went out to the mound. I was excited."

Things started well for the young left-hander, as he struck out the first Cardinal he faced. After handing out a base on balls, Nuxhall then collected another strikeout for out number two. He was feeling pretty good, until he glanced over and saw that Stan "The Man" Musial was striding to the plate. That's when the wheels began to fall off.

Musial laced a sharp single, and Nuxhall suddenly realized where he was—standing in the center of Crosley Field, pitching to the best team in the league rather than the 13- and 14-year-old kids he was accustomed to facing.

"Guess then is when I was really nervous," he said, a couple of days later. "Things just weren't going right. I walked the next three men...I don't know who they were. Y'see, sir," he apologized to the *Washington Post* reporter who was interviewing him. "I don't know all their names yet."

Nuxhall couldn't collect another out, allowing five runs on two hits and five walks. With the score 18–0, McKechnie took Nuxhall out of the game in favor of another youngster, Jake Eisenhart.[1] When asked what McKechnie told him when the manager came to the mound, Nuxhall said, "I know he said something, but I was so numb emotionally I can't recall a thing."

After the game, Nuxhall was despondent, but the importance of the moment eventually dawned on him. "Yep, I'm lucky," he admitted. "Never thought that at 15 I'd be pitching in the big time. Guess lots of kids would like to do that."

Nuxhall successfully retired two of the first three hitters he faced, but wouldn't get a third batter out until eight years later. His eventual return to the majors, however, was followed by a solid 15-year career spent mostly in Cincinnati.[2]

"I was in awe of all of it," Nuxhall remembered later. "I always looked back and wondered what might have happened if I had gotten the third out instead of the walk. It was during the war, and the talent was slim, and they were using just about anyone they could get. I wondered that if I had gotten the third out, if I might have stayed a little longer."

Sixty years after his historic debut, Joe Nuxhall remained one of the most beloved figures in Cincinnati sports history. After his playing career ended, "the Old Left-hander" embarked upon a magical four-decade run as a radio broadcaster for the Reds. Said legendary broadcaster Marty Brennaman, Nuxhall's partner in the booth for most

---

1. Eisenhart was just 21 years old, and that day marked his major league debut as well. Unlike Nuxhall, it also marked the end of his career, as Eisenhart never played in another big league game.
2. Nuxhall was 130–109 in his Reds career. When he retired, he had pitched in more games than anyone in franchise history.

of those years: "In a business that breeds egomaniacs, Joe Nuxhall is the rarest of the rare. I've never seen him be anything but nice to his fans, and their numbers are beyond comprehension."

A Cincinnati legend, indeed, and it all dates back to a quiet afternoon in June of 1944.

45

CINCINNATI FLAMETHROWERS

In the 2020s, 100 mph fastballs barely raise an eyebrow. Triple digit heaters are as common at the ballpark as Cracker Jack. But it wasn't always like this; as recently as 2008, only 20 major league pitchers threw a pitch at 100 mph or above. Combined, all pitchers threw just 214 such fastballs (of 714,122 total pitches thrown that year).

By 2023, the frequency of 100 mph pitches had jumped over tenfold, to 3,880, thrown by 64 different pitchers. These numbers keep climbing, despite the institution of a pitch clock.

Not that long ago, Reds fans could regularly watch one of the tiny handful of men who could throw a baseball that hard. It was the most electrifying fastball the game had ever seen, which came, of course, from the left arm of Reds closer Aroldis Chapman. Despite the steady stream of fireballers in the years since, Chapman remains the King of Velo. His 105.8 mph (170.2686 km/h) fastball, thrown in San Diego on September 24, 2010, still holds the Guinness World Record for fastest baseball pitch. But Chapman wasn't the first Reds flamethrower, and he wouldn't be the last.

Tony Mullane

Tony Mullane, a colorful (and morally bankrupt) pitcher in the 1880s, was known for having one of the game's best fastballs. That turns out to be a bit of a dubious honor, given that Mullane was also known for helping erode a rule then in effect requiring underhand pitching. If you're one of the first guys to throw the ball overhand, your pitches are likely to be among the fastest.

Johnny Vander Meer and Ewell Blackwell

In the 1930s and 40s, Johnny Vander Meer and Ewell Blackwell were known to bring elite heat. At least one source estimated Vander Meer's fastball at 100 mph, while The Sporting News put it more colorfully, describing the Dutch Master's fastball as "machine gun bullets" and looking to the batter like "hummingbird eggs." Blackwell didn't throw as hard as his contemporary, Bob Feller, but his "hopping" fastball was enhanced by his "terrifying" sidearm delivery, and still ranked among the elite of his era.

Jim Maloney

Eclipsed by the Big Red Machine era that he just missed, and virtually unknown to the last three generations of Reds fans, Jim Maloney was the team's ace throughout the 1960s. Barely 20 years old when he debuted in 1960, Maloney had joined the ranks of the NL's elite pitchers by 1963, and had a seven year run as good as any Red. Unfortunately, chronic arm problems—and a freak achilles tendon injury—pushed him out of the game completely by age 31.

Maloney's fastball was unquestionably dominant. Henry Aaron said that Maloney was the hardest thrower in the league, and both Sandy Koufax and Bob Gibson ranked Maloney atop the league. "I don't throw as hard as Jim Maloney," Gibson said "Nobody throws harder than Maloney." Speaking from 60'6" downrange, Johnny Bench agreed, saying that he never caught a pitcher who threw harder—a statement that takes on even more weight when you remember that Bench spent a night each summer sampling the NL's elite at the All-Star game.

Historians admire Maloney, too. In their 2004 book, *The Neyer-James Guide to Pitchers*, Rob Neyer and Bill James listed Maloney's among the best 25 fastballs in baseball history; and as having the sixth-best fastball in both the 1960-64 and 1965-69 timeframes. Only Gibson, Koufax, and Pittsburgh's Bob Veale joined him on both the decade's lists.

Results? Maloney threw two no-hitters, plus another start where he didn't allow a hit until the 11th inning.[1] Add five other one-hitters and nine two-hitters, and you've got yourself a truly overpowering starter. The numbers agree. Among starters in the 1960s, only Koufax struck out more men per nine innings. Maloney still holds the Reds franchise record for career strikeouts. Soto, Rijo, Arroyo, Harang, Cueto—over five decades of increasing strikeout rates, no one could catch him.

As the details of his career have faded into memory, Maloney's fastball has achieved almost Bunyan-esque proportions. One unsourced

---

1. Maloney threw 187 pitches in that game. Completely unrelated, Maloney made a mere five starts after his 29th birthday.

report says that Maloney was clocked at 99.5 in 1965; others round the number up to 100, though rarely with any detail. Those stories then lead to claims that Maloney actually "threw 112 mph," based on data showing that the speed of a fastball decreases roughly ten percent between the mound and the plate.[2]

Maloney has jokingly dismissed the 112 mph story as "fake news," and even questions whether he definitely threw 100 mph. Without radar guns at the ballpark, "[t]here was no way of knowing" how hard anyone actually threw. But Maloney ultimately allowed that on his good days, he threw as hard as anyone in baseball at the time.

Gary Nolan

Another one of baseball's all-time "coulda been" stories is Gary Nolan. Debuting for the Reds in 1967 at just 18 years old, Nolan was a power pitcher, relying on his fastball to strike out 206 pitchers in 226 ⅔ innings. But like Maloney, heavy workloads, a remarkably unsympathetic Reds front office, and bad luck plagued Nolan for the rest of his career. By 1970, he had been forced to reinvent himself as a changeup/curveball specialist. Nolan was good at that, too, going 15-5 with a 1.99 ERA for the 1972 pennant winners. But ultimately, the injuries took their toll and Nolan was effectively finished at 29.

Tom Seaver

No chapter on fastballs could omit Tom Terrific. Seaver threw 98 mph as a young star on the Mets. While Seaver was remarkable for his durability and good health—he made at least 32 starts every year until he turned 35—his truly blazing fastball was largely gone by the time he joined the Reds in 1977.

Rob Dibble

Rob Dibble was the first real Reds fireballer from the era where radar guns were more or less ubiquitous, and he knew how to light up that gun. A big (6'4" 230 lbs) righthander, Dibble spent two years in the low minors as a starter, striking out just 4-5 men per 9 innings. But once he

---

2. Maloney's pitch, assuming it was measured via radar, was measured at or near the plate. Modern technology measures the speed when the ball leaves the pitcher's hand. (See "How Fast is Fast," below).

was moved to the bullpen, Dibble threw all-out, all the time, bumping up his strikeout rates as he moved up through the system.

By the time he arrived in Cincinnati in 1988, Dibble's fastball was hitting three digits with regularity. Paired with an exploding 90 mph slider, Dibble was dominant from the start, striking out nearly a batter per inning as a rookie - and going up from there. In 1989, Dibble set a record by striking out 12.8 batters per inning pitched, then went on to break his own record in 1991 and 1992.

In between, of course, Dibble joined with two other hard-throwing relievers to win a World Championship as the Nasty Boys. Lefthanders Randy Myers and Norm Charlton both threw in the mid-90s, still elite velocity in the early 1990s.

Dibble touched his greatest speed in 1992, when he registered 101 mph on the Candlestick Park radar gun, a figure that was (for a time) the fastest measured pitch in a major league game.

Aroldis Chapman

Growing up in the province of Holguín, in the town of Cayo Mambí, on Cuba's eastern shore, Chapman actually dreamed of being a boxer. One day, some local kids needed another player for their neighborhood baseball game, so they asked Aroldis—just nine years old, but already tall—if he wanted to play. Boxing was in Chapman's rear-view mirror from that day forward.

Chapman played first base almost exclusively until age 15, when a coach noticed Chapman's strong arm and thought to try him as a pitcher. He never went back to first base. Within three years, Chapman was a starting pitcher for the Holguín team in Cuba's national league, dazzling baseball fans across the small nation with a blistering fastball that had already been clocked in the triple digits. Fame and riches awaited the lanky left-hander, but only if he could escape Cuba.

After one defection attempt and a suspension from Cuba's national team, Chapman eventually returned and dazzled onlookers at the 2009 World Baseball Classic. All the while, however, he waited quietly for another opportunity to present itself.

That opportunity came almost 15 months after Chapman's first defection attempt. Shortly after arriving in the Netherlands for a tournament with the national team, Chapman told his roommate he was going out to smoke. Instead, he stepped out of the hotel lobby and into a car that was waiting for him. With only his passport and a pack of cigarettes to his name, Chapman rode off into freedom.

After a lengthy dance with agents and scouts and big league executives, Chapman signed a multi-million-dollar contract with Cincinnati. He made his debut in late 2010, and by 2012 had established himself as perhaps the greatest closer in baseball. That year, Chapman saved 38 games with a 1.51 ERA, striking out 122 batters in just 71.2 innings. At midseason, he was named to the first of four consecutive NL All-Star teams.[3]

By this time, there was a name for the buzz that went up around the ballpark whenever Chapman entered a game, as fans eagerly anticipated seeing that world-class fastball. It was called "Chapmania," and no Reds fan was immune.

During his six seasons with the Reds, Chapman was a valuable contributor to three playoff teams, posting a 2.17 ERA to go along with 146 saves. That save total was good for fourth on the all-time franchise list, but no pitcher in Reds history was ever as dominant. Chapman averaged more than 15 strikeouts per nine innings as a Red, a ratio that dwarfs every other pitcher in club history.[4]

During that span, Chapman's cool and unflappable demeanor on the mound contributed to a reputation as an unstoppable force unlike anything baseball had ever seen. During spring training in 2014, however, it appeared that Aroldis had met his match. A line drive off the bat of Royals catcher Salvador Pérez—after a 99 mph offering by Chapman—hit the pitcher in the face and he crumpled to the mound. The stadium fell silent, as trainers and coaches rushed to his aid. Soon Chapman was carried off the field on a stretcher, and the exhibition game was abandoned.

Chapman had suffered a skull fracture above his left eye, and he underwent emergency surgery to insert a titanium plate. Amazingly, Chapman returned to the Reds nearly two months later, showing no ill-effects from the frightening injury. His first pitch was a 100 mph strike, and Chapman struck out the side in the ninth inning to pick up the save.

---

3. Chapman is one of only six Reds pitchers to be selected to four or more All-Star Games. The others are: Ewell Blackwell (6), Paul Derringer (6), Bob Purkey (5), Bucky Walters (5), and Johnny Vander Meer (4).

4. Chapman averaged 15.4 strikeouts per nine innings as a Red. Rob Dibble ranks a distant second (among pitchers with at least 200 IP as a Red) at 12.4.

HOW FAST IS FAST?

The complicating factor in comparing fastballs across history is that different radar guns and other technology measure the ball's speed at different points on its journey from the pitcher's hand and the catcher's mitt. Over time, advancements have let us measure velocity closer and closer to its fastest point, at the pitcher's release. That's where MLB's current Statcast system looks, using "a series of high-resolution optical cameras along with radar equipment."

In 2010, when Chapman threw his record fastball, the league used a three-camera system called Pitch/FX, which measured the ball about 50 feet from the mount. According to Baseball America's JJ Cooper, MLB retroactively converted Pitch/FX measurements to the new system—a change that actually gave Chapman an additional 0.7 MPH.

And both of those methods are "faster" than the old ways. While experts differ on the details and degree, most agree that the methods of the 1960-80s understate the fastballs of the past. The 2015 documentary Fastball attempted to reconcile these differences, and create a true apples-to-apples comparison. Their verdict was that Nolan Ryan, not Chapman, threw the fastest-ever fastball at 108.5 MPH, followed by Bob Feller at 107.6.

Later that season, Chapman set an all-time baseball record by striking out at least one batter in 49 consecutive relief appearances.

Just more than a year after returning from that scary injury, Chapman was one of the Reds' two representatives at the 2015 All-Star Game held in Cincinnati. Moments after the final out of the eighth inning, a sellout crowd heard the Rage Against the Machine song "Wake Up" begin to blare through the Great American Ball Park loudspeakers. As they had done so many times before, Reds fans leapt to their feet to celebrate the entrance of the "Cuban Missile," as Aroldis emerged from behind the center-field fence and jogged to the mound.

On the national stage, Chapman did not disappoint. He struck out each of the three AL All-Stars that he faced; 12 of his 14 pitches were clocked at 100 mph or faster. One fastball hit 103 on the radar gun. After whiffing Yankees first baseman Mark Teixeira for the third out, Chapman walked off the mound showing a rare hint of a smile as he looked around at the 43,000-plus who were wildly applauding one of the most unique talents in baseball history. Chapmania, indeed.

Hunter Greene delivers a pitch against the Milwaukee Brewers in May 2022.

(Joe Robbins/Icon Sportswire/AP Images)

In 2015, his final season with the Reds, Chapman threw the 62 fastest pitches recorded by any pitcher in the big leagues. Alas, with the club belatedly starting a rebuilding process following two losing seasons, Chapman was traded to the Yankees for four minor leaguers after the 2015 season. He then moved on to the Chicago Cubs, where he earned a 2016 World Series ring.

Hunter Greene

The fiery comet currently streaking across Cincinnati skies is Hunter Greene, a phenom who threw 102 mph, appeared on the cover of *Sports Illustrated*, and was drafted #2 overall—all before he was old enough to vote.

After battling back from Tommy John surgery, Greene reached the majors in 2022, and quickly set fire to radar guns and fans' imaginations. In only his second career start, Greene unleashed 39 triple-digit fastballs, the most ever recorded; the previous record had been 33. Through August 2024, Greene had thrown a remarkable 437 pitches at 100 mph or more, already ranking twelfth in the era of official MLB speed measurements. Perhaps more incredible, Greene ranked first among starting pitchers. Spots 1–11 (as well as 12–19) belonged to short relievers, who can afford to throw their hardest for a few pitches a night.

Unlike Dibble, for whom the phrase "maximum effort" may have been coined, Greene's fastball is most commonly described as "easy gas." His motion is consistent and unhurried. His arm action is clean. And when going well, Greene almost seems to will the ball to a precise spot. He takes a leisurely windup and suddenly the ball appears in the catcher's glove on the outside corner.

As odd as it may seem, Greene's 102 mph fastball may not be his best pitch. He throws his slider almost 40% of the time. That pitch, thrown in the mid to upper 80s, has excellent break—and Greene has the command to put it in any spot he wants.

Greene took a big leap forward in 2024, developing into a certified ace while being named to his first All-Star team at the age of 24. If he can remain healthy, Hunter may eventually be remembered as the Reds best fireballer.

46

THE SEASON THAT WASN'T

As the '80s dawned, there was reason to hope that the Big Red Machine still had a little gasoline left in the tank. In 1979, the Reds had won yet another division title—their sixth of the decade—before falling to the eventual World Series–champion Pittsburgh Pirates in the playoffs.

The following season, Cincinnati won 89 games, but key injuries to the pitching staff resulted in a third-place finish. Still, the Reds ended the 1980 season just three and a half games out of first, and manager John McNamara, who had replaced legendary skipper Sparky Anderson after the 1978 season, had reason to be optimistic about 1981.

"If we can keep them healthy," said McNamara, "I don't see any reason why we can't win it."

These weren't the same old Reds of the mid-1970s, though; the roster had undergone a transformation. After César Gerónimo was dealt to Kansas City in January 1981, only four members of the Machine's vaunted "Great Eight"—Johnny Bench, Dave Concepción, Ken Griffey, and George Foster—remained in Cincinnati.

In place of the departed stars was a group of talented twenty-somethings. Ray Knight was an All-Star third baseman, and center fielder Dave Collins was one of the most prolific base-stealers in baseball, with 79 steals in 1980. The right side of the infield featured Dan Driessen and Ron Oester, both future inductees into the Reds Hall of Fame.

The pitching staff had been completely turned over from the glory years. Not a single pitcher on the 1981 roster had been a member of the 1976 World Series–champion Reds. Tom Seaver was still one of the biggest stars in baseball. He was joined by four highly regarded youngsters—Mario Soto, Bruce Berenyi, Frank Pastore, and Mike LaCoss—all under the age of 26. Soto was a budding ace and, with Seaver, he gave the Reds a formidable one-two punch at the top of the rotation.

The (somewhat) new-look Reds opened the season with a 3–2 victory over Philadelphia before 51,716 expectant fans at Riverfront

Stadium.[1] The excitement was short-lived; by the second week of May, the Reds were just 14–14 and in third place.

An eight-game winning streak, beginning with a walk-off win against the Cubs on May 12, bumped the Reds into second place. Just when things had started to go Cincinnati's way, however, disaster struck—or so it appeared. Late in the month, Johnny Bench broke his ankle sliding into second base. At the time, Bench was hitting .343. He wouldn't return to the lineup until the end of August.

Undeterred, the Reds ran off another seven-game win streak, culminating in a brilliant complete game 5–2 victory by Seaver over his former team, the Mets. The win, on June 11, improved Seaver to 7–1 with a 2.06 ERA and it seemed like he was on his way to yet another outstanding season at the age of 36. Even better, the Reds had pulled to within one-half game of Los Angeles in the standings.

The following day, the season was interrupted after a unanimous vote of the Executive Board of the MLB Players' Association. The players were on strike.

The threat of a players' strike had been looming all season long. At issue was the question of compensation for teams who lost players to free agency. During the 1970s, the players had won a number of hard-fought battles that resulted in the creation of the arbitration process and free agency. Stung by those defeats, owners tried to push back, demanding new rules requiring compensation to any team that lost a player in free agency. That compensation, according to the scheme dreamed up by owners, would be that each team signing a free agent would have to give up a player of comparable ability to the team who lost the free agent. The players understandably balked at these conditions, which would have placed a substantial roadblock to true free agency. Making matters worse, Ray Grebey served as the owners' chief negotiator. Grebey had gained some amount of acclaim as a hard-nosed negotiator for General Electric during its own employees' strike, and MLB's owners snatched him up in 1978.

Grebey lived up to his reputation in the weeks leading up to—and during—the strike, refusing to surrender an inch to the players. Time and

---

1.   Newly elected President Ronald Reagan had been scheduled to throw out the first pitch on Opening Day, but nine days before the game, Reagan was wounded in an assassination attempt by John Hinckley outside the Washington Hilton Hotel.

again, the players offered compromises, and every time, the hard-line Grebey urged ownership to reject those proposals.

Grebey's fatal mistake was underestimating the resolve of the players' union as the strike dragged on. Finally, with club owners losing millions of dollars in revenue each week, Grebey was forced to blink. On July 31, the owners agreed to a compromise solution that barely resembled their original demand. It was another significant victory for the players, but it came at a huge price. Players lost more than $28 million in total salaries during the strike, a number dwarfed by the $72 million financial hit taken by ownership.

"I don't think it's a laughing matter," said Seaver, "but it will be one of the most unusual, nonsensical parts of my career. It's just ironic that one little man comes out of General Electric, or wherever Ray Grebey came from, and messes with our game."

With the strike over, everyone began the process of picking up the pieces. The Reds gathered at the University of Michigan for an abbreviated training camp.[2] While teams around the league were working on their conditioning, the owners were hatching another nutty scheme, this one involving the playoffs.

Under the proposal, the teams in first place at the time of the work stoppage would be declared "champions" of the first half. Each division would crown a second-half champion as well, based only on teams' records after returning from the strike. At the end of the season, the two half-season "champions" would play each other in a best-of-five series for the right to move on to the League Championship Series.[3]

Since the Reds had finished a half-game behind Los Angeles in the first half, they would need either to win the second half, or finish with the best overall record behind the Dodgers. Later, John McNamara would call it a "lame-brain idea," but the playoff scheme was approved by the owners on August 6. The Reds, Cardinals, and Phillies were the only National league teams to vote against the split-season format.

Reds president Dick Wagner hated the idea. Not only did it leave the Reds out in the cold, and devalue the full season, it created perverse incentives—the Reds now had a vested interest in seeing the first-

2. On the University of Michigan's baseball team that year was a tough young third baseman named Chris Sabo. Over the next two years, Sabo would be joined in the Wolverines infield by shortstop Barry Larkin and first baseman Hal Morris. All three players would play vital roles for the Reds' next championship team in 1990.

3. If a team won both halves, they would play the team with the second-best record for the full season.

half champion Dodgers win the second half (if the Reds couldn't do it themselves).

Wagner's concerns quickly became obvious to everyone else (managers Tony La Russa and Whitey Herzog openly contemplated throwing games, or forfeiting them, to ensure a postseason spot), and the postseason format was hastily modified: If the same team won both halves, their opponent would be the second place team from the second half only. It didn't really eliminate the game-throwing risk, but it made it less likely. However, it was even less fair to the Reds, as it gave them zero credit for winning 35 games before the strike, a fact not lost on Wagner.

After the resumption of play, Cincinnati lost three of their first four games, but rebounded to post another strong half of baseball. Seaver didn't skip a beat, finishing with his last great season. In April, he recorded his 3,000th career strikeout, and at seasons' end, Seaver had a 14-2 record and a 2.54 ERA. Soto had a breakout year as well, going 12-9 with a 3.29 ERA and 10 complete games.

On the offensive side of the ledger, George Foster had another excellent season, hitting 22 homers with 90 RBI in only 108 games. Dave Concepción was named Reds MVP by the local baseball writers after hitting .306/.358/.409 and playing his usual stellar defense at shortstop. After returning late in the season, Bench finished at .309 with 8 home runs in 52 games.

It wasn't enough. On October 3, the Houston Astros clinched the NL West second-half title, with the Reds stuck in second place once again, a game and a half back. On the season, Cincinnati finished with a 66–42 record, the best mark in the major leagues. But because they hadn't finished in first place in either half, they were shut out of the playoffs.[4]

"If I wasn't a grown man, I think I'd go cry on a curb or a park or somewhere," said McNamara. "You strive for this thing all your life and lose it because of this."

On the final day of the regular season, Soto pitched a brilliant one-hit shutout, striking out nine Braves. Before the game, with the entire city upset over the injustice of the best team in baseball being left out of the playoffs, the Reds unfurled a huge pennant reading "Baseballs [sic] Best Record 1981."

---

4.   The Cardinals—who, like the Reds, had voted against the split-season format—finished with the second best full-season record in the National League, but also failed to win the East in either half and therefore didn't qualify for the playoffs.

CINCINNATI REDS

Said backup catcher Mike O'Berry: "It's tough to take when you think you're the best team and the playoffs start and you're sitting home watching it."

What they watched was even more infuriating. After qualifying for the playoffs despite a full-season record that was four games worse than Cincinnati's mark, the Dodgers went on to win the World Series. For years, Reds players would insist that 1981 could have been the third championship for the Big Red Machine.

Whether the Reds would have won is pure speculation, of course. But what is clear is that the story of the Machine could easily have been even more impressive. For the five-year stretch after the 1976 championship, the Reds compiled the best winning percentage in the National League, but were unable to reach another World Series.

The disappointment of 1981, in what could have been a very special season, marked the official end of the glory days. Ken Griffey and George Foster were traded during the off-season as Wagner committed to a complete rebuild. The Reds collapsed, losing 101 games in 1982, and wouldn't have another winning season until 1985.

It's not often that the Reds were able to compile the best record in the major leagues, but thanks to the strike and the wacky playoff system, the 1981 club has gone down in history largely as a forgotten team.

"When you come down to it," said John McNamara, "it really was the season that wasn't."

AND HE DIDN'T EVEN START

Over nearly a century and a half, the Reds have had dozens of great hitters. From Bid McPhee and Sam Crawford at the turn of the 20th century to Junior Griffey and Joey Votto in the 21st, the Reds have never lacked for historic hitters.

But none of them ever had a day as impactful as the half-night of work Art Shamsky put in on a late summer's Friday in 1966.

It was a down year for the Reds, their first losing season in six years, and one of only two sub-.500 years between 1961 and 1981. The biggest problem, of course, was that Frank Robinson was winning the Triple Crown for Baltimore instead of the Reds, having been traded for Milt Pappas and two others over the winter.

The Reds entered the day in sixth place in the 10-team NL. Manager Don Heffner had been fired over the All-Star break, and his 33-year-old replacement, Dave Bristol,[1] had the Reds creeping back toward the vicinity of contention, cutting their deficit from 16 games to nine in the prior month. The Pirates, on the other hand, were in the thick of the pennant race, arriving in Cincinnati leading the Cubs by two games and the Dodgers by three.

This game was loaded with talent. Four Hall of Famers (plus the Hit King) took the field at Crosley: Tony Pérez for the Reds and Willie Stargell, Roberto Clemente, and Bill Mazeroski for the Pirates. The stars definitely shone that night, but this story is about a man who didn't take the field until the eighth inning: Art Shamsky.

Growing up in St. Louis, Shamsky loved baseball (and the Cardinals), but didn't consider himself an exceptional player. He didn't even try out for the high school team until his senior year, and only hit about .300 that year. Shamsky was just 16 when he graduated, though, and after playing ball for a year at the University of Missouri, he signed with the Reds.

Shamsky was sent to Geneva of the New York-Penn League, where he met fellow Reds prospects Pérez and Pete Rose. Shamsky, still only 18,

---

1. Shamsky had played for Bristol (then a player-manager) at two different stops in the minors.

hit well (.271/.407/.482), and was promoted the following year to Class B Topeka, while Rose and Pérez spent another year in Class D. While slender, Shamsky was a real power prospect, averaging 18 home runs a year as a very young minor leaguer, topping out at 25 as a 22-year-old in AAA.

Breaking into the big leagues in 1965, he was forced into the difficult role of pinch-hitter, starting only 12 of the 64 games he played. His rookie year also established Shamsky's career-long reputation as a platoon player—he faced right-handed pitching 98 times, but had only eight plate appearances against southpaws.

By 1966, with Robinson gone, Shamsky stepped into the role of the Reds fourth outfielder. He started 66 games, and came off the bench for another 33. August 12 was one of the latter.

The pitching matchup could've been a good one. Both Pittsburgh's Bob Veale and the Reds' Sammy Ellis had been All-Stars in 1965. Veale was having another good year (entering the game at 12-7 with a 2.89 ERA), but Ellis wasn't...to say the least. He entered the game with a 9-14 record and 5.02 ERA.

Neither man helped his numbers on this night. In the bottom of the first, Deron Johnson followed a Rose walk with a home run, putting the Reds ahead 2-0.

Ellis actually looked strong at first, retiring the first six Pirates he faced. But in the third, things fell apart. Mazeroski singled and catcher Jesse Gonder homered, tying the game. The Pirates scored twice more on a Clemente home run, and led 4-2.

Rose tied it again with his 12th homer in the fifth, but the seesaw quickly moved in the Pirates' favor, as third baseman Bob Bailey homered over the center-field fence to lead off the top of the sixth, making the score 5-4. In the bottom of the inning, the Reds took a 6-5 lead with a fairly pedestrian combination of singles and a sacrifice fly.

Cincinnati's Joe Nuxhall took the mound in relief to start the seventh. After retiring the first two Pirates, Nuxhall hit Matty Alou with a pitch and then gave up Bailey's second homer of the night. The Pirates again led, this time 7-6.

Let's take a breath for the seventh inning stretch. To this point, we've had a fairly exciting mid-summer slugfest. The teams had combined for

13 runs, 14 hits, and five lead changes. But now things were about to get really interesting.

Through a double-switch, Shamsky entered to play left field in the top of the eighth. His first turn at bat came in the bottom of that inning, with the Reds trailing by a run. Shortstop Leo Cardenas had led off with a single, and one out later, Shamsky blasted a ball high over the center-field fence, giving the Reds an 8–7 lead with just one inning left.

Reliever Don Nottebart, who'd replaced Nuxhall, wasn't able to hold that lead. On for his second inning of work, Nottebart retired Mazeroski, but then faced legendary pinch-hitter (and Reds Hall of Famer) Jerry Lynch. Lynch did what he frequently did: Hit a huge pinch-hit home run, breaking his own career record of 18 pinch-hit homers, and tying the game at 8–8.

The Reds went down in order in the bottom of the ninth against Roy Face, the Pirates longtime ace fireman. In the top of the 10th, Stargell hit a solo homer to give the Pirates a 9–8 lead and an 82 percent Win Expectancy.[2]

No worries: Art Shamsky came through again in the bottom of the 10th, hitting a game-tying solo homer.

The Reds then loaded the bases with one out, but weren't able to push across the game-winner.

Twenty-one-year-old lefty Billy McCool took the mound for the Reds to start the 11th, and immediately walked Mazeroski. Face, hitting for himself, bunted into a double play, erasing the baserunner. Not content with the gift, McCool then walked catcher Jim Pagliaroni *and* Matty Alou. Bob Bailey doubled to center field, scoring both runners for his fourth and fifth RBIs of the night. McCool finally escaped the inning, but the Pirates led 11–9.

By this point, most of the 25,477 ticket-buyers were still in attendance, and many may have felt that Shamsky could again save the day, if he only got a chance. The newly minted hero wasn't due up until fourth. With two outs—and the Pirates Win Expectancy now at 99 percent—Johnny Edwards coaxed a walk. Pirates manager Walker Cooper went to his bullpen, calling on Billy O'Dell, an effective veteran and more importantly, his only left-handed reliever.

---

2. For more on Win Expectancy, look to the A Note on Statistics section before Chapter 1.

Though he rarely faced lefties, this was a different type of night for Art Shamsky. After falling behind in the count 2-2, he launched a long fly ball into the right-field bleachers, just inside the foul pole. It was his third homer, and the Reds were again tied. The Pirates had just blown their sixth different lead, three of them upended by Art Shamsky.

Unfortunately, Shamsky didn't come to the plate again. Both clubs went down in order in the 12th, but in the 13th, the Pirates cobbled together two singles, two intentional walks, and a Cincinnati error into three runs. The Reds couldn't score, and the Pirates won 14–11.

It was the most impactful single performance in Reds history, but Art Shamsky begged off Reds radio's *Star of the Game* program. His manager approved. "When you lose there are no stars," Bristol told *Sports Illustrated*.

Shamsky wasn't the star the following day, either. He didn't even play. Bristol put him back on the bench for Saturday's game, as the Reds faced Pirates left-hander Woodie Fryman. On Sunday, Shamsky finally resurfaced as a pinch-hitter with one on and two out in the seventh inning, and the Reds trailing 1–0. What did he do? He homered in his fourth consecutive at-bat, tying the record for home runs in consecutive plate appearances.[3]

Shamsky's power surge wasn't a complete fluke. He only had 54 hits in 1966, but 21 of them were home runs. His Isolated Power (ISO) of .291 was tied with Willie McCovey for second-best in the NL, ahead of Willie Mays, Hank Aaron, and Willie Stargell.

Shamsky was traded to the Mets after the 1967 season. Though he earned his greatest fame—and a World Series ring—as a member of the Mets 1969 championship team, he still holds a unique place in Reds history.

---

3. Shamsky was removed in a double switch and the Reds bullpen blew the lead again.

48

2012
NL CENTRAL
CHAMPS

The 2010 Reds had flamed out, getting swept by the Phillies in the Division Series, but the future looked bright for 2011. Cincinnati had two budding superstars in Joey Votto (the 2010 NL MVP) and Jay Bruce (25 home runs as a 23-year-old), and some of the best young pitching talent in baseball: Johnny Cueto, Homer Bailey, and Mike Leake were all 25 or younger.

Reds general manager Walt Jocketty largely stood pat in the 2010–11 off-season, and the result was a flat, mediocre 2011 season. The pitching could generously be described as lousy, and season-long black holes at shortstop and left field put a drag on an otherwise-solid offense.

The next off-season, Jocketty took decisive action to fix the team's holes, in hopes of avoiding the franchise's 11th losing season in 12 years.[1] He acquired a talented young starter—24-year-old Mat Latos—and one of the better relievers in the game—lefty Sean Marshall—in separate trades. Jocketty then added another reliever, signing closer Ryan Madson to a reasonable one-year, $8.5 million contract. That acquisition was accompanied by the announcement that flame-throwing setup man Aroldis Chapman would be moved to the starting rotation.

Finally, Jocketty signed journeyman left fielder Ryan Ludwick (.237 and 13 HR in 2011) to a bargain deal, with the expectation that Ludwick would contend with Chris Heisey for the left-field job.

These dramatic moves appeared to put the Reds back on the map, as many of the so-called experts named the Reds among potential pennant contenders. But before the season even started, Jocketty was forced to tear up his Plan A and improvise.

Madson, who had been lights-out as Philadelphia's closer the year before, reported to spring training with elbow discomfort. He insisted this was something he worked through every spring, but this time was different. Madson needed season-ending surgery before he even pitched

---

1. At least some of the holes. An aging Scott Rolen was still being penciled in to play third base and bat fourth, despite missing all but 65 games in 2011.

in a single exhibition game for Cincinnati. The Reds designated Marshall their closer, and scrapped the Chapman-to-the-rotation plan

Just before Opening Day, Jocketty and owner Bob Castellini dropped the biggest news: the Reds had signed Votto to a 12-year, $251.5 million contract extension—the longest guaranteed deal in major league history. Five days later, they signed Brandon Phillips to a six-year, $72.5 million extension, locking the second baseman up through 2017.

Once the season finally got under way, manager Dusty Baker spent a couple of months trying to figure out his bullpen. Marshall struggled early (opponents hit .301 against him through May), while Chapman dominated, not allowing an earned run until June 7 and striking out 52 men in his first 29 innings pitched. So, in late May, Chapman became the full-time closer, while Marshall regained his form in the setup role (a 1.74 ERA after May 20, with opponents hitting just .191/.259/237 against him). Perhaps coincidentally, the Reds limped to a 20–19 start with Marshall as closer; after Chapman took over, they were 77–46.

One thing Baker *didn't* have to worry about was his starting rotation. Before the season, an anonymous scout had told a reporter that the Reds biggest problem would be a "lack of innings from their starting pitchers, and how much pressure that puts on their bullpen." That guy couldn't have been more wrong. The Reds' Opening Day rotation—Cueto, Latos, Bronson Arroyo, Bailey, and Leake—started 161 of the team's 162 games.[2]

While the Reds' record over the first six weeks was forgettable, there was one all-time great moment. On Mother's Day, Votto homered three times, including a walk-off grand slam.

By June 29, the Reds were eight games over .500 and had a one-game lead over Pittsburgh. The pitching had been great, but Votto was the story. He was hitting .354/.476/.639, with 14 home runs and 33 doubles in the season's first 76 games. Votto had been elected to start the All-Star Game, and was cruising toward a second MVP Award in three seasons. Then he jammed his left knee sliding into third base.

After trying to play through the injury for two weeks (including the All-Star Game), Votto finally had surgery on July 17. While initially projected to miss just three to four weeks, Votto ended up missing seven

---

2.   The answer to the trivia question is Todd Redmond, who started the second game of a mid-August doubleheader, in the middle of a stretch of 33 games in 33 days.

weeks in the heart of the season...and, impossibly, the Reds went 33–16 without their best player, extending their NL Central lead from one game to 8.5.

How? First, their run prevention, already excellent, improved. Cincinnati's team ERA in July was 3.03, and they played exceptional team defense, with plus defenders at the four most crucial positions: catcher, shortstop, second base, and center field.

"Hitting has ups and downs, pitching has ups and downs," said right fielder Jay Bruce. "Defense is our constant. It's comforting for the hitters, for the pitchers, for everyone. Defense doesn't slump."

But how could the offense fill a Votto-shaped hole for 49 games?

The bulk of Votto's at-bats went to rookie Todd Frazier, who finally got his chance at age 26. Frazier started 36 of those 49 games at first base (and started another 11 for Rolen at third). Over that stretch, Frazier hit a Votto-like (or at least Votto Lite) .300/.347/.500.

Ludwick was even better, hitting .342/.406/.651, with 14 home runs and 36 RBI. Bruce also had a helpfully timed hot streak, hitting .284/.366/.611, with 13 homers and 34 RBI. Phillips (.310/.337/.483), catcher Ryan Hanigan (.304/.407/.353), and even Chris Heisey (.304/.324/.536) stepped up.

The crisis even led Scott Rolen back to the fountain of youth for one last drink. He hit .301/.398/.496 while Votto was out of the lineup.[3]

To keep their focus over the long season, the Reds had set an internal goal of winning every series, with the thinking that winning two of every three games would result in a pretty good record at the end of the season. (In fact, it would lead to a 108–54 record. Very good.) To serve as a reminder, one of the players secured a gold trophy cup, which traveled with the club during the second half of the season. In Chicago, it was the "Windy City Cup." When playing San Francisco, it became the "Golden Gate Cup," etc.

The 2012 Reds were a fun team to watch, even without Votto's methodical majesty. Frazier and Ludwick were outgoing and boisterous, and Phillips added to his decade-long defensive highlight film. The Reds were aggressive on the basepaths, not in stealing bases but in going first-to-third on a single (a point of particular pride for the 37-year-old Rolen).

---

3. For the rest of the season, Rolen hit just .210/.264/.337.

Votto returned from the disabled list on September 4, claiming to be fully recovered. His on-base skills were as good as ever (.505 OBP after his return), but the injury sapped almost all of his power. In his final 105 plate appearances, Votto only managed eight doubles and no home runs.[4]

For whatever reason, Votto's return coincided with a team-wide slump: the Reds hit only .230 in September. They scored the fewest runs in the National League for the month, but their pitching and defense carried them to a 16–12 record.

Throughout September, the Reds and Nationals battled each other for the best record in the majors. The Reds, in fact, were the first team in either league to clinch their division, locking things up on September 22. In the season's final week, Homer Bailey pitched one of the finest single games in club history, no-hitting the Pittsburgh Pirates, walking only one, and striking out 10. With a Game Score[5] of 96, the game ranks as the best nine-inning pitching performance in Reds history.

In contrast to the excitement on the field, the Reds organization experienced a scary moment away from the diamond. Dusty Baker was forced to watch both the clinching victory and Bailey's no-hitter on television, as he'd been hospitalized with an irregular heartbeat (and later suffered a mini-stroke while in the hospital). Baker missed 11 games, and was still dealing with fatigue into October.

The Reds faced the San Francisco Giants in the Division Series, matching Baker against his old team, and the hungry Reds against the 2010 World Series champions. Baker penciled in a rotation of Cueto, Arroyo, Latos, and Bailey.

Cueto's 19 wins were the most by a Reds right-hander since Jack Billingham in 1974, and his 33 starts led the league. He started Game 1 by striking out Giants center fielder Angel Pagan, and got ahead of second baseman Marco Scutaro 0-2.

Then, six pitches in, Cueto was struck with severe back spasms, forcing him to leave the game. The postseason was five minutes old and Dusty's grand plan had already been thrown out the window. Back

---

4. Looking at it another way: Through June 29, Votto's Isolated Power (ISO), a simple measure of a hitter's raw power, was .285. Afterward, it was .099. For reference, Ryan Braun led the 2012 NL with a .276 ISO; Bronson Arroyo managed a .063.

5. Remember, Game Score is a metric that measures a pitcher's effectiveness in any given start. In general, a game score of 50 is average and the closer a pitcher gets to 100, the more impressive the outing. The highest nine-inning game score in baseball history (105) was Kerry Wood's 20-strikeout, one-hit performance for Chicago in 1998.

in Cincinnati, fans (who were still processing Roy Halladay's 2010 NLDS no-hitter) thought, "Here we go again." And this in a season where no member of the rotation missed so much as one start.

Given just seconds to reconfigure his entire pitching rotation, Baker pushed exactly the right buttons. Mat Latos had pitched three days earlier, so he was the best choice...but he worked on a starter's routine and would need 15–20 minutes to warm up. So Baker called on reliever Sam LeCure as a stop-gap—he knew LeCure could get ready quickly and wasn't rattled by pressure situations.[6]

LeCure finished the first inning and pitched a scoreless second, calming the waters and giving Latos a chance to warm up. Drew Stubbs led off the Cincinnati half of the third with a single, and one out later, Phillips launched a moon-shot home run to left-center.

Baker then called on Latos, who had already thrown his standard bullpen session earlier that afternoon. Latos performed brilliantly, giving the Reds four innings of one-run relief,[7] and handing a 3–1 lead over to the real bullpen. Marshall, Jonathan Broxton,[8] and Chapman finished it off, and the final was 5–3. The Reds had flirted with disaster, but ended up with their first playoff win in 17 years.

The Game 2 matchup made Reds fans nervous, though. The Giants' young starter Madison Bumgarner (16–11, 3.37 ERA) had utterly dominated the Reds at GABP earlier that summer, pitching a one-hit, 10-strikeout shutout—the best start in his career, to that point.

Arroyo would start for the Reds. He had plenty of postseason experience, but it wasn't all that comforting to Reds fans. In 11 postseason games, his ERA was 6.04. Baker's original plan had been for Arroyo to start the second game in San Francisco's spacious AT&T Park, while letting Latos, a strikeout pitcher, start Game 3 at GABP.

Once again, Baker's decision worked out perfectly, as Arroyo threw 7⅓ innings of one-hit, shutout baseball, and the Reds took their revenge on Bumgarner and the San Francisco bullpen, winning 9–0.

The Reds returned home to an ecstatic Queen City, needing just one win to clinch the series and move on to the League Championship Series.

---

6.   For example, LeCure had held hitters to a .130 batting average with the bases loaded, to that point in his career.

7.   Baker pulled Latos after 57 pitches, in hopes that he could start either Game 4 or 5.

8.   After the season, the Reds re-signed Broxton to a three-year, $21 million contract, hoping he would close and Chapman would move to the rotation in 2013. But Chapman wanted to stay at closer, and so Broxton became a very expensive setup man...then spent much of 2013 on the disabled list before being traded away in mid-2014.

CINCINNATI REDS

They had dominated the Giants on their own field, and history was on their side—38 of the 42 teams who'd taken a 2–0 lead in a five-game series had gone on to win. To complete the picture, the Game 3 pitching matchup was in the Reds favor. Homer Bailey (13–10, 3.68) had finished the season hot, with a 1.85 ERA over his final seven starts, including that no-hitter. The Giants countered with 35-year-old journeyman Ryan Vogelsong (14–9, 3.37), who had struggled with a 5.45 ERA over the same stretch of time.

Things started well for the Reds, as they scored a run in the bottom of the first. The Giants stole a run of their own in the third, scoring without getting a hit.[9] In fact, Bailey held the Giants hitless until Scutaro singled with two out in the sixth. But as dominant as Bailey was (one hit, 10 strikeouts in seven innings pitched), Vogelsong and four San Francisco relievers were just as effective—the Reds managed just one infield single after the first inning. Marshall and Chapman threw perfect innings after Bailey was lifted for a pinch-hitter, and the game went into the 10th inning, still tied 1–1.

Broxton took the mound for the Reds, and gave up quick singles to Hunter Pence and Buster Posey. Broxton rebounded by striking out two Giants in a row, but then the Reds defense, which had been its pride and backbone all season, betrayed them.

Broxton's first pitch to Giants' backup shortstop Joaquín Árias was an inside fastball that Hanigan simply missed.[10] The ball kicked to the backstop and both runners advanced, putting the go-ahead run on third base. With the count 1-2, and the chilly crowd of 44,501 on their feet, Broxton got Árias to hit a two-hopper to Rolen at third. Rolen, veteran of 17 seasons and owner of eight Gold Gloves for defensive excellence, bobbled the short-hop for an error. Posey scored and the Giants led 2–1. The Reds went down quietly in the 10th, and the Series moved to a fourth game.

Cincinnati had failed to take advantage of Bailey's brilliant outing, and now Dusty Baker had some more maneuvering to do. Cueto had been ruled out for the Series, so the question was who would start Game 4.[11] Mike Leake took the mound, but he definitely wasn't the answer.

---

9. The sequence went: HBP, walk, sacrifice bunt, sacrifice fly.
10. The play was scored a passed ball. Hanigan had only three during the regular season.
11. The Reds successfully petitioned MLB to place Cueto on the disabled list and activate Leake, who hadn't been on the original postseason roster.

Ángel Pagán hit Leake's second pitch a dozen rows deep into the right-field bleachers.

San Francisco's starter was veteran left-hander Barry Zito, and he had his own shaky start, walking three Reds in a row to force in a run in the first. But Leake gave it right back, surrendering a two-run home run to Gregor Blanco in the second, and two more runs in the fifth. By the time all the damage was done, the final score was 8–3.

Latos, the surprising hero of the Series opener, returned for the finale. His opponent was Matt Cain, who'd taken the loss in Game 1. Both pitched well through four innings, scattering a few baserunners but avoiding any real threats. Latos' fastball was lively and his breaking ball sharp. The intense, sometimes-emotional pitcher was confident and staying within himself.

How quickly things can change.

Blanco led off the fifth inning, and Latos quickly got ahead in the count 0-2. When Latos didn't get the strike three call he wanted from umpire Tom Hallion, the pitcher was visibly irritated.[12] When Blanco later singled, Latos began to stew. (This just as the TBS television crew chose this time to air an interview with Reds pitching coach Bryan Price, taped between the fourth and fifth innings. Price described Latos as "locked in," and in control of his emotions.)

When his first two pitches to Brandon Crawford—both borderline—were also called balls, Latos' focus was essentially gone. After arguing with Hallion between pitches, Latos grooved a nothing, 90-mph fastball—well below the 93 to 94 he'd been throwing all day—and Crawford pulled it into the corner in right field for a triple. Blanco scored easily and the Giants led 1–0.

Poker players use the term "on tilt" to describe a player whose emotional frustration gets the best of them, leading to bad decisions and a cascade of negative outcomes. It's a self-defeating mental state that's very hard to escape, and it's a job made even harder when your sure-handed shortstop (Zack Cozart in this case) fails to handle a high chopper and a second run scores.

Visibly steaming, Latos then walked Scutaro on four pitches, and gave up a single to Pablo Sandoval. Baker considered pulling Latos at that point, but decided to let Latos face Posey, who would soon

---

12. The pitch was inside.

be named the 2012 NL MVP. Posey had also homered against Latos in Game 1.

"We discussed it and he just made a couple of bad pitches and he still had plenty left in the tank," Baker explained afterward. A million armchair managers felt differently.

Latos got ahead of Posey, two balls and two strikes. The Cincinnati crowd, nervous and discouraged but still hopeful, got to their feet to encourage a strikeout. Latos threw a 94-mph fastball down the heart of the plate, and Posey crushed it, hitting a majestic 434-foot grand slam that silenced 44,142 fans long before the ball landed in GABP's second deck. Latos never even turned his head to watch it. He just collected a new baseball and waited for Dusty Baker to come out and formally remove him. Nearly 15 minutes had passed since Latos first began to visibly lose his composure.

As Marty Brennaman told the Reds radio audience, "All of a sudden, it's six to nothing ballgame." Most listeners would've added a coda: "... and that ballgame is over."

But the Reds themselves didn't feel that way. Phillips took a bite out of the lead with a two-run double in the bottom of the fifth. Ludwick led off the sixth with a solo homer, followed by a Bruce walk and a Rolen single. With nobody out, Hanigan came to the plate as the potential tying run. With the count full, Baker sent the runners, trying to keep out of the double play. Hanigan—who finished 2012 with a minuscule 10 percent strikeout rate—took strike three, and Bruce was thrown out at third. Rally killed.

The Reds got two baserunners on in both the seventh and the eighth, but couldn't score. In the ninth, Cozart walked and Votto singled to bring the tying run to the plate for the fourth consecutive inning. Ludwick singled in a run, but Bruce flew out and Rolen struck out to end the game, the series, and the Reds' 2012 season.[13]

The record book may label the 2012 Reds as the first team to blow a Division Series after leading 2–0, but we prefer to remember them as a 99-win team[14] that had one of the most resilient, entertaining seasons in the last 40 years.

---

13. The strikeout also closed the book on Scott Rolen's career. Rolen didn't bother announcing his retirement, but he never played again. He would be inducted into the Hall of Fame in 2023
14. Including the postseason.

THE
OUT-OF-NOWHERE
1999 REDS

The 1999 Reds didn't win the World Series. They didn't have a roster filled with Hall of Famers. They didn't even make the playoffs. Yet they're one of the more beloved Reds teams of the last 30 years.

To understand why, you must first understand the state of baseball in the late 1990s. The 1994–95 players' strike had fundamentally damaged baseball's bond with its fans—a problem felt acutely in Cincinnati, where average attendance dropped from 32,164 in 1994 to 22,144 in 1998.

But it wasn't just the strike, or the fact that the Reds had offered fans a long stretch of mediocre, uninteresting baseball. Even team captain Barry Larkin felt it. "When I was growing up, there was a lot of pride in the Reds," he said before the 1999 season. "We lost that feeling. I want to see it come back to Cincinnati."

To understand the 1999 Reds, you have to realize that Reds fans had lost hope. They felt like the game was rigged against them. They'd watched big-budget teams like the Yankees, Braves, and Indians dominate the postseason, while the Reds cut payroll dramatically. Fans had listened to a constant drumbeat of poor-mouthing and anti-marketing, from baseball commissioner Bud Selig to Reds general manager Jim Bowden, all the way down to the local columnists and talk radio shouters. "Teams like the Reds have no hope," was the constant refrain.

It turns out that this was mostly hooey—a dual-purpose propaganda weapon deployed in the owners' long-running war with the players' union, and also in their campaigns to secure public funding of new stadiums in places like Cincinnati, Pittsburgh, and Milwaukee. But people usually believe what they hear, particularly when almost everyone is singing the same tune.

So that's how Reds fans felt as the 1998 season ended. Bowden, however, was never one to go without a fight. He'd spent the past two seasons shedding payroll, but stockpiling young talent. He'd given opportunities to promising infielders Pokey Reese and Aaron Boone, and traded for top prospects Paul Konerko, Dmitri Young, and Sean Casey.[1] The Reds had developed an excellent young reliever in Danny Graves, and had more arms in the pipeline.

But Bowden was never known for his patience, and in November 1998, he made two trades designed to jumpstart the rebuilding process. First, he traded second baseman Bret Boone and pitcher Mike Remlinger to the Braves for pitcher Denny Neagle, outfielder Michael Tucker, and a prospect. Boone was coming off a season in which he hit a career-high 24 home runs and won a Gold Glove, but Neagle was a mainstay of the best rotation in baseball, winning 52 games over the previous three seasons. The Reds had added a number one starter, and had cleared second base for Reese.

Bowden wasn't done. The next day, he traded Konerko (who was blocked by Casey at first base) for 25-year-old White Sox center fielder Mike Cameron, who was fast and had a reputation for good defense, but had hit just .210 in 1998.

"With our payroll limitations the way they are," Bowden said, "we're giving the fans a good team to watch. I think if these guys produce the way they're capable, we can surprise some people."

Another move was likely, as the additions of Tucker and Cameron gave the Reds five starting-quality outfielders. Many suspected that veteran Reggie Sanders (and his $3.7 million salary) would be the one to go, as Bowden searched for a conventional cleanup hitter.

On February 2, 1999, Bowden found his big bat, acquiring slugger Greg Vaughn from the Padres in exchange for Sanders and two prospects. The trade didn't make the Reds younger or cheaper, nor was it a long-term move—Vaughn would be a free agent at the end of the 1999 season. But Vaughn had finished fourth in 1998 MVP voting, hitting 50 home runs for the pennant-winning Padres.

Despite Vaughn's key role with the 1999 Reds, his biggest mark on Reds history was breaking the team's ban on facial hair, which had persisted at least since the mid-1960s. Vaughn told Bowden, "I'm just going to show up at spring training with my goatee. When you traded for me, you got the goatee, too." The Reds couldn't argue with that logic, and just before spring training, announced the elimination of the ban.

---

1. The Casey deal was especially Bowden-ian (dramatic and controversial), since it happened the day before Opening Day 1998 and sent Dave Burba—the Reds' scheduled Opening Day starter—to Cleveland.

Young and Reese walked into the clubhouse wearing neatly-trimmed goatees and big smiles. "There are some ugly people without facial hair," Young said, rubbing his goatee. "And I'm one of them."

Vaughn also arrived at spring training with a bearing that discouraged foolishness. "I'm pretty intense on the field," he explained. "My attitude is, only one thing matters, and that's getting the 'W.' I'll be the first one to jump on a player if he's not giving his all."

The press was focused on the power, but the Reds quickly learned that Vaughn would also make a major contribution in the clubhouse, where he befriended and mentored the young talent that Bowden had assembled. Four everyday starters—Casey, Reese, Boone, and Young, plus Opening Day starting pitcher Brett Tomko and co-closer Danny Graves—were all born within 18 months of one another. Between Larkin and Vaughn, the youngsters had two thoughtful, uncompromising, and highly respected veteran teammates on whom to rely.

They also had 68-year-old manager Jack McKeon, a surprisingly perfect fit for the Reds young roster. "I spent 17 years managing in the minor leagues with young kids," he said. "I understand them. I'm patient with them. I don't yell at them and I don't rant and rave."

Despite all this, the Reds struggled out of the gate, finding themselves in last place entering play on May 3. Neither Vaughn (.203) nor Larkin (.182) were hitting, and the Reds had just been manhandled by the Braves, managing only four runs and 10 hits in a three-game series sweep.[2]

Vaughn called a closed-door clubhouse meeting. He was concerned that the Reds didn't feel they belonged on the same field as the Braves. "There was no name-calling and no finger-pointing," he said. "The hitting and the pitching is going to come, but the rest of it has to stop. We have to want to win, think we're going to win."

The next night, the Reds opened an 11-game homestand against the Diamondbacks. After blowing an early lead, Cincinnati entered the ninth tied 3–3. Boone led off with a bunt single, and Reese sacrificed him to second. The next two hitters walked to load the bases, and Cameron, riding an 0-for-13 streak, ripped a ball to deep right field. It struck the wall, just short of a grand slam, but good enough for a walk-off win. "This one was won by the kids—Cameron, Boone, Reese," McKeon said.

---

2. And the Reds hadn't even faced future Hall of Famers Greg Maddux or Tom Glavine in the series.

The next night, it was the veterans' turn, as Larkin and Vaughn combined to score five runs, with Larkin's sixth-inning home run (scoring Vaughn) being the difference-maker in a 6–4 win over Arizona. Those two wins launched the Reds on a 21–8 stretch that pulled them to within 1.5 games of first place Houston.

This was Reds fans' first full season with the real Sean Casey. His 1998 debut season had been derailed just three days after he arrived from Cleveland, when he was hit in the eye by an errant throw during batting practice. Casey only missed a month, but he struggled on his return, and spent a few more weeks in AAA. But once he recovered, Casey announced himself as one of the better young hitters in the league, hitting .300/.394/.498 in the second half.

He improved on those numbers in 1999, hitting .332/.399/.539 with 25 home runs, 99 RBI, 103 runs scored, and 42 doubles. But more than the numbers, Casey captivated teammates and fans alike with his genuine, open personality. Not since Sparky Anderson had Cincinnati seen a character like this: an elite performer who was eminently approachable. He was a grown-up kid who was still awed by his surroundings, and down-to-earth enough to consider "nice" to be the highest of compliments. Like Sparky, Casey lived by the very simple lessons taught by his father: Everyone deserves respect. Treat people the way you want to be treated.

First nicknamed "The Mayor" for his chatterbox nature at first base, Casey gave the title real meaning by embracing the entire community and never forgetting a name. "He's the nicest guy in baseball," Graves once said. Larkin called him the most sincere person he'd met in the game. "He's too good not to be true," Larkin said.

Casey was real, as was Larkin. Playing a career-high 160 games, the 35-year-old Larkin enjoyed his last great season, hitting .293/.390/.420 with 30 steals and still-excellent defense.

Pitching coach Don Gullett was again exceptional in papering over holes in the pitching staff. This time, he had to deal with the fact that four-fifths of the Reds' Opening Day rotation was either hurt or ineffective in the season's first half.[3] Yet Cincinnati's ERA (3.99) ranked third in the league as of the All-Star break. How did they do it? Retreads

---

3. Here's how the Opening Day rotation performed up to the All-Star break: Tomko: 5.42 ERA; Neagle: 8.17; Pete Harnisch: 3.42; Steve Avery: 4.53; and Jason Bere: 6.85.

Mike Cameron (top) is congratulated by Pokey Reese after Cameron scored the winning run on a base hit by Mark Lewis in the bottom of the 10th inning in a July 1999 game against the Diamondbacks. (AP Photo/David Kohl)

Steve Parris (5–1, 3.86 in the first half) and Ron Villone (4–2, 3.42) were surprisingly competent, and the Reds had baseball's best bullpen.

The old-school McKeon ignored "modern" rules about bullpen usage—he actually *managed* his pen, choosing pitchers based on the game situation, matchups, and who had the hot hand. On the season, seven different Reds earned multiple saves. Graves led the team in the category with 27, but he entered the game in the ninth inning (or later) in only 28 of his 75 appearances. He pitched 111 innings, including 41 multi-inning outings.

Young Scott Williamson—on his way to winning the 1999 Rookie of the Year Award—threw 93⅓ innings of relief, with a 2.41 ERA and 107 strikeouts. He wasn't strictly an eighth-inning setup man, either; Williamson saved 19 games, and over half his outings were for multiple innings. Rubber-armed Scott Sullivan threw 113⅔ innings in 79 games, pitching 57 times with zero or one day's rest. Together, the three young relievers combined for 318 innings pitched, with a 2.86 ERA and 254 strikeouts.

But by mid-July, it was evident that the Reds needed pitching help. Bowden was desperately working to add another starter, if he could somehow convince managing executive John Allen to bump up the payroll. (Allen had been named the team's "managing executive" in 1996, and had operational control from the time of owner Marge Schott's suspension until sale of the Reds was finalized.) [4]

Bowden also hoped for an internal boost when Neagle returned from the disabled list—the big off-season acquisition had started the year 0–6 and had pitched just 31 innings in the first half. And Bowden prayed that Pete Harnisch could keep pitching through the pain in his shoulder. He was leading the team in wins, innings, and ERA, but nobody knew how long he could keep it up.

"It is clear to everybody, we don't have five solid starters to run out there," McKeon said. "Poor Pete Harnisch is going out there and pitching on guts. We want to win, want what we've done so far to keep going. These guys have busted their tails. But you can't win without pitching, no matter what."

---

4. In April 1999, Schott sold the Reds to a group led by billionaire Carl Lindner, who paid $67 million for controlling interest in the team. The sale needed approval of baseball's other owners, which came in June.

So Bowden kept hustling, and came up with a deadline deal to acquire veteran Baltimore right-hander Juan Guzman in exchange for two prospects.[5] Guzman brought an 85–75 career record, but also a $5.25 million salary—Bowden had to go back and wheedle some cash out of the Orioles to (partly) make up for the payroll hit before Allen and ownership would sign off.

Before Guzman could take the mound for the Reds, Neagle finally returned on August 4 and provided a huge boost, holding the Rockies to three hits and a run over six innings. Second time out, he threw seven innings of one-hit baseball against the Pirates. In all, Neagle went 8–2 with a 3.11 ERA in August and September.

Guzman's first start was just as promising, as he went eight innings in a 2–1 loss to the Rockies. "If he pitches like that, we'll win most times," McKeon said. Guzman went on to make 12 starts for the Reds with an excellent 3.03 ERA.

In just a week, the Reds' starting rotation had been reshaped from an imminent disaster into a strength. The position players recognized the difference. "You see five guys now who can win any day of the week," Casey said. "You feel like if you get four or five runs on the board, we've got the game."

The Reds played great baseball down the stretch, going 38–21 in August and September. They hit (.277/.349/.471, 83 home runs), pitched (3.80 ERA), fielded (just 18 unearned runs), and ran (56 steals) as well as anyone over that 57-game stretch, but they couldn't quite pull ahead of the Astros to stay.

The Reds and Astros entered play on October 1 tied for first in the Central, with both clubs two games ahead of the New York Mets for the NL's sole wild-card berth. The Reds headed to Milwaukee for a three-game, season-ending series. It was October baseball, in every sense of the phrase. Win the series, and you keep playing. Lose it, and things would get complicated.

Outwardly, the Reds welcomed the opportunity to take charge of their own destiny. "It's nice knowing that you control everything," Boone said. "It's on us." But at least one veteran thought the pressure of the

---

5. One was B.J. Ryan, a 23-year-old left-hander, who immediately joined the Baltimore bullpen and went on to a long career in the American League.

pennant race was starting to wear on the young roster. "I think guys are kind of drained," Larkin said.

To their credit, the Brewers weren't just playing out the string in a lost season. The Reds jumped out to a 3–0 lead in the opener, but Milwaukee battled to tie it in the eighth, then won on a 10th-inning walk-off single. Meanwhile, the Mets were beating the Pirates and the Astros were losing to the Dodgers.

Because the Reds held the tiebreaker over Houston, they still controlled their destiny: if they won the last two games, they'd make the playoffs. No such luck. The Brewers knocked Guzman out of Saturday afternoon's game with a seven-run second inning, and coasted to a 10–6 win. This time, the Mets and the Astros both won.

The Reds had brought 108 bottles of champagne to Milwaukee on Friday night. Now it looked like the bubbly would be coming back on the chartered jet, unopened. "Guys are trying maybe a little too hard," Vaughn said after Saturday's game.

That night, McKeon led a contingent of Reds coaches, staff, and players to mass at Old St. Mary's Catholic Church in downtown Milwaukee. Looking for hope wherever he could find it, McKeon took heart in the fact that the bishop was "pinch-hitting" for the regular parish priest, and was "wearing his big red hat!"—a sign that providence favored the Redlegs.

Everything came down to Sunday, game 162. Harnisch took the mound for the Reds. He'd been the starter the last time the team won, way back on Tuesday. As the teams readied for the 3:05 PM start, the rains fell in Milwaukee. The playoff picture, however, cleared up considerably as the Mets and Astros played their early afternoon games. Unfortunately, both clubs won, making the Reds' playoff outlook as gloomy as the Wisconsin weather.

There was no longer any good scenario. Lose Sunday's game and the season is over. Win, and the Reds would play the Mets in a one-game playoff, Monday evening in Cincinnati. Meanwhile, the rains fell, and fell, and fell. Water filled the warning track like a moat, and the outfield wasn't much better. On any other day, the game would have been postponed, but because the Division Series was set to start on Tuesday, there was little choice but to wait it out.

And so they did, for 5 hours and 47 minutes. Though the Brewers announced a crowd of 55,992 at County Stadium,[6] only a few hundred were still on hand when the game began at 9:52 PM. The game was mercifully brief. The Reds scored five runs in the third inning (including Vaughn's 45th home run of the year)[7] and locked up a 7–1 win in just two hours and 36 minutes. They would play another day. Or rather, they would play another game later that same day—the Reds' do-or-die playoff game with the Mets started in Cincinnati in less than 19 hours.

Reds fans were ready—the game sold out in 7.5 hours (54,621 tickets, including standing room), the culmination of a long, long comeback from the 1994–95 strike. The Reds hadn't sold out their postseason games in 1995, and even with the exciting 96-win team, Cinergy Field had only two sellout crowds in all of 1999 (one being Opening Day).

The packed house had little to cheer about, unfortunately. New York's veteran lefty Al Leiter was near-perfect, allowing just one Cincinnati hit (and no baserunners beyond first base) through the game's first eight innings. The final was 5–0. It was just the third time all year that the Reds had been shut out.

But as the Mets celebrated on the Cinergy turf, Reds fans refused to leave. They didn't want to part with this special team—this season that everyone saw as a gift—so they stood in the chilly ballpark on a late Monday night and they cheered. The players returned for an encore. Vaughn came onto the field and tossed hats into the crowd. Others tossed batting gloves. Catcher Eddie Taubensee thanked the grounds crew, while Casey high fived fans.

But the same awareness that provided joy, also led to sadness. By the time Casey made it back to the clubhouse, he was inconsolable. "It's not that we lost," Casey said. "It's emotional 'cause you look around the locker room and you still don't want it to be over. There's so many great guys in this room. I don't want it to end."

Taubensee felt the same way. "It's not just losing this game, but losing this team."

---

6. It was technically the largest regular-season crowd in Brewers history, although nowhere near that many people showed up. The game was originally supposed to be the final game at Milwaukee County Stadium, but a tragic construction accident delayed completion of Miller Park until 2001.

7. Vaughn's 45 home run season still ranks sixth in Reds history.

Had they won just one more game, the 1999 Reds may have been remembered as one of the most successful teams in the organization's history; as it is, they still rank as one of the most surprising and magical.

"I wouldn't take a day back," said Young. "Not one day."

Anyone who watched them that summer agrees.

1972 WORLD SERIES

After winning the 1972 pennant over the Pirates in dramatic fashion, the Reds were headed back to the World Series, hoping to make everyone forget their loss in the 1970 Series. Their opponent would be the Oakland A's.

The Athletics franchise hadn't been to a World Series since 1931, but owner Charlie O. Finley had finally rebuilt them into a contender, putting up five consecutive winning seasons and back-to-back AL West titles, before finally making it back to the World Series by beating an aging Tigers team in the 1972 ALCS.

The '72 A's had power, at least for that era. Their 134 home runs led the AL; today it would rank near the bottom of the league. Mike Epstein hit 26; Reggie Jackson had 25. Joe Rudi and Dave Duncan each hit 19.

On the mound, the A's had colorful names with gaudy numbers. Jim "Catfish" Hunter went 21-7 with a 2.04 ERA and finished fourth in Cy Young voting. John "Blue Moon" Odom had a 15-6 record and a 2.50 ERA. Lefty (and nickname-less) Ken Holtzman went 19-11 with a 2.51 ERA.[1]

Encouraged by the iconoclastic Finley, the A's were everything the Reds were not, at least on the surface. The A's wore bright gold and green uniforms, white spikes, and three different types of caps.

Like the Reds, the A's long had a rule against facial hair, but when attention-loving star Reggie Jackson arrived at spring training 1972 with a mustache (and announced plans for a full beard), Finley tried reverse psychology: he encouraged several other players to grow their own mustaches, figuring that Jackson would lose interest when he was no longer unique. Finley outfoxed himself, though—he found that he loved the look and saw it as a way to make his *team* stand out. He scheduled a "Mustache Day" at the ballpark for Father's Day 1972, and offered $300 to any Athletic who grew a mustache by the big day.

The contrast in styles was mostly a superficial thing—something for each team's fans to feel superior about. But the media immediately

---

1. These numbers were good, but remember that the average ERA in the AL that season was 3.06.

turned a baseball series into a civil war of generations, lifestyles, and geography—the "Hairs vs. Squares" Series. One Bay Area writer framed the Series as a morality play, with Oakland representing freedom, and the Reds not just symbols of a repressive world, but active participants in it. He called Sparky Anderson a "short haired freak" and "one of the troglodytes of the sport."

The Reds may have believed their traditional style to be superior to the A's "Sunday School softball" look,[2] but to their credit, they never much made it about character, or even performance. "Look," Anderson said, "hair don't have nothing to do with the way you play ball.... It's got nothing to do with being morally superior, either. I just don't like long hair on a ball player. You've got to have discipline and this is one place to get it."

That discipline talk wasn't just coach-speak. The A's had real issues. Shortstop Bert Campaneris had been suspended for the final three games of the ALCS, after throwing his bat at Detroit pitcher Lerrin LaGrow in response to being hit in the foot with a pitch. Across the clubhouse, pitcher Vida Blue was fuming about the fact that he hadn't gotten a start in the ALCS, and was openly welcoming a trade. He and Odom had nearly come to blows in the A's clubhouse *during the pennant-winning celebration,* after arguing about something else.

Oakland later proved to be one of modern baseball's true powerhouses, winning five consecutive American League West titles and three World Series in a row. But in October 1972, the Reds were the overwhelming favorites, particularly after Jackson was ruled out for the Series after pulling a hamstring in the ALCS.

In Game 1, the A's sent Holtzman to the Riverfront Stadium mound to face Gary Nolan. It was a rematch of one of the great pitching duels of the early '70s. On June 3, 1971, Holtzman, then with the Cubs, had no-hit the Reds. Nolan, for his part, allowed only a single unearned run in eight innings.

Game 1 also introduced one of baseball's all-time surprise postseason heroes, in Oakland catcher Gene Tenace. Converted from the outfield in the minors, the 25-year-old Tenace had only secured Oakland's starting catcher job in the season's final month. Though he'd hit well enough to close the season (.377 OBP in September), Tenace's

---

2. All credit to Bob Howsam for that one. The man passionately hated white cleats.

season totals were lousy (.225/.307/.339, and only 5 home runs), and he went stone cold in the ALCS, going just 1-for-17.

But on this night, on the game's biggest stage, Gene Tenace was every bit the immortal, homering in his first two World Series at-bats (the first man ever to do it).[3] Tenace's home runs gave Oakland a 3–2 lead, and Holtzman, Rollie Fingers, and Vida Blue made it last, holding the Reds scoreless after the fourth.[4]

Game 2 pitted Catfish Hunter against the red-hot Ross Grimsley. Grimsley wasn't nearly as sharp as he'd been in the NLCS, but he did battle. Oakland notched five singles in the game's first two innings, yet managed only one run. In the third, Grimsley left a fastball out over the plate to Oakland left fielder Joe Rudi, who deposited it deep into the green seats in left-center. Hunter protected that 2–0 lead into the ninth. He surrendered a run on a couple of hits, but Fingers came on to slam the door.

After a travel day and a rainout, Cincinnati sent Jack Billingham to the mound in Oakland for Game 3; Oakland countered with Odom. Both were brilliant. Through six innings, neither team had scored. The Reds had one hit and Oakland two.

The Reds finally broke through in the seventh. Tony Pérez singled, and was bunted to second. César Gerónimo hit a soft single to center, where the ball nearly came to a halt on the wet outfield grass. Center fielder George Hendrick picked it up and sidearmed the ball in to Campaneris, conceding the run. Meanwhile, the wet grass claimed a victim in Pérez, who fell flat on his face rounding third. Campaneris could've thrown Pérez out easily, but he never knew what was happening behind his back.

That was the only run Billingham (who went eight innings) and reliever Clay Carroll would need. The Reds won it 1–0.

Game 4 was another classic. Gullet faced Holtzman, in a battle of left-handers. Tenace homered again, giving the A's a 1–0 lead in the fifth. Holtzman protected that lead until the eighth, when Dave Concepción singled and advanced to third with two outs. Blue again came in to

---

3. Atlanta's Andruw Jones would match the trick as a 19-year-old in 1996, and Houston's Kyle Tucker did the same in 2022.

4. Though one of baseball's best young starters, and the 1971 AL Cy Young Award winner, Blue pitched mostly out of the bullpen in the 1972 postseason, making four appearances in the five-game ALCS, and another four in the World Series. His 2⅓ inning outing in Game 1 of the World Series came just two days after he threw four scoreless innings to save the A's pennant clincher.

INSIDE THE MOMENT

Nobody knew it at the time, but Johnny Bench played through the pennant race and postseason in a state of deep personal anxiety. After a routine x-ray in early September, Reds doctors noticed a spot the size of a half dollar on Bench's lung. Bench, who had never smoked and was just 24, kept things quiet and tried not to imagine the worst-case scenario. Playoff adrenaline and a young athlete's sense of invincibility got him through.

Under this pressure, Bench hit .286/.384/.610 in September, including a run of seven homers in seven late-season games to secure the league home run and RBI titles (and along with them, his second MVP trophy). In the postseason, Bench hit .293/.375/.537.

That December, Bench had exploratory surgery, where the doctor was also able to remove the growth. The operation was painful and the recovery was long, but the growth was benign—caused by coccidioidomycosis, an often-asymptomatic fungal disease known as "Valley Fever."

relieve, and promptly walked Joe Morgan. Bobby Tolan then yanked Blue's first pitch down the right-field line for a double, easily plating Concepción and Morgan (who was running on the pitch). Pedro Borbon retired the A's in the eighth, and the Reds were just three outs away from evening the Series.

Oakland sent Gonzalo Márquez up to pinch-hit with one out in the bottom of the ninth. The Reds scouting report said that the left-handed Márquez was a pull hitter, but Sparky let shortstop Dave Concepción ignore the scouting report and play Márquez as an opposite field hitter.[5] Márquez, of course, hit a bounder right where the scouting report said Concepción should have been positioned, putting the tying run on base. Three consecutive singles later, the A's had a walk-off win and a 3–1 Series lead. Anderson never forgave himself for letting a player override Ray Shore's scouting report.

Through four games, the Big Red Machine had only scored six runs. The top of the lineup was ice-cold (Rose, Morgan, and Tolan were

---

5. Like Concepción, Márquez was a Venezuelan. Concepción was certain he knew Márquez's tendencies better than the scouting report.

a combined 4-for-44), and the Reds were suffering an overall power outage (just three doubles and no home runs).

Both trends turned around quickly in Game 5, as Rose jumped on Hunter's first pitch for a laser-shot home run. But in the second inning, Reds starter Jim McGlothlin gave up a three-run home run to—guess who?—Gene Tenace, for his record-tying fourth blast of the Series.

In the fifth, with the Reds trailing 4–2, Morgan came to the plate with two outs, still hitless in the Series. The fact is that Morgan had injured his foot in Game 4 of the NLCS. Unable to sleep because of the pain, Morgan had the Reds team doctor inject his heel with novocaine before NLCS Game 5. He then taped the entire ankle to stabilize it and compensate for the lack of sensation. Morgan had tried to keep the injury quiet, both to avoid excuse-making and to hide the weakness, but by this point, the injury was a story. What the public didn't know was that Morgan's heel was actually feeling much better.

This time, he drew a walk and headed to first. He broke for second with a great jump. Tolan swung, flaring a single to right-center field. Morgan never broke stride and scored easily without a throw. That's right, Joe Morgan had scored from first base on a routine single. "A play like that gave me as much satisfaction, maybe more, than if I had homered or driven in a run with a hit," Morgan remembered.

The Reds tied the game in the eighth on a near replay: Morgan walked again, stole second, and scored on a Tolan single. Morgan's bat still hadn't showed up, but his eye (two walks), legs, and brain had led to two crucial runs, and kept the Reds' hopes alive.

Thanks to singles by Gerónimo and Rose, and some lousy Oakland defense, the Reds eked out a go-ahead run in the top of the ninth.

After Tenace walked to lead off the ninth and a sacrifice bunt attempt failed, Oakland sent Blue Moon Odom in to pinch run for Tenace. Sparky brought in Billingham, only two days removed from his Game 4 gem. Oakland countered with pinch-hitter Dave Duncan, who singled to move Odom, the tying run, to third with one out.[6]

The next batter, Campaneris, lifted a high popup behind the first base bag, and Morgan caught the ball about three steps into the outfield grass. Morgan figured that Odom would try to score—Morgan's one supposed weakness was his throwing arm—but as he pivoted to

---

6. The A's pinch-hitters went an absurd 6-for-8 in the three games played in Oakland.

throw, his feet went out from under him on the still-wet Oakland grass. Fortunately for Morgan, he caught himself, popped up quickly, and made an easy throw to Bench, who had the plate blocked and tagged Odom for the game's final out.

Game 6 was the Series' one and only blowout.[7] Vida Blue finally got the start he'd been demanding, and he probably wished that he'd kept his mouth shut. The Reds touched him up for three runs in 5⅔ innings, and added a five-run seventh inning against the Oakland bullpen. Final score: 8–1. Improbably, the Reds had rallied from an 0–2 deficit and tied the Series.

It came down to Game 7. On the mound, it was a rematch of Game 3: Odom and Billingham, who had combined to pitch 15 innings of six-hit, one-run, 18-strikeout baseball in their first matchup.

Oakland Manager Dick Williams made one big change. The Reds had been running wild on the bases, stealing a combined six bases in winning Games 5 and 6. Williams wanted Duncan back behind the plate, but he obviously couldn't bench Tenace (.300/.364/.900 through the first six games). That meant that Epstein (still hitless for the Series) went to the bench while Tenace shifted to first base.

A sellout crowd of 56,040—at the time, the largest crowd ever to attend a baseball game in Cincinnati—packed Riverfront Stadium. Defense cost the Reds in the first, when Tolan misplayed a short line drive into a triple. Two batters later, a Tenace chopper took a funny hop off a seam in the AstroTurf, then bounced off third baseman Denis Menke's glove, giving Oakland a 1–0 lead.

Meanwhile, Odom was handling the Reds, and Williams looked like a genius when Duncan threw out Morgan trying to steal second.

The Reds tied it in the fifth when Pérez doubled and scored on a sacrifice fly.

Borbon took over in the sixth inning, and gave up a leadoff hit to Campaneris. Two outs later, the Reds elected to pitch to Tenace, who once again made them pay, roping an RBI double down the left-field line. Pinch runner Allan Lewis replaced Tenace, who jogged off the field with a World Series slugging percentage record (.913) and a certain Series MVP, as long as Oakland held the lead.

---

7. Every other game was a one-run affair.

Bando followed with a long blast to straightaway center. Tolan may have had a chance at it, but as he reached the warning track, he dramatically collapsed with a pulled hamstring, while the ball rebounded off the center-field wall. Lewis scored, and Oakland's lead was 3–1.

Rose led off the home eighth with a single off Hunter. Left-handed Holtzman came on to face Morgan, who doubled down the line. The tying runs were in scoring position with nobody out. Fingers came in for the sixth time in the Series, to face Joe Hague, pinch-hitting for the injured Tolan. Hague popped out, and the A's walked Bench (and his 40 regular season home runs) intentionally.

That brought up Pérez, who already had 10 hits in the Series. His sacrifice fly plated Rose and moved Morgan to third. Bench stole second, putting the go-ahead run in scoring position, but Menke flew out to short left to end the rally. Fingers retired Cincinnati in the ninth, and the Reds came up just short of winning their first Series since 1940.

Nobody spoke much in the Reds clubhouse afterward. Just thinking about the loss would make Morgan sick, years later. But for Howsam and the Reds front office, the long-term plan was working as they hoped. All the pieces of the Big Red Machine were in place, and the future still looked bright.

[Acknowledgments]

We started this book nearly twenty years ago, and looking back, we probably wouldn't have been able to complete it then. At least not for guys with day jobs. We would have spent hundreds of hours driving back and forth to Cincinnati and Cooperstown, to dig through newspaper archives, old books, and other ephemera.

But this book was largely completed from our own homes. Searchable archives for most major newspapers are now available online—the same is true for *The Sporting News*, *Sports Illustrated*, and other publications that were vital in the game's early days.

Google Books allows you to search the full text of millions of books, magazines, and newspapers. While Google doesn't always contain the full text of each book (respect for authors!), little-heralded inter-library loan services can bring anything you need to your local branch, with just a click of a mouse.

Baseball-Reference.com has the complete box score and play by play from almost every game ever played. That site, plus FanGraphs. com, can answer any statistical question. Hundreds of regular folks have uploaded old game videos onto YouTube, letting us see the people and moments we wrote about. The Society for American Baseball Research (SABR) provides research tools, great publications, and a community of supportive, fellow-minded baseball fans. Their Biography Project, with more than 8,000 different entries, is an invaluable resource (even if they don't have an entry on Elly De La Cruz, yet).

A huge debt of gratitude is owed to all the incredible writers at various newspapers—especially the *Cincinnati Enquirer* and *Dayton Daily News*—who have covered the ins and outs of Cincinnati Reds baseball for over 150 years.

We'd like to specifically thank the staff at the Powell branch of the Delaware County (Ohio) District Library, who handled dozens of

SearchOhio and OhioLINK deliveries with a smile; John Erardi, who gently waved us off one particular research dead end; and Todd Justus, Teds Peterson, Joel Luckhaupt, Jordan Dotson, and Nate Dotson for valuable editorial suggestions. Former Reds general manager Dick Williams and former Reds catcher Joe Oliver provided valuable insight and behind-the-scenes stories, and we'd be remiss if we didn't mention them here. Thanks, guys.

We would also like to pay tribute to several of the legends featured in this book, who have died since the first edition: Pete Rose, Joe Morgan, Frank Robinson, Tom Browning, Chuck Harmon, and Nino Escalera.

When Chad founded RedlegNation.com in 2005, we thought we'd amuse ourselves with a forum slightly more robust than Bill Lack's old CINTIRED email list-serv. We never dreamed it would lead to writing in other outlets, covering the Reds regularly, and even this book. Thanks to all the writers and editors at Redleg Nation who inspired, informed, and pushed us over the last decade-plus. Thanks as well to the entire community at The Riverfront that has sprung up around our long-running Reds podcast. We look forward to enjoying many more seasons obsessively following the Reds with this crazy family of loyal fans.

We extend special thanks to Chris Welsh for writing the foreword to this edition, as well as to Josh Williams, Jesse Jordan, and the rest of the great folks at Triumph Books, who rescued this project from a bad situation, and helped nurse it into a product that makes us all proud.

Finally, we must thank our coworkers and friends and especially our families, who inspired us, shared our fandom, and lately, have suffered through way too many months of dad holed up in his office, or sitting on the couch with a notepad in his lap. Thank you, thank you, thank you.

[Selected Bibliography]

Newspapers
Chicago Tribune
Cincinnati Enquirer
Columbus Dispatch
Dayton Daily News
Los Angeles Times
New York Times
Washington Post
USA Today

Websites
Baseball-Reference.com
BleacherReport.com
ESPN.com
MLB.com
RedlegNation.com
Sabr.org/bioproject
RedReporter.com
Fangraphs.com

Periodicals
Baseball Magazine
Cincinnati Magazine
The Sporting News
Sports Illustrated

Books

—Anderson, Sparky, and Dan Ewald. *They Call Me Sparky*. Sleeping Bear, 1998.

—Anderson, Sparky, and Si Burick. *The Main Spark*. Doubleday, 1978.

—Angell, Roger. *Five Seasons: A Baseball Companion*. New York: Simon and Schuster, 1977.

—Armour, Mark (Editor). *The Great Eight: The 1975 Cincinnati Reds*. University of Nebraska Press, 2014.

—Armour, Mark L., and Daniel Levitt R. *In Pursuit of Pennants: Baseball Operations from Deadball to Moneyball*. University of Nebraska, 2015.

—Asinof, Eliot. *Eight Men Out: The Black Sox and the 1919 World Series*. Holt Rinehart & Winston, 1963.

—Bass, Mike. *Marge Schott: Unleashed*. Sagamore Pub., 1993.

—Bench, Johnny, and William Brashler. *Catch You Later: The Autobiography of Johnny Bench*. Harper & Row, 1979.

—Bradley, Leo H. *Underrated Reds: The Story of the 1939–1940 Cincinnati Reds, the Team's First Undisputed Championship*. Fried Pub., 2009.

—Brosnan, Jim. *Pennant Race*. Harper, 1962.

—Browning, Tom, and Dann Stupp. *Tales from the Cincinnati Reds Dugout: A Collection of the Greatest Reds Stories Ever Told*. Sports Publishing, 2012.

—Buckley, James. *Perfect: The Inside Story of Baseball's Twenty Perfect Games.* Triumph Books, 2012.

—Carmichael, John P. (Editor). *My Greatest Day in Baseball.* Grosset & Dunlap, 1963

—Cieradkowski, Gary. *The League of Outsider Baseball: An Illustrated History of Baseball's Forgotten Heroes.* Touchstone, 2015.

—Conner, Floyd, and John Snyder. *Day by Day in Cincinnati Reds History.* Leisure, 1983.

—Cook, William A. *Big Klu: The Baseball Life of Ted Kluszewski.* McFarland & Co., 2012.

—Davis, Eric, and Ralph Wiley. *Born to Play: The Eric Davis Story: Life Lessons in Overcoming Adversity On and Off the Field.* Viking, 1999.

—Devine, Christopher. *Harry Wright: The Father of Professional Base Ball.* McFarland & Co., 2003. Thomas Dunne, 2014.

—Epstein, Dan. *Stars and Strikes: Baseball and America in the Bicentennial Summer of '76.*

—Erardi, John, and Greg Rhodes. *The First Boys of Summer.* Road West Publishing, 1994.

—Erardi, John, and Greg Rhodes. *Opening Day.* Road West Publishing, 2004.

—Erardi, John, and Joel Luckhaupt. *The Wire-to-Wire Reds: Sweet Lou, Nasty Boys, and the Wild Run to a World Championship.* Clerisy Press, 2010.

—Ewald, Dan. *Sparky and Me: My Friendship with Sparky Anderson and the Lessons He Shared about Baseball and Life.* Thomas Dunne, 2012.

—Faber, Charles F., and Zachariah Webb. *The Hunt for a Reds October: Cincinnati in 1990.* McFarland & Co., 2015.

—Feldmann, Doug. *The 1976 Cincinnati Reds: Last Hurrah for the Big Red Machine.* McFarland & Co., 2009.

—Freedman, Lew. *Game of My Life, Cincinnati Reds: Memorable Stories of Reds Baseball.* Sports Publishing, 2013.

—Frost, Mark. *Game 6: Cincinnati, Boston, and the 1975 World Series.* Hachette Books, 2009.

—Guschov, Stephen D. *The Red Stockings of Cincinnati: Base Ball's First All-Professional Team and Its Historic 1869 and 1870 Seasons.* McFarland & Co., 1998.

—Griffey, Ken. *Big Red: Baseball, Fatherhood, and My Life in the Big Red Machine.* Triumph Books, 2014.

—Honig, Donald. *Baseball When the Grass Was Real.* University of Nebraska Press, 1975.

—James, Bill. *The New Bill James Historical Baseball Abstract.* Free Press, 2003.

—James, Bill, and Rob Neyer. *The Neyer/James Guide to Pitchers.* Fireside, 2004.

—Jordan, David. *Pete Rose: A Biography.* Greenwood, 2004.

— Koppett, Leonard. *The Man in the Dugout: Baseball's Top Managers and How They Got That Way.* Crown, 1993.

—Lawson, Earl. *Cincinnati Seasons: My 34 Years With the Reds.* Diamond Communications, 1987.

—Glbson, Bob and Phil Pepe. *From Ghetto to Glory: The Story of Bob Gibson,* Prentice-Hall, 1968.

—Light, Jonathan Fraser. *The Cultural Encyclopedia of Baseball, 2nd Edition,* McFarland & Co., 2005

—Linkugel, Wil and Edward Pappas. *They Tasted Glory: Among the Missing at the Baseball Hall of Fame.* McFarland & Co., 1998.

—Luckhaupt, Joel. *100 Things Reds Fans Should Know & Do Before They Die.* Triumph Books, 2013.

—McCoy, Hal. *The Real McCoy: My Half-Century with the Cincinnati Reds.* Orange Frazer Press, 2015.

—McCullough, Bob. *My Greatest Day in Baseball, 1946–1997.* Taylor Publishing Co., 1998.

—Moffi, Larry, and Jonathan Kronstadt. *Crossing the Line: Black Major Leaguers, 1947 - 1959*. U of Iowa, 1994.

—Morgan, Joe, and David Falkner. *Joe Morgan: A Life in Baseball*. W.W. Norton, 1993.

—Posnanski, Joe. *The Machine: The Story of the 1975 Cincinnati Reds*. William Morrow, 2009.

—Preston, Joseph G. *Major League Baseball in the 1970s: A Modern Game Emerges*. McFarland & Co., 2004.

—Rathgeber, Bob. *Cincinnati Reds Scrapbook*. Jordon & Co., 1982.

—Reidenbaugh, Lowell, Joe Hoppel, and Mike Nahrstedt. *The Sporting News Selects Baseball's 50 Greatest Games*. Sporting News Pub., 1986.

—Rose, Pete, with Hal McCoy. *The Official Pete Rose Scrapbook*. Signet, 1985.

—Rhodes, Greg, and John Erardi. *Big Red Dynasty: How Bob Howsam & Sparky Anderson Built the Big Red Machine*. Road West Publishing, 1997.

—Rhodes, Greg and John Snyder. *Redleg Journal: Year by Year and Day by Day with the Cincinnati Reds since 1866*. Road West Publishing, 2000.

—Ruby, Jeff, and Robert Windeler. *Not Counting Tomorrow: The Unlikely Life of Jeff Ruby*. Black Tie Productions, 2013.

—Schmetzer, Mark. *Before the Machine: The Story of the 1961 Pennant-Winning Reds*. Clerisy Press, 2011.

—Schmetzer, Mark and Joe Jacobs. *The Comeback Kids*. Clerisy Press, 2010.

—Smith, Daryl Raymond. *Making the Big Red Machine: Bob Howsam and the Cincinnati Reds of the 1970s*. McFarland & Co., 2009.

—Sugar, Bert Randolph. *Baseball's 50 Greatest Games*. Exeter, 1986.

—Vrusho, Spike. *Benchclearing: Baseball's Greatest Fights and Riots*. Lyons Press, 2008.

—Walker, Robert Harris. *Cincinnati and the Big Red Machine*. Indiana University Press, 1988.

—Werber, Bill and C. Paul Rogers. *Memories of a Ballplayer: Bill Werber and Baseball in the 1930s*. Society for American Baseball Research, 2000.

—Wheeler, Lonnie and John Baskin. *The Cincinnati Game*. Orange Frazer Press, 1988.

[About the Authors]

Chad Dotson has helmed Reds coverage at *Cincinnati Magazine* since 2014; he's also the founder of both Redleg Nation (redlegnation.com) and the long-running Reds podcast, *The Riverfront*. His Substack newsletter about Cincinnati sports and culture can be found at chaddotson.com. Dotson lives in Richmond, Virginia, with his wife, Sabrina. He's @dotsonc on X.

Chris Garber spends his days as an advertising and intellectual property lawyer and his summer nights as a Reds fan. He was a contributing editor and featured writer for Redleg Nation for over a decade, and is a regular guest on The Riverfront podcast. A graduate of Ohio University's E.W. Scripps School of Journalism and William & Mary Law School, Chris lives near Columbus, Ohio, with his wife, Katie, and their three children.